UNIVERSITY OF WYOMING

COMPLIMENTS OF
ELLBOGEN CENTER FOR
TEACHING AND LEARNING

COE 307
307-766-4847

www.uwyo.edu/ctl

Teaching Defiance

Stories and Strategies for Activist Educators

A Book Written
in Wartime
by
Michael Newman

Foreword by
Stephen Brookfield

JOSSEY-BASS
A Wiley Imprint
www.josseybass.com

Published by Jossey-Bass
A Wiley Imprint
989 Market Street, San Francisco, CA 94103-1741   www.josseybass.com

Jossey-Bass books and products are available through most bookstores. To contact Jossey-Bass
directly call our Customer Care Department within the U.S. at 800-956-7739, outside the
U.S. at 317-572-3986, or fax 317-572-4002.

"Warty Bliggens the Toad" from *The Lives and Times of Archy and Mehitabel* by Don Marquis,
© 1927, 1930, 1933, 1935, 1950 by Doubleday, a division of Random House, Inc. Used by
permission of Doubleday, a division of Random House, Inc.

"Mon sombre amour d'orange amère" from *Elsa* by Louis Aragon. © Editions Gallimard.
Used by permission.

Library of Congress Cataloging-in-Publication Data
Library of Congress Cataloging-in-Publication Data

Newman, Michael, 1939-
  Teaching defiance : stories and strategies for activist educators / Michael Newman ; foreword
by Stephen Brookfield. — 1st ed.
    p. cm. — (The Jossey-Bass higher and adult education series)
  Includes bibliographical references and index.
  ISBN-13: 978-0-7879-8556-1 (cloth)
  ISBN-10: 0-7879-8556-2 (cloth)
  1. Social action—Study and teaching. 2. Reformers. I. Title. II. Series.
  HN29.N47 2006
  303.48'4—dc22   2006004175

Printed in the United States of America
FIRST EDITION
HC Printing   10 9 8 7 6 5 4 3 2 1

The Jossey-Bass

Higher and Adult Education Series

Contents

Part Four: Insight and Action

Part Five: Defiance and Morality

Foreword

It is a pleasure to be able to write this Foreword and to introduce the provocative work of Michael Newman to a North American audience. Although Mike has an impressive body of published work to his credit, and although two of his books have won the Cyril O. Houle World Award for Literature in Adult Education, this book marks the first time a North American publisher has made his work available for educators in the United States and Canada.

Teaching Defiance is a book that will become iconic in the field, the kind of text that will cause major reverberations and that people will be talking about for years to come. I predict it will have a long shelf life as a classic text, one that chronicles the insights and passions of an adult educator with a worldwide reputation for articulating a view of the field that is uniquely conceived and expressed. In this book Mike argues that adult learning is a tool people can use to create genuinely participatory economic and political structures and to recognize when political leaders are trying to hoodwink them. Put simply, there is no one else in adult education who puts this case as powerfully and lyrically as Mike Newman. His work flows beautifully, with a fluid and pleasing mix of dramatic personal story, pertinent theoretical analysis and extensive practical illustration.

Reading *Teaching Defiance* generated strong feelings of envy in this writer. I only wish I had it in me to write something so powerful, accessible and convincing. About a year ago in fact I started to write a piece on the role that adult education should be playing in promoting true dialogue around the U.S.-led coalition's invasion of

Iraq. I was prompted by some of the same outrage that lies behind *Teaching Defiance*. After several weeks work, I had the beginnings of a first chapter but just couldn't seem to capture the right tone of immediacy and distance, activism and theoretical analysis, autobiography and biographical illustration that I was trying for. So I scrapped the project. Now I know why I abandoned my book. Without my being aware of it someone was doing what I was trying to on the other side of the world but with much greater experience and assurance than I could muster. *Teaching Defiance* is the book that I was trying to write but couldn't, and it is one the field sorely needs. Mike argues a principled and informed case that reinserts adult education where it started and where it belongs—in the tradition of a strong, truly democratic movement that uses education to help the citizenry stay critically alert to the ever-present dangers of demagoguery, brainwashing, secrecy at the highest levels and ideological manipulation. In North America this is the tradition of Myles Horton, Eduard Lindeman and Moses Coady that is so often espoused but rarely acted on. *Teaching Defiance* rekindles a fire of citizen involvement and justifiable outrage that needs fanning.

This is a book that addresses all kinds of ideas—for example the way that hatred of, and anger at, injustice are positive catalysts for change—that will disturb the field as a whole. But this will be an enriching and productive disturbance, one grounded in equal measure in theoretical illumination and practical vignettes. Although theoretically fluent, Mike never strays too far from the field of practice. Just when mentions of Habermas, Sartre or Camus threaten to leave us behind, we collide with the dramatic stories of the opening batsmen of the Australian cricket team, the art student with the candles and lighter fluid, a theater of the oppressed piece developed by car thieves or the autobiographies of Gandhi and Mandela. Just when we feel the book might become only a personal polemic, Mike provides us with some highly detailed descriptions of his own practices—role plays, critical incidents, simulations, dialogue sessions, metaphor analysis, meeting guidelines—that will encourage readers to experiment with their own adaptations of these.

There is so much in here that will be immediately familiar to North American readers in terms of situations experienced, types of individuals encountered (colleagues, superiors and students), crises endured and practices tried, that I have no doubt but that people will be glued to the text as I was. The use of examples of individuals and practices from around the globe (including South Africa, France, England and so on) is a particularly positive benefit of the text, providing a refreshing alternative to the American-bound nature of many adult education texts in the field. In a globalized era more of our books need to be written with this breadth of perspective.

Some may feel that this is too controversial a text. I personally can't think of anything more timely or necessary. Certainly, ideas such as defiance, rebelliousness or the positive aspects of hate and anger will undoubtedly disturb and annoy some readers. But this is the reality of the time we live in, as well as the reality of adult educational practice. Anyone who has worked in the field will have been faced with some of the situations and dilemmas Mike describes— particularly since so many adult educators work within marginalized settings where they are constantly fighting for a fair share of resources, battling incomprehension or outright hostility from superiors, developing programming around crisis situations that bedevil adults' lives, seeing the connections between adults' private troubles and wider social and political forces and so on.

People are hungry for a book that springs from passionate conviction and a sense of outrage, that gives hope, illumination and useful ideas in equal measure, and that is as accessible as a *New York Times* best seller. *Teaching Defiance* is that book.

Stephen Brookfield
Minneapolis-St. Paul, 2006

Preamble

Three preliminary comments, and then my thanks:

First, I am Australian and examples given in this book are often Australian ones. I make no bones about this. But there are references to France, the United Kingdom, South Africa, the United States, Jamaica, India and elsewhere and it is my intention that the discussion should be of relevance to activist educators everywhere.

Second, I acknowledge the negative implications of the word *defiance*. The word suggests a reaction, a response to the initiatives of others. But this book was written in wartime when Australian so-called "defense" forces were in Afghanistan and then Iraq, and when a small group of people in powerful positions in a limited number of countries were pursuing their own agendas with little consultation or care for people of other views. Defiance does seem an appropriate stance for this age. If we are to live out our lives as original and creative beings we need to take control of our moment, and a large part of taking control of our moment will involve defying others. This book is for those who want to learn and teach how to do this.

Third, in this book I discuss different kinds of action and that leads me to discuss the use of violent action. For the most part I try to do this dispassionately. But I do not want to imply that I condone the use of violence. I am appalled and repelled by violence, whether it be the execution of a convicted murderer, the use of deadly military force, a mindless street mugging, or the monstrously organized violence committed by bombers in a bar in Bali or an underground train in London. However, I do believe that if we want to adopt anything other than a knee-jerk reaction, if we are to adopt a coherently worked-out moral position to guide our own thoughts and our own actions, if we are to work out how we can counter the barbarous, the unjust and the malign, then we need to confront and discuss violence. And that is what I have tried to do.

And now my thanks:

I want to acknowledge the people who have knowingly and unknowingly contributed to my writing this book, and so I say thank you to all the people with whom I have worked, who have shared their ideas and their practice with me and who through their conversation, example and writing have made me think; to all the participants in classes, training courses and workshops who have experienced, commented on and contributed to the processes I describe in this book; and to the people who have read and commented on the draft manuscript (or parts of it). They are my partner Joelle Battestini, our daughter Alicia Battestini, and our son Frank Newman; my colleagues, comrades and friends Kathleen Galvin, Jane Clarke, Sharon Holmes, Astrid Von Kotze, Jane Dawson, Peter Willis, Phil Drew, Pitika Ntuli, Kate Collier, Sally MacKinnon, Celina McEwen, Rick Flowers, Arthur Wilson and Stephen Brookfield; and David Brightman and Cathy Mallon of Jossey-Bass. Over a coffee somewhere some time ago David encouraged me to write this book and then followed me up with occasional e-mails to make sure that I did. Cathy displayed wonderful patience, and an understanding of my particular quirks as a writer, as she guided me through the copyediting and production phases. Finally I need to thank—but the word is not strong enough—Billy's mother for giving me permission to tell Billy's story and use Billy's name. Of course, having said my thanks, I need to say that any confusions, inconsistencies or errors remain mine.

Michael Newman
February 2006

About the Author

Michael Newman is a consultant and author in the field of adult education. He has a Ph.D. from the University of Technology, Sydney (UTS). An Australian, he worked as a community education worker in inner London for eight years, then as warden of an adult education college for four years. After his return to Australia, he was director of the Metropolitan Region of the Workers Education Association of New South Wales, a national trainer for the Australian Trade Union Training Authority, and a senior lecturer in adult education at the University of Technology, Sydney for twelve years.

At UTS, he taught in both postgraduate and undergraduate programs, specializing in subjects related to adult teaching and learning, social action and popular education. He retired from his full-time post with UTS in 2001 but remains an honorary associate of the university and a research fellow of the university's Centre for Popular Education.

He has been a visiting scholar for brief periods in Canada, South Africa, the Netherlands, Thailand and New Zealand. Two of his books have won the Cyril O. Houle Award for Outstanding Literature in Adult Education, awarded by the American Association of Adult and Continuing Education.

Part One

MAKING A START

1

TAKING SIDES

At its heart this book is about choice. It examines how we can help ourselves and others understand that we do have choices, and then learn how to make defiant choices. I argue that we can do this by using rational discourse, nonrational discourse, and that magical mix of the rational and nonrational, the telling of stories. In this first part, I introduce the idea of teaching defiance. In the next part, I deal with themes which run through the rest of the book. These include rebelliousness, defiance, consciousness and choice. In the third part, I look at ways of using rational discourse to help people analyze, communicate and negotiate for personal and collective change. In the fourth part, I look at how we can use nonrational discourse to encourage insight, and to turn insight into action. And in the final part, I look at how we can use storytelling to help ourselves and others construct our own moralities, and so choose acts of defiance which we can justify.

Using Theory

As must already be obvious, this book is a polemic. I will put a case. I will take sides. I will argue that activist educators should teach people to make up their own minds and take control of their own lives. I will argue that we should teach ourselves and others to be defiant.

Of course, if I am adopting the style of a polemicist, I should tell you at the outset what makes me tick. So . . . I subscribe to the Marxist idea that we generate our consciousness in dialectical rela-

3

tionship with our social and material world. We make ourselves by living in and responding to a context. I like Anthony Giddens's claim (1991, 52, 53) that our self-identity is not given but "has to be routinely created and sustained in the reflexive activities of the individual."

I understand that we are utterly alone but that our existence as conscious beings depends on the company of others. We are trapped inside our own awareness and can only ever communicate imperfectly with the world outside. And yet it is through this imperfect communication that we construct our being. It is through this troubled, sensuous encounter between the self and the world (Allman, 2001) that we create, and then develop, the ways in which we feel and think.

I am an existentialist to the extent that I believe that we have choice. To say that we can do nothing even in the face of what appear to be insurmountable odds is to deny our humanity. I like Sartre's insistence (1984, 572–573) that we do not receive our goals "from outside" or from "a so-called inner nature." We can choose our "ultimate ends," give character to our being and make manifest our freedom.

I like Camus's idea of the absurd. There is nothing to believe in, no ultimate truth, no deity or set of absolute principles to give us direction, and yet we spend our lives behaving as if there were. We stand "face to face with the irrational" yet feel a "longing for happiness and reason" (Camus, 1975, 31–32). Absurd though it is, we will spend our lives striving to give purpose to a purposeless existence.

So I like the critical theorists' retreat from the idea of the enlightened rational being to the ideas of aesthetics and egalitarian communicative action (Rasmussen, 1996). Our search for some kind of meaning will be through an examination of values. And our search for that elusive purpose will be through talk.

And I like Habermas's tripartitions (Habermas, 1972; see also Dallmayr, 1996, 85–86). We exist simultaneously in objective, social and subjective worlds. We live according to the three value spheres of science, ethics and self-expression. We construct our being through relationships which are subject-to-object, subject-to-subject and subject-to-self. And we grow by engaging in instrumental, interpretive and critical learning.

Faced with isolation, choice, absurdity, a loss of the rational and the challenges of living in multiple worlds, we need to learn and teach what in eighteenth-century English was described as "bottom." Imperfectly translating this into twenty-first-century English, I believe we need to teach and learn a combination of feistiness, character, courage and perseverance.

Taking Control of Our Moment

I have said elsewhere (Newman, 1999) that I like watching professionals at work, be they a glass worker swabbing out molds with consummate physical grace, a rock guitarist playing a searing, silvery solo or a skilled and committed union educator delivering a course on workers' and other human rights. Professionals, whether paid or not, know what they are doing. They make the right choices. They are in control of their moment.

"Freddie" Ayer was an English philosopher and I like him too, in good part because, at the age of seventy-seven and just two years before his death, he intervened to stop the then heavyweight boxing champion of the world from harassing a supermodel at a social event in New York (Rogers, 1999, 344). But I also like him for some of his philosophical ideas. Ayer (1971, 104–106) called himself "a logical empiricist" and argued that all "genuine propositions" other than tautologies draw their significance from the fact that they can be verified with reference to a "sense-experience." As a start to this book, therefore, I want to look at two consummate professionals and their encounter with an intense and artificially heightened experience. I am not going to pretend to apply the kind of rigor to the process that Ayer would want, but as I write this book I will use practical example, anecdote and description of this kind to "verify" some of the propositions I make. And I realize that for this first practical example I have chosen the game of cricket, and so I must ask those who are not familiar with cricket to imagine a tennis player on the receiving end of a series of massive serves, or a baseball batter stepping up to face an unforgiving pitcher or an exponent of karate facing a sustained and furious attack.

Matthew Hayden and Justin Langer are the opening batsmen for the Australian test cricket team. As I write, the Australian team is the best in the world, so Hayden and Langer are amongst the best batsmen in the world. Opening batsmen are a special breed. They walk out onto the field to face the fast bowlers of the other side. The bowlers are fresh and the ball is new, rock-hard and shiny. As the batsman on strike takes up his position, he faces the prospect, if he survives, of having the ball bowled at him for several hours at speeds of up to 150 kilometers per hour. The ball has a raised seam around it. It can curve in the air. As it hits the surface of the wicket, it can change direction. It can jag in towards the batsman or sheer away. It can skid through at groin level, or it can rear up towards the batsman's rib cage, heart or head. The batsman can respond in a number of ways. He can hook, pull, cut, drive, glance or block the ball, or let it go through to the keeper. From the moment the ball leaves the bowler's upstretched arm the batsman has a fraction of a second in which to judge how he will respond. The slightest mistake and he will snick a catch to the waiting fielders, or miss the ball and have it crash into his body or shatter the stumps behind him.

Television coverage of cricket is sophisticated, and sometimes in slow-motion replay the camera will zoom in on the batsman's gaze. When Hayden and Langer are on song, these close-ups are electric. They are close-ups of people under a fierce, ritualized attack. They are close-ups of people making lightning choices. They are close-ups of people who are intensely aware and utterly in the present. These are professionals in full control of their moment, and you can see a glorious, bloody-minded defiance in their eyes.

Facing Up to Our Futures

We have no control over our past. We can use it, interpret it, learn from it and even rewrite it but the fact of it mockingly remains. I am Australian and Australia was once officially racist. Our immigration policy was unashamedly referred to as "the White Australia policy." There is no escaping this unsavory fact.

We have no guaranteed control over our future. We can try to influence it by learning, planning and taking action, but events happen which can divert the whole course of our lives. On September 11, 2001, passenger planes were flown into buildings in the cities of Washington and New York in the United States, killing everyone on board and thousands on the ground and changing the world.

Our pasts direct us forward, obvious futures rush back to meet us, and others wait unseen to waylay us, like footpads in a dark alley. All we have is the present, a moment in which we can choose, in which we can either give in to our pasts or face up to, deal with and defy some of our futures.

Making Up Our Own Minds

In Australia in the 1970s progressive political leaders broke free from our racist past and vigorously promoted multiculturalism. Migrants were accepted from all parts of the world. Legislation was introduced to redress previous systemic inequities and promote equal opportunities in employment. People became more tolerant of differences in sexual preference. Diversity was celebrated.

Some twenty years later and this momentum for tolerance and equity abated. Now difference was treated with suspicion. In the 1990s Australia introduced stringent border protection to prevent asylum seekers arriving on our shores, and began putting those people who did slip though the cordon into mandatory detention. The treatment of these refugees was harsh. The camps were inhospitable and prisonlike. Whole families including young children were imprisoned for months and even years while their claims to refugee status were examined. Many of these refugees were from the Middle East, and many were Muslim.

In public pronouncements about the arrival of refugees, some of our political leaders obscured the differences between refugees and terrorists. Old prejudices were awakened and new prejudices fed. And, although the treatment of refugees was given wide coverage in the mass media and there were vigorous protests and demonstrations, the government clearly judged that a majority would support its actions against these frightened, desperate people, or that we would not care.

In Australia in 2003, as the United States, the United Kingdom, and Australia prepared to go to war in Iraq, opposition to the war grew. On a Sunday in February 2003 more than 250,000 people gathered in the center of Sydney in protest against the war. Similar protests took place across Australia, and yet the prime minister and his government ignored these calls and committed Australian servicemen and servicewomen to the war in both supporting and combat roles. Once the invasion of Iraq was under way, there were more demonstrations and marches, but the numbers were less. Again the government judged that a sufficient number of people would remain unconcerned.

There was a truculence in the tone and style of a number of our mass media commentators and columnists. They scoffed at people who disagreed with their viewpoints. They replaced careful argument and debate with ridicule.

Someone else's future was being laid out for us. Imaginative, alternative ideas were being ignored. Australia is a small country on the other side of the world. We did not have to invade Iraq. Instead of promoting the idea of war, our political leaders could have tried to prevent it. Drawing authority from the fact that they represented a successful multicultural country, they could have stepped onto the international stage and offered to broker encounters and discussions with a view to helping the various parties seek ways to ensure peace.

Drawing authority from Australia's long-standing relationship with the United States, our leaders could have tried to help the policy-makers in Washington understand why so many people resented their influence and actions in the world.

But our leaders took us to war, secure in the knowledge that a majority of the population would say either "There's nothing I can do" or "Who cares?" A hegemony of the Gramscian kind had been established: a majority of the population allowed a small number of our political figures to make up our minds for us.

Critical Thinking

It is common enough these days to hear people say that we should teach critical thinking, but this injunction has become a platitude. There was a time when critical thinking derived from critical theory. This kind of critical thinking involved separating out "truth" from "ideology." It meant analyzing human activity in terms of power and refusing to take the words, ideas, injunctions and orders of others at face value. It meant not letting others make up our minds for us. It meant abandoning the search for some fixed set of principles and adopting a stance of informed and continual critique. Critical thinking was not a neutral activity. Like the critical theory from which it sprang, critical thinking was associated with the pursuit of social justice.

But the term has been domesticated. In the 1970s and 1980s, as enrollments dropped in traditional university departments of philosophy, the teachers in those departments went looking for work and offered to teach critical thinking in other departments. Often what they taught was Aristotelian logic and its extensions in modern scientific reasoning. This may have been no bad thing but, away from their own philosophy departments and teaching trainee geologists, architects, doctors and engineers, these teachers were required to focus on logical process and were much less likely to encourage a condition of constant intellectual skepticism. "Critical thinking" became a feature in educational publicity and a common objective or item of content in many curricula. But it was no longer critical thinking in the pursuit of social justice.

In 1980s and 1990s, teaching critical thinking became a feature of programs in human resource development and workplace learning, and the concept was reduced to a corporatist competency. Now critical thinking was to be found as just one in a list of higher-order competencies, capabilities or capacities, alongside others such as "the ability to work in a team" and "a desire to produce high quality products" (Gonczi, 1992, 4).

Instead of this domesticated kind of critical thinking, I propose that we teach people how to resist.

Stating a Mission

If I go looking for a mission for activist adult educators—those people who are committed to helping themselves and others live out their lives through their learning—then it will be this. Our job is to help people become truly conscious, understand the different worlds we live in, and develop a morality in the face of the evident amorality of our universe. It is to teach people how to make up their own minds, and how to take control of their moment. It is to teach choice. It is to help ourselves and others break free from our pasts, plan for the futures we want and resist the futures we do not want. Our job is to teach defiance.

Finding Examples

Adult educators working in different contexts already teach defiance. In an interpersonal communication workshop people learn how to listen and speak effectively, how to avoid and resolve misunderstandings, and also how to assert themselves. In a program for people who have left school early, young adults engage in a combination of leisure activities, work experience and instruction in job-seeking skills in order to confront and counter some of the effects of their disadvantaged backgrounds. And in a trade union course in occupational health and safety, activist members learn the information and strategies needed to take on managers who otherwise might be tempted to cut corners on safety. Although not normally expressed in this way, the purpose in each of these adult education activities is to help people learn how to defy others who might be laying out unwanted futures for them.

There are times when adult educators can seize the opportunity to teach defiance. I know of a middle-class woman who enrolled in a noncredit adult education course in silversmithing. She was in her sixties at the time and faced an unchallenging future dictated by her social class. She had joined the course as a diversion, but she quickly demonstrated an aptitude for working with silver and her tutor encouraged her. He suggested further, more serious study, and by the time the woman was in her seventies she was designing, making, exhibiting and selling silver jewelry. She had her own workshop at the back of her house, her own business and, for the first time in her life, her own career. Her silversmithing tutor had helped her turn that initial class of two hours a week into an act of defiance.

In the above examples, the teaching and learning of defiance, even when acknowledged, is secondary or incidental. In communication skills workshops, the aims often have more to do with boosting the participants' confidence in social and professional encounters, that is, they have to do with the participants' "personal growth." In the program for early school leavers the major aim is to get the participants into employment. In the occupational health and safety course, the aim is to make workplaces safer. And for the tutor and students in that silversmithing course, the aims were to teach and learn the basics of designing and making small pieces of silver jewelry.

In the mid-1980s I designed an educational course whose overt aim was to teach defiance. I was a trainer with the Australian Trade Union Training Authority (TUTA), a national organization with training centers in each state providing courses for members of unions in organizing, negotiating workplace agreements, representing members and other trade union skills. Over several weeks I wrote the curriculum for a two-week course provisionally called "Powershift." The course was to be offered to experienced union activists and would help them develop the necessary skills and knowledge in order to challenge the authority of management in a workplace. Through the use of training sessions, case studies, and role-play, participants would devise ways of shifting some of the power to the shop floor so that workers could have a greater say in the ways their workplaces were organized and in how the profits from their work were distributed. The skills to be learned included analyzing problems, managing meetings, mobilizing a workplace, campaigning and negotiating agreements. There were to be information sessions on work organization, company finances, company structure, common and not so common company practice and the current state of Australian industry and the Australian economy. I set the role-plays within a scenario of a middle-sized Australian enterprise expanding into the Asian-Pacific market. The participants were to develop their campaigns around the introduction of new technologies and a management drive for increased productivity.

The course itself was based on a shift of power from the trainers to the participants. At the outset the trainers would be in control but as the course progressed the participants would gradually take over. In the first week the trainers and visiting experts would provide input sessions, and these would interrupt the scenario in order to inform the participants and allow them to take the scenario further. As the course entered the second week, the input sessions would be reduced in number and participants would spend an increasing amount of time in the scenario. What input sessions there were would be decided on by a course committee and provided by participants drawing upon their own resources and the center's information services. And in the last few days of the course, the scenario would dominate. On the final day subgroups would outline their findings and put their proposals to the trainers and the other

Figure 1

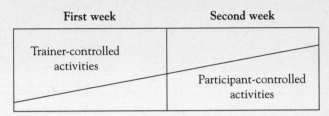

From Trade Union Training Australia Inc. (TUTA). Used by permission.

participants, as if they were committees reporting to a general meeting of workplace members. Figure 1 represents this shift of control.

The course never took place. TUTA underwent major restructuring itself. The director of my center, who had supported me in the writing of the course, moved on to another position in TUTA. And some months later I too moved on, to another organization altogether.

Now, a good number of years on and I am writing this book. In a way I am taking up where I left off, but my aim is to investigate how adult educators working in any context can make the teaching of defiance not secondary nor incidental nor just one of several aims, but central to our work.

Part Two

REBELLIOUSNESS AND DEFIANCE

2

REBELLIOUSNESS

Cultural Rebelliousness

Australians are said to be irreverent, disrespectful and intolerant of people with airs and fancies. As with most generalizations about national character it is difficult to say whether this is true, since history has also shown Australians—within their own borders at least—to be peaceable, essentially law-abiding and so, by definition, respectful of authority. However it is certainly true that a remarkable collective irreverence was in abundant evidence close to a century ago in the behavior of the Australians who made up the Australian Imperial Force (the First AIF) and went off to fight in the First World War.

Great Britain entered the war against Germany on August 4, 1914. The Australian government declared war on Germany the following day, called for volunteers and young men from all over the country responded. They left their jobs in the cities, the working-class industrial suburbs and the country towns. They walked in from the bush to railheads and took trains to the capital cities on the coast. The Australian government had promised to send an initial force of 20,000 to Europe to be put under British command. This force was assembled within three months and the first convoy of transport ships began taking the troops to the northern hemisphere in November. These troops were destined to fight in the Dardanelles against the Turks and then to go on to fight on the Western Front in Europe. Australian men kept volunteering and were sent to join the forces already fighting. By the end of the war more than 330,000 Australians—from a total population in the Commonwealth of Australia of less than five million—had been involved in the forces, the vast majority of them in the army (Firkins, 1973; Gammage, 1974).

All these men were volunteers. And in the camps on the edges of the Australian cities, on the voyage to the other side of the world, then in the camps while they waited to go into the firing line, they were irreverent, disrespectful and intolerant of people who adopted airs and fancies.

Bill Gammage wrote a history of the First AIF based on the diaries and letters of approximately one thousand Australian soldiers who fought in the front lines. Of their attitude in the holding camps around cities like Melbourne and Sydney before they were shipped overseas, he says:

> They remained incorrigibly civilian, for they were not and did not wish to become regular soldiers. They were young men answering their country's call; they would fight willingly, but they saw no point in the rigours and inanities of parade ground discipline, and until they reached the front they considered the army a job which should be regulated by the conventions attached to any employer-employee relationship [Gammage, 1974, 26].

The men left camp at the end of the day without thinking of seeking permission and reported back for work the next morning as they would in any normal job. They treated their officers "with easy familiarity" and viewed rebuffs "as proof of malice or want of intellect in their seniors." They argued with their noncommissioned officers and "retained the right to be ruled by their own judgement" (Gammage, 1974, 26).

An Irish teacher was in awe of the lack of discipline in his new comrades, and wrote:

> They break camps when they list, brushing aside any resistance in the shape of, say, special guards with fixed bayonets, etc.; and for some time now they have decided that the Government has no

right to charge them fares in the railways up to Sydney—so they simply don't buy tickets; they laugh at the ticket-collectors and sometimes bundle them off the trains if the trains slow up passing a station! [Gammage, 1974, 27]

Towards the end of 1915 the authorities imposed a stricter regime in camps near Sydney and early in 1916 several hundred soldiers marched "under the control of leaders they had appointed" from Casula Camp to Liverpool Camp where they confronted the military authorities. In other contexts they could have been considered deserters or charged with mutiny but Gammage comments (1974, 28) that "their actions were those of strikers stating legitimate grievances and expecting redress, and apparently the authorities did not think this unnatural."

On the trip to the other side of the world the troops took matters into their own hands. In mid-1915 when a transport ship called into Colombo, the soldiers were refused leave, took it in any event and were fined. When the ship put to sea again, they rioted at the price of fruit in the ship's canteen, pushing officers about, assaulting the military police and booing the commanding officer. And they rioted at Alexandria. Here again the men were ordered to remain on board but, as one of them later wrote,

> immediately ropes were thrown from the decks to the pier and down slid the men, like sheep one starts and away go the rest. Soon the side of the boat was covered with ropes . . . the officers tried to prevent this but had to give it up. Armed guards were placed on the piers, but they were useless [Gammage, 1974, 35].

That first force of 20,000 was placed in camps outside Cairo. Again they saw no reason to stay in camp after the day's training and continued to go absent without leave. Patsy Adam-Smith, another chronicler of the exploits of Australians on and off the battlefields of the First World War, tells of a group of soldiers trying to get back to camp late one night. The last tram was packed and there were no places for them. The men acquired a donkey, put their most inebriated member on it, created a diversion and purloined the tram for themselves. The account from which Adam-Smith quotes (1978, 48) ends with these words: " . . . we leapt on board taking the donkey with us. The donkey was put off at the next stop."

Even in camp, discipline could be eccentric. Gammage tells the story of a captain accompanying a brigadier one evening and coming across a guard on duty eating a pie. "Hotly he ordered the soldier to present arms, at which the man asked the brigadier to hold his pie while he performed the required ritual" (Gammage, 1974, 38–39). This last story has the ring of the apocryphal about it, but it symbolizes nicely the soldiers' attitude towards pointless demonstrations of authority.

Not all the exploits of the troops could be described as innocent skylarking. They included drunkenness, brawling and, close to the troops departure for the landing at Gallipoli, serious rioting. On Good Friday 1915, when some units learned that they were to leave for the front, a number of men went into the Haret el Wasser, the red-light district of Cairo, to settle some scores. There had been growing resentment over the large number of cases of venereal disease resulting from the soldiers' patronage of the brothels there, the allegedly poor quality of the drink provided and the spiraling prices for both kinds of service. The men sacked several of the houses, throwing bedding, clothing and furniture into the street, piling them up and setting them alight. A building and a number of balconies caught fire and the men then cut the hoses of the local fire services when they arrived. A full-scale riot developed when British military police arrived and fired their pistols, wounding several soldiers. The military police were attacked with rocks and beer bottles and were forced to withdraw. With the mob "in dangerous disorder" the Lancashire Territorials were summoned and stood across the road with fixed bayonets. The rioting subsided and the soldiers slowly dispersed (Gammage, 1974; Adam-Smith, 1978).

Even when the soldiers were in dangerous disorder they were not engaged in a rebellion or revolution. They were not staging an uprising aimed at seriously challenging authority, let alone overthrowing and replacing that authority. Nor were they questioning the reason for their being there. Adam-Smith and Gammage quote letters and diary entries that suggest the men, far from mutinying, were eager for those in authority to get them to the front so that they could fight the enemy.

Australia had no standing army to speak of before the outbreak of war. There were few existing military traditions, and the masses of men who suddenly found themselves thrown together to make up the army drew on other codes of behavior. If they were from the cities, many of them would have been in jobs where unions were influential and the authority of the employer regularly questioned. If they were from the country, then many would have been from family properties and were used to working on their own or in small groups and making their own decisions. These men, then, brought with them an independence of spirit and a distrust of authority which were part of their makeup. Theirs was a cultural rebelliousness, essentially larrikin in nature and, beyond challenging the more ludicrous features of military discipline, without any clear purpose.

Political Rebelliousness

But rebelliousness can be purposeful and political in intent. A celebrated example is Rosa Parks's refusal to give up her seat to a white passenger in that bus in Montgomery, Alabama, in the United States on December 1, 1955. On the surface of it, the story is straightforward. Parks, employed as a seamstress at a department store, caught a bus home after work. The seating on the bus was segregated, with seats for whites in the front, seats for blacks at the back, and some seats in the middle which black people could use if they were unoccupied. Parks sat in one of these. Three stops later more white people boarded the bus and the driver ordered Parks to vacate her seat for a white man. Parks refused. The driver called the police and Parks was arrested. Her arrest led to a citywide boycott of the buses by black people for 381 days and brought a local pastor, Dr. Martin Luther King Jr., to national prominence as a leader of the civil rights movement. Parks challenged her conviction and the matter finally went to the U.S. Supreme Court where, on December 20, 1956, the court ruled that Montgomery's segregated bus seating was unconstitutional. The boycott was seen as the first of the many subsequent boycotts, marches and mass demonstrations for civil rights in the United States and, because of this, Parks is sometimes referred to as "the mother of the civil rights movement" (Lewis, 1965; Branch, 1988).

When Parks got on that bus she was tired and wanted to get home. She had not intended to confront the driver and the law, yet she did, and there are several histories behind her actions.

First, as a child Parks had witnessed terrible violence against black people.

Second, she had had a run-in with this particular bus driver several years before.

Third, in some respects Parks may have been an ordinary, middle-aged working woman, but she was also an activist. She had been the local secretary of the National Association for the Advancement of Colored People, doing the unsung office paperwork, recording the incidents of racial discrimination which were reported to the association, and interviewing people with complaints. Some of these people had witnessed killings.

Fourth, Parks was not the first person to be arrested for refusing to relinquish her seat. At least two others had been arrested at different times during the preceding months, but local activists had felt that neither was the right person around whom to build a campaign. They felt Parks was, and moved quickly to hold meetings, call the boycott, and set up a new organization called the Montgomery Improvement Association, with King elected as its president.

And fifth, some weeks before she refused to give up her seat on that bus, Parks had attended a residential workshop at the Highlander Institute, a small independent center committed to education for social action. At Highlander Parks had met like-minded people, white as well as black, and she said that the encounter made her realize for the first time that there could be a unified society with people "of different races and backgrounds" living in peace and harmony (cited in Horton, 1990, 149–150).

In one sense Rosa Parks's rebelliousness could be interpreted as a simple refusal to be humiliated by the bus driver again. But of course it was much more than that. Her action was premised on her personal story, her years as a quiet and determined activist, her informed beliefs, her friendships, and her experience at Highlander. It was a courageous act and it gave rise to momentous events. Her rebelliousness may have been spontaneous in the moment of its happening, but it was prepared for and highly political in its nature and circumstance.

Systemic Rebelliousness

Rebelliousness can be part of the order of things, an organized and commonly repeated strategy. I remember meeting a senior official of a blue-collar union which covered people operating heavy machinery on building sites and in factories and mines. The union was reasonably small but powerful nonetheless because its members held key positions in their workplaces. If a crane driver refused to climb the dizzying heights to the cabin of his crane above a city building site, most of the significant work on the site would come to a halt. If the operators refused to maintain the machinery in a mine controlling the lifts and the ventilation, all work stopped. The official told me with a wry smile that he had trained as a librarian but had taken a break and traveled to the north of Australia where he took a casual job as a machine operator on a large site, joining the union in the process. He liked the job and the union, stayed, was elected workplace representative and in due course was elected a full-time official.

Union officials are often depicted as troublemakers. This comes about because they turn up at workplaces where there is trouble.

But their job is to troubleshoot rather than trouble-make. Their job is to curb the excesses of bosses, stop exploitation, ensure a safe workplace, get a good deal for their members and get people back to work, since it is only by getting the site working effectively that their members will earn their wages.

This union official was good at his job. He was a tough man, and the managers and bosses he encountered were hard people too who were often under pressure and therefore tempted to cut corners on safety, employ people ignorant of their rights and push the work-force as hard as they could. Encounters between the official and managers, particularly at the outset of a dispute, were often less than polite. This former librarian said that he enjoyed a job which paid him "to march onto a site and be rude."

In Australia at the time I met this official, industrial relations disputes could be taken to a tribunal called the Commonwealth Conciliation and Arbitration Commission. The commission's job was not, as in a court of law, to find the truth but rather to settle the dispute, and in order to get a matter before the commission a union or employer had to prove that there was a dispute in the first place. A common way for unions to make this clear was to call a stoppage, often a twenty-four-hour strike. If this were successful, then the union's officials could go before the commission having established that their members meant business. It was a ploy to put pressure on the commission, was understood as such by all parties involved and so was, in effect, the use of a systemic rebelliousness.

Rebelliousness and Rebellion

A state of rebelliousness is very different from an act of rebellion, but clearly one can lead to the other. People who spontaneously resist some act of authority may find that their actions draw other people in and that these other people then take action themselves. Events gather a momentum and what began as a protest becomes an uprising. This happened in France in 1968, in what became known as *les événements*, when student protests at one university early in May triggered demonstrations, rioting, strikes and other forms of civil disobedience across the country. By the middle of the month these events had brought much of the country to a standstill and were seriously threatening the stability of the government (Feenberg and Freedman, 2001).

Of course the events occurred in a context. There was an intellectual climate in France which encouraged ideas of self-determination and action against authority. Amongst the established thinkers, Jean-Paul Sartre had examined questions of consciousness, choice and action. Albert Camus had challenged any purpose others might set for us and had insisted that the citizen take priority over the state. And Simone de Beauvoir had challenged the patriarchal character of society. Amongst the "newer" thinkers, Michel Foucault questioned the Enlightenment's concepts of knowledge and rationality and suggested that the old certainties which went with them were at an end. France is a country where philosophy is taught in *lycées* (state secondary schools) as well as universities, and these thinkers were discussed within the formal curricula. Outside the classroom Marxism in its different guises remained a strong influence and many university campuses had active political groups espousing revolutionary doctrines.

There was a climate of industrial unrest in France. The economy was faring well but industrial workers were not sharing the benefits. Discipline, particularly in the car factories, was tough and work was organized in the Taylorist mode. There had been waves of strikes in the preceding year and in the months leading up to May. Police had been called to some of the strikes and, when they cleared a Peugeot factory in 1967, two workers had been killed (McMillan, 1992, 181).

There was an established pattern in France from the Revolution on of political action in the streets. More recently the Algerian struggle for independence from France had caused deep divisions. During the 1950s and into the 1960s there had been demonstrations, bombings, an attempted assassination of the president and, at one moment, real fear of an insurrection by parts of the armed forces. More recently still there had been demonstrations and counterdemonstrations over the American involvement in the war in Vietnam, and in March 1968 six student activists were arrested for bombing the windows of the Parisian offices of an American corporation.

And there was a climate of extreme dissatisfaction on many university campuses. The French education system was centralized and inflexible. Much of the teaching was traditional, impersonal and authoritarian. Recent "reforms" had been imposed without consultation, increasing the frustration of both students and teachers. The campuses were often appallingly overcrowded, and this overcrowding was resolved by a draconian system of exams in which large numbers of students were failed at the end of each year.

In the months leading up to May there had been student unrest on the university campus at Nanterre on the outskirts of Paris. The campus had been opened in 1964 to take the overspill from the Sorbonne inside Paris. Nanterre was large, soulless and already overcrowded. Students were disaffected and there had been a succession of mass meetings and protests, a sit-in, and arrests. Towards the end of April the university decided to discipline some of the student leaders.

On May 3 students gathered at the Sorbonne in the quartier latin in Paris to discuss the events at Nanterre. Their numbers swelled and the university authorities called the police. Arrests were made, and a battle between police and students developed in which a large number of people were injured and hundreds more were arrested. Courses were suspended and the national students' union and the lecturers' union called a strike in protest. In the week that followed the protests grew. On May 6 there were more battles between the police and students. Students overturned cars and built barricades. The police used tear gas and the students responded with cobblestones and Molotov cocktails. Hundreds of people were injured and hundreds more were arrested. Thousands of students marched the next day. Red and black flags were hung from the Arc de Triomphe. The protests and agitation continued, students from

the lycées joined in and, as the days went by, the numbers of protesters increased. On May 10 tens of thousands of people marched
along the Boulevard St. Germain to the Sorbonne. The police were
out in force. Once into the streets around the Sorbonne, the protesters constructed barricades. The police assaulted the barricades
and a long night of rioting followed in which cars were burned,
hundreds were arrested, and hundreds of protesters and police were
injured. The major federations of unions called a general strike for
May 13, and hundreds of thousands of students and workers took to
the streets of Paris. Students occupied the Sorbonne and the École
des Beaux-Arts. Students at the École des Beaux-Arts began producing thousands of posters which were distributed to protesters
and pasted up all over the central areas of Paris. The protests spread
to towns and cities outside Paris. Workers began striking in large
factories, and some of these strikes became occupations. In Paris
students occupied the Théâtre de l'Odéon. Industrial strife, demonstrations and battles with the police escalated, and by May 20 up to
ten million workers across France were on strike (Feenberg and
Freeman, 2001). Rail and air services were at a halt. Ferries were no
longer running on the English Channel. Mail was not being deliv-
ered and newspapers were not being distributed. On May 24 President de Gaulle announced that he would hold a referendum but
rioting continued overnight and an attempt was made to torch the
Stock Exchange. On the following day workers in the state radio
and television services went on strike. Other groups, such as doctors, shop assistants, lawyers, workers in the arts industries and even
professional footballers, began making demands (Brown, 1974, 14).
Starting with unrest on a single campus, events had developed over
a period of just three weeks to a point where the country was in
near paralysis.

Rebellion occurred but a revolution did not. The powerful
Communist Party of France, supposedly a revolutionary party, had
remained aloof from the students, depicting them as spoiled young
members of the bourgeoisie. And because many of the workers who
occupied their factories were unaligned, the Communist Party had

kept its distance from them as well and so lost the opportunity to push for workers' control (autogestion). Instead of making a grab for power either on the streets or in the workplace, it had supported the unions in what was essentially a conventional claim for improved wages and conditions.

In the final days of May the unions negotiated an agreement with employers and the government for wage increases averaging 10 percent across the country and for an increase in the minimum wage of a third. The minister for education resigned. On May 28 the Prime Minister, Georges Pompidou, ordered the army to position tanks on the outskirts of Paris. On May 29 the largest union body, the Confédération Générale du Travail (CGT), organized a demonstration in Paris of hundreds of thousands of people, effectively taking the initiative for the demonstrations away from the students. Together these actions outmaneuvered other union and political bodies which had been positioning themselves to establish an interim government to fill any power vacuum that might occur.

On May 30 President de Gaulle went on radio and television to withdraw the idea of the referendum, dissolve the Assemblée Nationale and announce elections in June. There were demonstrations across the country in support of de Gaulle, with an estimated half a million people marching in Paris.

In early June most of the strikes came to an end. Fuel became easily available again. Road and rail services resumed. Police removed workers from some of the occupied factories, and students from the Odéon and the Sorbonne. The election campaign started on June 10. There were some violent incidents but life gradually returned to a kind of normality.

Some features of French society and life were changed. Pay and conditions for workers improved. Certain formalities of address, enshrined in the language until then, were relaxed, affecting the way people in workplaces and other social contexts related. In the next few years elements of the French education system were liberalized, and some aspects of French systems of governance were decentralized. French thought, in the form of poststructuralism and postmodernism, developed apace in the writings of people like Foucault, Jean Baudrillard and, later, Jean-François Lyotard. But in terms of the immediate events of May 1968 in France, perhaps they were really over in July when the counting for the election of the Assemblée Nationale was completed and it became clear that the conservative parties had increased their majority (Brown, 1974; Feenberg and Freedman, 2001; Gildea, 1996; Greenland, 1998; McMillan, 1992).

Reports of the events on the streets of Paris in May 1968 vary in emphasis (McMillan, 1992). Undoubtedly there were moments of real and ugly violence. The crude brutality of the Compagnies Républicaines de Sécurité (CRS), a paramilitary arm of the French police forces, shocked many. There were stories of beatings in police cells. And many people, both police and demonstrators, were hospitalized as a result of injuries sustained in the street battles. But Bruno Bontempelli, a Parisian friend of mine and now an established novelist, was a twenty-year-old at the time and he recalls the events as "une grande fête," a huge and magnificent party. He acknowledges the danger but stresses the madness, the excitement and the fun of it all. Another friend, Bryan Willis, an Australian this time, got into the building of the École des Beaux-Arts and joined in with the people producing all those posters. He talks of a small group of serious people in a room upstairs apparently planning the revolution but says they were out of tune with the general atmosphere of risk, exhilaration and adventure. He tells the story of going out one night to paste up posters:

> We came round the corner and there was a busload of CRS (special riot police) standing around smoking fags. We hurried across the road but on the other side there was another bunch of them having a fag. We were caught between the two. They looked at us, thought "What have we got here?" and started moving towards us. Just at that moment, a car pulled up and the girl I was with wrenched open

the door and told the little bald bloke at the wheel that the flics [cops] were after us. She jumped in the front and I jumped in the back. Now if that was in England, the driver would have said, "I think those policemen want to talk to you, can you get out of my car?" But that guy just took off. At that moment he was Alain Delon, he was Belmondo. That's the French for you. Wonderful [cited in Greenland, 1998].

And I was there too! My girlfriend was French and I was summoned to Paris by her anxious father who told us to get the paperwork done so that I could marry his daughter as soon as possible. He thought that he might lose everything in the turmoil and apparently wanted to secure her future by getting her married to an Australian currently living none too well in London. By some miracle I got a seat on what the booking clerk said was the only flight by any airline that day into France. The plane landed at a military air base and buses took us into Paris where my girlfriend met me. We went directly to the town hall of the seventh arrondissement to begin the paperwork, and I realized that if town halls all over the country were open then the country was actually functioning at an everyday administrative level, and that the kind of descent into anarchy my girlfriend's father feared was not happening. I did witness a massive demonstration the next day, red and black banners aloft, swinging its cheerful way down the rue de Rivoli and into the Place de la Concorde. And my now fiancée and I went into the Sorbonne in the early hours of the morning where we listened to workers in blue overalls addressing a ragtag mob in one of the courtyards, and then wandered through the buildings, coming upon a lecture theater full of people engaged in excited debate and another housing an impromptu concert of second-rate jazz. The mood was febrile, energetic, elated and, yes, Bruno is right, one of fun. Bryan captures it in his description of the little bald bloke at the wheel of that car. The month was a display of opportunistic, astonished rebelliousness.

Rebelliousness and Revolution

It did not happen in France in 1968, but rebelliousness *can* lead to revolution. Rebelliousness can be more than an exhilarated mood producing disorder and chaos. It can, as Mahatma Gandhi showed the world, be turned into a coordinated strategy with which to challenge the might of an empire. If we define revolution as the overturning of a government, then the nonviolent action—the coordinated rebelliousness—which Gandhi urged people in the Indian subcontinent to use in the 1920s, 1930s and 1940s played a significant part in achieving just that. In 1947 Great Britain relinquished its colonial rule in the subcontinent and withdrew.

The process leading to this revolution was a long one, lasting over five decades. Gandhi began developing his nonviolent action in Durban, South Africa, where he had gone in 1894 as a young man to practice law. The newly autonomous government of Natal intended to disenfranchise the Indians living there and Gandhi, at the age of twenty-three, helped found the Natal Indian Congress to resist these moves, using lobbying and the law as his tools. From then until 1914 Gandhi moved between his native India, England and South Africa but spent the majority of this period in South Africa, encouraging Indians to take different kinds of action and beginning to think through his ideas on resistance. In 1904 he set up a law office in Johannesburg and, when the Transvaal government passed a law in 1907 requiring all Indians to register and be fingerprinted, Gandhi put into operation for the first time a process of resistance which he called *satyagraha*.

The word *satyagraha* is made up of two Gujarati words and carries the ideas of truth and force or essence of being. It has been variously translated or described in English as "non-violent struggle," "militant non-violence" and even "war without violence" (Sharp, 1979, 4, 23, 24). Writing of that first campaign, Woodcock (1972, 39) says that Gandhi wanted to offer resistance by people who were not afraid to be violent but who chose to be nonviolent. It was to be overt resistance without hostility. The aims would be limited and clearly articulated, and the tactics used to achieve them would be announced ahead of time. One of the aims would be to convert the opponent by the example of "suffering willingly endured." Gandhi distinguished between passive resistance, which he saw as "a resistance of the weak," and satyagraha, which he described as "resistance of the brave" (Sharp, 1979, 99, 105).

The campaign lasted from 1907 to 1914. Tactics included picketing, filling the jails by sending large numbers of traders without licenses into the streets, organizing huge gatherings at which registration cards were burned, coordinating tax strikes and industrial strikes, and organizing demonstrations and marches by women, who were arrested in the hundreds, again creating a bureaucratic nightmare for the authorities. Gandhi was arrested twice over this period. The government responded violently to a strike by miners, and Gandhi held a mass meeting to mourn those who were killed. At that meeting he abandoned European dress and appeared shaven and barefoot. At a key moment Gandhi called off a satyagraha so as not to clash with a strike by railway workers, winning their sympathy and the admiration of many others. Public opinion now forced the South African authorities to negotiate and in 1914 the Indian Relief Act was passed, removing discriminatory laws affecting Indians.

Gandhi returned to the much vaster arena of India where, from 1914 to independence in 1947 and his assassination in 1948, he promoted his form of nonviolent activism as a means of struggle, as a way of life, and even as a means of defense for a whole country and an alternative to war. He had no desire for political leadership in conventional terms. However, during that period he won both national and international recognition as a political force to be reckoned with and viceroys in India and even the government in London were obliged to deal directly with him.

Gandhi proved an astute political strategist, able to inspire, mobilize, organize and choose the right historical moment. He engaged in localized satyagraha, enlisting and training local lawyers and others as activists whom he called *satyagrahis*, organizing strikes and protests, and fasting in order to strengthen his supporters' resolve and shame his opponents, whether they were mill owners or the local British authorities, into making concessions. In 1919 he coordinated his first national satyagraha against the Rowlatt Act, a law which introduced draconian penalties for sedition and the possession of seditious materials. Committees were set up all over India to manage the campaign. Merchants closed their shops and workers stopped work. Satyagrahis offered themselves for arrest by breaking one of a list of oppressive laws, such as contravening the salt tax law by making salt on the seashore, or selling banned texts and an unregistered newspaper Gandhi had produced for that purpose. Millions of Indians took part. The authorities responded in some places with violence, but in many other places the campaign was conducted without violence and demonstrated just how widespread the nationalist movement was. The Rowlatt Act was never invoked.

Gandhi was arrested and imprisoned in 1922, released in 1924 and briefly assumed the presidency of the Indian National Congress for a year. In 1927 he organized another major satyagraha. The British government had set up a commission on possible constitutional changes without consulting the Indians. In keeping with his belief that satyagraha should have a limited objective, Gandhi chose not to target the commission but to attack the overtaxing of peasants in the area of Bardoli. The satyagraha took the form of a tax strike. Some 84,000 peasants in the area withheld their taxes. Satyagrahis, merchants and workers across the country took action in support. Initially the government responded by making large numbers of arrests but it finally conceded, released everyone who had been arrested and, after an inquiry, reduced taxes on the peasant farmers and paid compensation to people whose goods had been seized.

In 1929 the Indian National Congress called for complete severance from Britain and the British Empire and Gandhi was appointed to lead another nationwide satyagraha. This time he surprised even his close allies by opting instead for an apparently individual satyagraha. On January 26, 1930, he published the Indian

Declaration of Independence, and on March 12 he began what became known as his salt march. Again he chose an apparently limited objective, to walk the 241 miles from Sabarmati Ashram to Dandi on the coast where he would gather up salt and so break the salt tax law. He set off with seventy-nine volunteers but was quickly accompanied by a crowd, which grew as the days passed. Gandhi had notified the viceroy of his intended march and the viceroy had decided not to intervene, thinking the march would fail. Indian, then British and American, journalists began reporting the march. On April 6 Gandhi reached the coast and, watched by thousands, picked up a piece of salt. This symbolic act was followed by action across India. People began harvesting and selling salt themselves, Indian legislators and officials resigned from their posts, people stopped work, newspapers ceased publication rather than accept censorship, and there were processions and demonstrations under the guidance of satyagrahis which for the first time were joined by large numbers of women. The government arrested thousands of people, and on May 4 arrested Gandhi. Noncooperation continued, and in January 1931 the viceroy called Gandhi to a meeting at which they agreed to a face-saving pact allowing the private production of salt, releasing the tens of thousands of people who had been imprisoned, and agreeing to round-table talks to be held in London to discuss giving constitutional government to India. In 1935 Indians were given self-government at the provincial level. The Indian population had been stirred by the events surrounding the salt march, and the English population had been made aware of some of the injustices perpetrated in India in their name.

For the remainder of the 1930s Gandhi withdrew from the immediate struggle for independence and concentrated on trying to improve the status and condition of the "untouchables" in the Indian caste system. He returned to mainstream Indian politics in the early 1940s. Britain had taken India into the Second World War without consulting the provincial governments. These governments resigned, and the Indian National Congress offered to cooperate with Britain but only in return for complete independence. The viceroy refused and the congress asked Gandhi to organize another satyagraha. This time Gandhi organized a scheme of disobedience in which, one by one, Indian leaders defied a British regulation which prevented them from expressing their views on the war. The disobedience snowballed and thousands were arrested. Following Gandhi's rejection of a British compromise, he and other leaders of the congress were arrested and interned. Gandhi was released in 1944, and from then until his death he worked to bring about an independence for India which would involve a reconciliation of the Hindu and Muslim sectors of the population and so avoid partition into two countries. In this he was unsuccessful, but on several occasions he intervened personally to stop intercommunal violence. In doing this he earned enemies as well as friends. His last days were spent in Delhi, where he had fasted and successfully brought to an end a period of terrible violence against minority communities. He was shot and killed as he was walking to a prayer meeting in the late afternoon of January 30, 1948 (Woodcock, 1972).

In what is almost a throwaway line in his biography of Gandhi, George Woodcock (1972, 95) writes: "Largely through his influence the British had grown weary of their empire." Nearly thirty years of recurring satyagraha led by this small, infuriating, eccentric, charismatic man dressed in his loincloth and with his "thin, small voice" and his millions of followers had simply become too much. To further infuriate the colonial power, no two instances of satyagraha were the same. This was in keeping with Gandhi's view of life itself as a continual experiment.

> Gandhi never set out to develop a fixed and final doctrine, but emphasized that his practice of *ahimsa* or nonviolence was always experimental, that his political struggle like his personal life was part of a continuing quest for truth as manifested existentially, a quest that could never end because human understanding was incapable of comprehending the absolute [Woodcock, 1972, 10].

Gandhi inspired in the leaders of the Indian National Congress, in hundreds of thousands of merchants and in millions of workers and peasants a mood, an attitude, a state of mind, a stance of continuous, creative rebelliousness. In doing so he challenged the authority of the largest empire in the world, building that challenge on an understanding that those in authority ruled only by virtue of the acquiescence, willing or enforced, of the population. By withdrawing the population's cooperation he cut off the most important source of the authorities' power. When the government responded to nonviolent action with severe repression, as it did on several occasions, it failed to strengthen its position but it did succeed in alienating ever more Indians and increasing doubts in England. Sharp (1979, 11) describes satyagraha as "a kind of political jiu-jitsu which generated the maximum Indian strength while using British strength to their own disadvantage."

In keeping with his idea of satyagraha as a continual experiment, Gandhi conducted each campaign carefully, and was always ready to call a satyagraha off if necessary, often achieving positive results in the process. In the first nationwide satyagraha, violent clashes occurred where there were no satyagrahis to maintain nonviolence in the face of assault. In later campaigns Gandhi used more volunteers and required of them "a discipline as rigorous as that of any guerilla movement" (Woodcock, 1972, 11). With this core of volunteers in place, he could then expect discipline from everyone in the campaign.

> There is no prima facie reason why under non-violence the mass . . . should be incapable of showing the discipline which in organized warfare a fighting force normally does [Gandhi cited in Sharp, 1979, 94].

Gandhi did not call for revolution in the form of a sudden and violent upheaval, but the rebelliousness he inspired was nonetheless revolutionary. Woodcock explains this apparent paradox:

Satyagraha accepts certain essential principles as beyond dispute, but its exponents develop these principles experimentally in the world of action where everything is relative and mutable, and in this sense the Gandhian philosophy is one of endless becoming, which makes it—in a somewhat different way from left-wing Marxism—a doctrine of permanent revolution [Woodcock, 1972, 79].

These ideas of permanent revolution and experiment are to be found in Gandhi's assertion that satyagraha should be a "creed," that is, a way of thinking and acting to be engaged in throughout life, and not a "policy" taken up for a defined political end (Sharp, 1979, 105). Gandhi himself did not have a set of clearly formulated ends in mind. He was not driven by a defined ideology, nor was he striving to establish some ideal form of society (Woodcock, 1972, 79). The means had value in themselves. The ends would emerge from the means and be consistent with them. So if the means were morally just, the ends would be too (Sharp, 1979, 69). But if Gandhi was open-minded about the ends, he had no doubts about the means. What was important above all else was to adopt a stance of dynamic, continuous, and generative rebelliousness.

3

INSPIRING REBELLIOUSNESS

Peaceful Protest

When hundreds of thousands of people took to the streets across Australia to demonstrate against the country's involvement in the war on Iraq, the demonstrations were peaceful and the demonstrators were for the most part law-abiding. Two of the marches were organized with schoolchildren as the main participants and they were boisterous. Some young men threw punches when a police officer pulled a Muslim girl's headscarf off, and some sections of the mass media used the word *violence* in their reports of the incident, but there was no damage to property and no one was injured. The organizers of the larger-scale demonstrations arranged the routes of the marches and the venues for the speeches in consultation with the police, and provided volunteer marshals to help control the crowds. When more people than were expected—many more—came to a march in Sydney, the organizers changed the route of the march, again in consultation with the police, and in the press the following day the police commissioner praised the demonstrators for their good behavior.

The commissioner had every right to be pleased since these kinds of so-called protest can actually reinforce the power of those people already in authority. Max Weber (1968, 53) defines power as the probability that a person or a number of people will be able to carry out their own will despite resistance. If we accept this definition, then an orderly, nonrebellious demonstration actually provides the resistance necessary for those in power to publicly display that power. They can either ignore the demands of the demonstrators, showing how unassailable their position is, or they can magnanimously concede, showing for all to see that it is they, the powerful, who have the capacity to respond to the demonstrators' demands and so resolve the conflict.

How, then, can we participate in the affairs of our community, state, country and world in ways which will prevent the authorities from so nonchalantly displaying their power? How can we unsettle those in power and actually make them take heed? As activist educators, how can we inspire rebelliousness?

Stories

We can tell stories. These stories do not need to be long. Their job is to illustrate a point upon which we can help people reflect and then move on to more learning.

We can tell stories of cultural rebelliousness. The story of the brigadier, the captain, the sentry and his pie will do. We can ask our learners: "Do you have similar stories?" "What does that tell us about the sentry?" "Was the sentry being mutinous?" "Should respect be earned?" and so on. Now we might tell the story of the march by those soldiers from the camp at Casula to Liverpool, drawing the distinction between individual and collective rebelliousness.

We can tell stories to encourage political rebelliousness. The story of the encounter between Rosa Parks and J. P. Blake, the bus driver, will do. We will need to give some background, but the story itself might concentrate on the actual exchange. Blake called out for the four people sitting in the row just behind the section reserved for whites to give up their seats. No one moved. Blake got out of his driver's seat and told them "more firmly" to move. The other three black people got up and moved to the back. Parks said she was not in the white section but in a no-man's land and did not have to move. Blake said that "the white section was where he said it was" (Branch, 1988, 129). It was in this instant that the civil rights movement in the United States was launched. Parks was not disputing the segregation of the seating in the bus. She had not taken a seat in the front section. Nor was she really making a point about the disputed area of seating. She was resisting the white driver's assumption of arbitrary power over the black people on the bus simply because he was white.

We can tell stories of systemic rebelliousness. My story of the librarian turned union official will do as a trigger. We can discuss his move from the calm and quiet environment of a library to the noise and dust and the sometimes crude and direct encounters with managers of open-cut mines and building sites. And we can speculate on the pleasure he found in preventing dangerous management practices, curbing the exploitation of migrant workers and getting the best deal he could for his members. We can look for other examples of systemic rebelliousness in watchdog organizations, the parliamentary activities of the Greens, independent advocacy groups like the National Council for Civil Liberties and the Australian Council of Social Services, and government agencies set up to monitor issues such as equity and human rights. We can examine the degree to which these different bodies have maintained a vigorous rebelliousness and the degree to which they have become domesticated. We can devise ways of rejuvenating the organizations that have become fixed in their ways, and we can dream up new organizations to monitor and challenge the actions of the powerful.

We can tell stories of rebelliousness leading to rebellion. Bryan Willis's story of the little bloke at the wheel of his car in Paris will do as a start. We can then expand the discussion to examine all the events in Paris in May 1968. Earlier in the year a commentator had written in one of the French papers that the French president and the French people were bored. Nothing was happening. How, just three months later, could the country have erupted into wide-scale rebellion? Just how stable is our own system? Could a sudden, unexpected disruption happen here? If our system is actually fragile, how might we protect it, and how might we use the fragility to trigger change? And just what do we want to protect, and just what do we want to change?

We can tell stories of rebelliousness leading to revolution. Gandhi's salt march will do this very nicely. We can describe this diminutive man in his loincloth and with his bamboo staff setting out from his ashram. We can describe how villagers along the way threw branches on the road for him to walk on, and how each night he addressed the ever-bigger crowds on the need for independence from Britain and the virtues of the moral life. We can describe how Indian commentators began comparing Gandhi's march with the epic journeys in the *Bhagavad Gita*. We can describe Gandhi's arrival at the coast, his ceremonial bathing and how Sarojini Naidu, the poet, raised her arms high and shouted, "Hail, Deliverer!" as Gandhi picked up the flake of salt. We can describe how Gandhi's defiance of British law unleashed acts of defiance across the country, and how in Peshawar men of a crack regiment, the Garhwali Rifles, refused to fire on the crowds, bringing back to the British authorities horrid memories of the Indian Mutiny (Woodcock, 1972, 73–75). We can acknowledge that another seventeen years passed before the British left India, but that Gandhi's salt march can be seen as the real beginning of that revolution. And we can ask ourselves and our learners who in our own country could command this kind of respect, and what kind of symbolic act would catch the nation's attention, inspire people to action and set in train events that might lead to significant change.

And there is no reason to stop there. We can imagine a perfect world, as a goal to strive for. We can ask who could command worldwide respect and speculate on what symbolic action she or he or they could take to prompt us to revolt against the excesses of the wealthy, the corrupt, the militaristic and the fanatics. What action could we take to make the populations of the world require of our leaders genuine efforts to combat poverty and genuine efforts to construct peace?

Using Frustration

Stories can make us laugh or cry. They can inspire or depress us. They can comfort or disturb us. Activist educators can use stories to evoke emotions and use those emotions to inspire rebelliousness. But sometimes we can make use of particular emotions or states of mind that are already there.

Rebelliousness, for example, can grow out of frustration. The process is not inevitable. Frustration can be a debilitating emotion. It comes about because we are constrained in some way and cannot have what we want or act as we wish. Clinical psychologist Stephen Diamond (1996, 25) describes frustration as "an existential concomitant to the human condition to which few—if any—are immune." If frustration is an experience common to us all, then it presents the activist educator with common opportunities to intervene, to prevent frustration from becoming a negative force, and to use it to inspire rebelliousness.

This process is likely to work best with a group of learners who share a common history, social class or community. The people in such a group might not know each other, but there would be some experience, characteristic or set of conditions that united them. We might be able to identify a shared frustration simply by asking, and then through a series of activities—individual reflection, pair work, small-group work and then a full discussion—get people to articulate that frustration. In all likelihood this process would not only help people express their frustration but also prompt them to begin exploring its causes. We would go on to identify what more we needed to know to be sure of these causes and to fully understand them. We might have to establish research projects and research groups. Research in a community or social action context is rarely disassociated from action, so this phase might well lead us into thinking about action, using the techniques of action research, and possibly engaging in action.

In the early 1970s I took up a post in an adult education institute in inner London and found myself able to set up evening courses on virtually any issue for which there might be a demand. The courses were noncredit and had no fixed curriculum, and I often appointed coordinators who were passionate about a cause and encouraged them to present courses which were as one-sided as they liked. Over the following few years I developed a program of "special studies" which included courses on "Alternative Societies," "Black Experience," "Women's Liberation," "Civil Liberties," "Our Planet," "Gay Studies" (renamed "Homosexuality-Changing Attitudes" after a struggle with the educational authorities), "Alternative Education," and "Irish Studies." The courses were successful, drawing good enrollments, creating vigorous discussion and inspiring some of the participants to engage in action. The "Alternative Societies" course spawned a welfare-rights group. The "Women's Liberation" course turned into a women's consciousness-raising group. And participants in the "Our Planet" course formed the West London Friends of the Earth. On reflection some thirty years later I realize that a number of these courses were constructed on a couple of associated frustrations. The coordinators and speakers were often people who had been frustrated by their lack of opportunity to have their voices heard, and the participants were often people who suspected they had been prevented from hearing the real story.

In these "special studies" courses the frustrations were already openly acknowledged, and the rebelliousness of spirit in both the speakers and the participants was usually already there. Those action groups formed quickly and easily. But sometimes frustration can be deeply embedded, and getting people to foreground and acknowledge it can be difficult. The frustration may express itself obliquely in conflict and dysfunction, or it may be denied and disguised in unproductive "busyness." We may have to get people to do a lot of talking. We may have to get people to do a lot of talking to each other. We may need to get them to tell their stories, and retell them. We may need to use role play and pose our questions obliquely during the debriefing. We might use metaphor.

I stumbled upon a profound frustration when using metaphors. The coordinator of a community center asked two of us to run a day-long problem-solving workshop for the center's management committee and staff. She told us that the center was close to dysfunctional. There were tensions within the management committee, and between the committee, whose members were volunteers, and the workers, who were paid. There were serious differences within the professional staff over philosophy and process. The center's own activities were on the wane, and some wanted to rebuild the center with a focus on direct action. Others seemed content to reduce the center's role to that of auspicing, that is, channeling funds to smaller community organizations.

We prepared for the day by interviewing as many of the workers and members of the management committee as possible and by reading through some of the center's files. When the day came, we had met most of the twenty-two people present and felt confident enough to forgo introductions. Without preamble I said that I had read the center's annual reports for the past few years and had formed an image of the organization as a ship. The ship had good steerage up and was cleaving its way through heavy seas, untroubled by the cross-currents or the occasional massive wave. Everything on board was in order. The brasswork was polished and the paint-work was spic-and-span. The captain was on the bridge, clearly in control and looking smart in his uniform. The navigator was in the navigation room doing his thing. In the engine room the engines were a poetry of motion and the engineer was there in his overalls, wiping his hands with a barely stained oilcloth because he had nothing else to do.

It may have been an unexpected start to the workshop but people did seem to be listening. I did not allow any time for a reaction and went straight on. But, I said, my colleague and I had also met and interviewed quite a number of the people present, and the image we had formed from those encounters was different. Again it was of a ship, but this time the ship had just enough steerage up to stop it from foundering. The brass was tarnished, and you could see rust everywhere. On the bridge the captain was drunk. The engine was beginning to come apart and the engineer did not know what to do. And the navigator had fallen overboard a couple of weeks ago.

My colleague wondered aloud if the listeners had any reactions to my images, and immediately someone said the center was not like that. Not like what? *The second image.* Is it like the first one? *Well, no.* So what is your organization really like? Some people seemed put out, angered even, by the bluntness of our image, and some may have been unsettled by the implication that the annual reports were fabrications. The discussion was animated. We let it run for a while and then interrupted, saying that if they did not like either of our images could they come up with their own? We asked them to break into groups and spend some time trying to find an image which worked.

Some twenty-five minutes later we came back into plenary session and heard the different images the groups had devised. When I ask for metaphors of an organization, I almost invariably get the image of a tightrope walker. I sometimes prevent this by giving it as an example of a metaphor when I am setting the exercise up. But I had not done so this time and, sure enough, the first group we asked said that their organization was like a tightrope walker. In an exercise like this the facilitator's job is to help people unpack their metaphors. My colleague and I began asking the group questions. Where is the tightrope walker? *In a circus.* Is the rope high up or one of those low, loose ropes close to the ground on which the walker sways from side to side? *It's a highwire.* Is the tightrope walker a man or a woman? *A woman.* How is she dressed? And so on. Sometimes in this kind of exercise a group has to go into a huddle before responding. They are refining the metaphor, but they know they are also revealing attitudes and information about the organization. In the process of unpacking, a moment usually comes when the discussion slips away from the metaphor and back into the real world. In this case the slippage occurred when I asked: "Is there a safety net?" The reply was immediate: *There was until the new gov-*

ernment was elected. The discussion may return briefly to the metaphor, but it usually now becomes wholly about the real world. If the exercise has been successful, then the discussion in this final phase will be franker and more productive because it is informed by the revelations, admissions and insights provided through the metaphor.

We helped the first group unpack their metaphor and then did the same for the next. We came to the final group and asked them what image they had chosen. This group was made up of the four Aboriginal workers employed at the center. We had let the groups form themselves and these four workers had quickly grouped together. Now one of them said they had not come up with an image. All they had done was talk. That's fine, my colleague said. Is there anything from your discussion you want to tell the rest of us? *Yes*, another from the group said, *we don't feel we can always do what we want. Sometimes we feel we are being told what to do and say*. But isn't that a bit like an actor in a play? *Maybe*. Can we go with the idea of an actor for a minute? *Maybe*. For example, if you are in a play, what kind of theater are you in? Is it a hall or more like a theater in the round? *It's in the round*. Is the audience on the same level as you or looking down at you? The rest of the people in the room were silent. *Looking down*. So if you sometimes feel as if you are speaking someone else's lines, who is writing them for you? *They are*, said one of Aboriginal workers, indicating everyone else in the room.

We had planned a number of different exercises and we did use some of them, particularly towards the end of the workshop, in order to tie things up a little, but the initial images had thrown up enough problems to keep people discussing for the rest of the day.

Miracles rarely happen as a result of workshops like this one. Changes may occur but they are usually some time down the track, and you can never be sure what part the workshop played in bringing them about. But my colleague and I did hear from the coordinator some weeks later that the chair of the management committee had resigned almost immediately after the workshop, that the management committee seemed to be functioning better, and that most of the workers at the center felt that the air had been cleared.

Channeling Dismay

There will be times when we can channel dismay into rebellious-ness. Dismay, too, can be a disabling emotion, more powerful and more sudden in its appearance than frustration. Dismay is a mixture of distress, fear and guilt, and our response is often flight or denial. So we drop the antique china plate and look in dismay at the shattered pieces on the kitchen floor. We are shocked by the gravity and the unexpectedness of the accident. We are immobilized, first by the shock and then, for some at least, by an internal struggle against the temptation to flee. This period of immobilization is often followed by intense action, in which we dispose of the evidence and make our getaway, or in which we own up to the disaster and set about making reparations. The impulse to flee is strong. A driver fleeing from an accident may not be inherently evil but simply disoriented by the accident and momentarily overtaken by dismay.

Dismay can occur in contexts other than a kitchen accident or a car crash. A young man plunged to his death from the roof of a storage shed under construction. He was not wearing a safety harness. People are regularly killed and injured at work and, although we should not accept a single death or injury in a workplace, sadly we often resign ourselves to these deaths, just as we do to the death toll on the roads. However, there were aspects of this young man's death that caused dismay rather than resignation. The young man was sixteen. He had left school in order to help with his family's finances. He was killed on his third day in the job. And there were allegations of negligence.

A call went out for action. I received an e-mail from my union urging its members to support the building unions at a midmorning rally in the center of Sydney. The e-mail said that the young man had deserved to live and that the building unions intended to ensure justice for him, his family and friends. It went on:

> Unions have been fighting for a long time for the implementation
> of a crime of industrial manslaughter. . . . We want laws that ensure

that if workers are killed due to negligence, bosses can and will be jailed. In New South Wales one worker dies every two days from accidents and workplace diseases. Enough is enough.

Some may be disturbed by the union movement's exploitation of this young man's death. But people had reacted with dismay rather than denial, and the trade unions used this dismay to engage in a public education campaign and urge their members to action.

Environmentalists in Australia have used dismay. In the campaign to save Fraser Island in Queensland in the 1970s and 1980s, adult educator and activist Ian Sinclair distributed aerial photographs of the devastation being caused by sand mining operations. In the campaign to stop the damming of the Franklin River in southern Tasmania, Bob Brown, a doctor turned full-time environmental activist, toured the country showing films of the wilderness under threat. The aim in each case was to cause dismay in the form of distress at the destruction or potential destruction, fear of a future in which this kind of destruction might be rampant, and guilt over our previous inaction. Sinclair backed up the aerial photographs with tours of Fraser Island for politicians, community leaders and activists so that they could experience at first hand the environment under threat. Brown and the Wilderness Society of which he was president established a blockade at the site of the dam, and hundreds of people from all over Australia and beyond traveled deep into the wilderness to engage in nonviolent direct action to prevent the dam from being built. Both campaigns channeled dismay into rebelliousness, and both were ultimately successful in saving areas of great natural beauty and ecological significance (MacKinnon, 2004).

Focusing Anger

We can inspire rebelliousness by focusing anger. Some of the processes may sound the same as those we use when getting people to express their frustration or channel their dismay, but frustration, dismay and anger are different emotions. Frustration is more a state of mind, and has usually come about as a result of some apparently intractable set of conditions. It can, in the first instance, render us passive. Dismay is an intense emotion often in response to an unanticipated event and can, in the first instance, immobilize us. Anger, however, is more often a response to something someone has done and is directed at the people we believe to be responsible. We will often know their names. Certainly anger can result in a brooding physical stasis, but our minds will run wild as we imagine all manner of things we might do. And, of course, anger can transmute into rage and erupt into action. That action may be disruptive but it will be the dynamic expression of a desire, a need, to have an impact on the people and the world around us.

The challenge for the activist educator is to help people translate their anger into forms of action whose impact will be useful. This educational activity has nothing to do with the kinds of workshop where people are sent into soundproofed rooms to pummel mattresses, or out into the wilderness to scream. Those workshops are about dissipating anger. Nor does this educational activity have much to do with anger management courses prescribed by doctors, social workers or magistrates for people whose anger has rendered them violent. Those courses are about getting dysfunctional people to cope and, more importantly, to stop them from destroying the lives of others.

Using anger to inspire rebelliousness is a meticulous activity. It involves fully functional people and a calculated encounter between emotion and intellect. One of the lowest-paid workers in a large organization was sacked. The sacking had been eighteen months coming. The worker, a quiet, unassuming man in his mid-thirties, was the general "gofer" in a particular section of the organization. He was the person colleagues asked to help carry things, move furniture, get recalcitrant printers and copiers working, set up displays and deal with minor computer glitches. The front line staff particularly appreciated him.

When it first became clear the worker was under threat, a number of his colleagues wrote letters of protest, but the organization ground its way on through various stages of warning, increasing the man's distress and making him retreat further into his shell. The organization sacked the man, but was forced by his union to keep him on through an internal appeals process. The organization then really sacked him.

A meeting was called and some thirty of the man's colleagues attended. The mood of the meeting was one of anger, and the organizers had to take the meeting through a number of stages. First they had to allow people to vent their individual anger. A number of people expressed their disgust at the treatment of this quiet man. One person talked of "evil." Then the organizers had to translate those individual expressions of anger into a coherent discussion and gauge the degree of collective anger. The discussion indicated that the anger was shared and that there was a consensus in the room. Then the organizers had to get the meeting to make a calculated collective decision on action. One person wanted to isolate the man's two immediate administrative superiors and refuse to work with them. Others argued that such an action would only increase the malaise that the man's sacking had created and that any action decided on had to be aimed at getting the man reinstated or effectively compensated. Others wanted to expose the perceived organizational weaknesses which had brought this situation about. And a number of people wanted the action to include strategies for reestablishing a spirit of goodwill in the organization. The meeting unanimously agreed to send a protest to the chief executive officer, and it is likely that this action contributed to a severance agreement brokered by the union and deemed satisfactory by the man at the center of the storm.

Anger and Rage

The organizers used people's anger to good effect, but they also had to make sure that it did not derail the meeting. Anger can be a destructive force, and when it manifests itself as rage it can become a form of temporary insanity. Diamond writes about rage in language normally reserved for descriptions of extreme religious experience or the effects of mind-bending drugs:

> To feel rage fully, to be totally filled with it, even temporarily overcome or possessed by it, is to know a type of ecstasy—a momentary loss of voluntary control, social inhibition, and self discipline; a surrender to animal instinct, as occurs during sexual orgasm; a direct— and sometimes purposely sought after—*participation mystique* in the daimonic powers of nature [Diamond, 1996, 15].

In Western European culture, anger and rage have not always been distinguished one from the other, and anger has often been seen as an emotion to be feared and therefore curbed. Plato, writing in Athens in the fourth century BCE, used an image of a charioteer and two horses to reflect the three aspects of the soul. One horse is beautiful, "upright and clean-limbed." The other is ugly, with "grey bloodshot eye," recalcitrant and uncooperative, "the mate of insolence and knavery." The charioteer represents reason, the beautiful horse the nobler aspects of the human spirit, and the ugly horse the ignoble impulses such as anger. To approach an object of his desire the charioteer must bring the recalcitrant horse under control and make it work alongside the other (Plato, 1975, 337–339). Seneca, in Rome in the first years of the first century CE, wrote of ways of "curing" anger. He described anger as "the most hideous and frenzied of all emotions" and argued that it was caused by unmet expectations, some of which were false or unattainable. He advocated a form of reasoned pessimism in which we examined our expectations, abandoned those we could not achieve, and anticipated disappointment and setback in those we could (de Botton, 2000). In Christian teaching anger was a sin, and religious devotion was seen as a way of overcoming it. In the age of the Enlightenment philosophers extolled the virtues of "the rational man"—in control of himself and his affairs and divorced from the cruder emotions. And already in this book I have sung the praises of Gandhi, who argued that a person swayed by passions such as anger would never find the truth. "And so," says social psychologist Carol Tavris (1982, 29), "for most of the twenty-five hundred years since Plato, the healthy individual was someone who did not fly off the handle, who was not, in Hamlet's felicitous phrase, passion's slave." Reason was placed in opposition to anger and given the job, if we return to the image of the charioteer, of reining it in and breaking its spirit.

Implicit in these ideas are the beliefs that human beings and beasts differ and that the difference is to be found in our use of reason and our ability to control emotion. But, as Tavris points out, Darwin muddied the waters. Charles Darwin's theory of natural selection and evolution applied to human beings and to beasts. We were animals too. In *The Expression of the Emotions in Man and Animals* Darwin (1965, 12) states that some of our expressions of emotion, "such as the bristling of the hair under the influence of extreme terror, or the uncovering of the teeth under that of furious rage, can hardly be understood, except in the belief that man once existed in a much lower and animal-like condition." Rage, that state of extreme emotion when we turn and confront our enemy with the intention of using our "utmost powers" to defend ourselves, is a basic emotion "animals of all kinds" use as a mechanism in our struggle for survival (Darwin, 1965, 74).

Darwin's ideas allowed Diamond 124 years later to argue that rage and anger are part of our makeup and to speak of rage as a positive existential experience:

> To feel real rage is to feel life pared down to its purest, simplest state: the rousing, rapturous flush of unfettered vitality, pristine purpose, and unshakeable will. It is at such moments that we are most alive [Diamond, 1996, 15].

If feeling anger is a natural human experience, then we need not be ashamed of it, nor try to suppress every expression of it. There will be times when anger, even intense anger, is justifiable. We may be maddened by an injustice, outraged at an irrational, dangerous or selfish act, or affronted by some absurdity. There are political leaders, bosses, gangs and individuals, cheats, abusers, molesters and polluters who do things about which it would be unnatural *not* to be angered.

Calculated and Creative Anger

Diamond (1996, 11) argues that rage occurs at a level of absolute intensity, whereas anger can exist in varying intensities. He uses the images of an "on-off switch" for rage and a "dimmer switch" for anger, suggesting that we can exercise control over anger but not so easily over rage. Diamond's ideas are borne out by the variety of words and phrases available to describe different intensities of anger. A person can be furious, annoyed or simply irritated, enraged, riled, pissed off or put out. And once we look at the language we can see that there are phrases to describe different types of anger as well. We can talk about experiencing a "white-hot anger" or "an icy anger," both equally intense but different in kind.

Tavris argues that Darwin was wrong to see rage in animals and anger in human beings as the same phenomenon, and in doing so echoes Diamond's ideas on control. Human beings, she says, can choose to simulate anger when we are not angry. We can choose to hide our anger behind a smile. We can grow angry at symbols and memories as well as at a current menace or danger. Even when our anger is apparently spontaneous, we have made a judgment—that a person's actions are insulting, or offensive, or unjust, or morally wrong:

> Human anger is far more intricate and serves many more purposes than the rage reflex of lower animals. We do not need to deny our mammalian, primate heritage, but we do not need to reduce ourselves to it either. Judgement and choice distinguish human beings from other species; judgement and choice are the hallmarks of human anger [Tavris, 1982, 36].

Once we recognize that anger involves judgment, we can see it is as a significant, and calculated, part of our human existence:

Anger therefore is as much a political matter as a biological one. The decision to get angry has powerful consequences, whether anger is directed towards one's spouse or one's government. Spouses and governments know this. They know that anger is ultimately an emphatic message: *Pay attention to me. I don't like what you are doing. Restore my pride. You're in my way. Danger. Give me justice* [Tavris, 1982, 45; italics in original].

Rage and anger can fuel the creative drive. "There exists as close (albeit much less obvious) a correlation between anger, rage and *creativity* as there does between anger, rage and *evil*," says Diamond (1996, 259; italics in original). He chooses to study this correlation in creative artists, but creativity is not limited to the arts, and we can see anger and rage motivating creative people in politics, sports, charitable service and social action. The captain of the Australian rugby team was criticized widely in the press. He had commented that strategy and skill were more important than passion in the game. Commentators took him to task, arguing that passion (and for passion read a simulation of the kind of rage Darwin was talking about) was far and away the most important element of this tough, bruising body-contact sport. Between two evenly matched teams, they argued, passion provided the inspired split-second judgments, the creative movements, which allowed one team to open up the play and breach the other team's defenses.

Using Anger

Activist educators can help people develop, articulate and explore their anger. There may even be moments when they can help people draw upon the energizing ecstasy of their rage. To make such experiences constructive, educators must help people manage this encounter between emotion and intellect. They can help people explore the causes of their anger, review the judgments upon which they have constructed their anger, and choose the level and kind of anger which will serve their rebelliousness. The process will be a delicate one in which educators seek to release and at the same time focus the passion and creativity of a potentially wayward emotion.

Both The Australian Manufacturing Workers Union and the Education and Campaign Unit of the Australian Council of Trade Unions run courses for union organizers and workplace activists in which they teach a three-stage organizing model described as "Anger-Hope-Action." Under the heading of Anger, the trainers and course participants examine formal and informal (visible and invisible) ways of getting workers in a particular workplace to name and analyze issues about which they feel most angry and then to clarify which of these issues are winnable. Under the heading of Hope, they examine ways of setting in place structures which enable effective communication in the workplace and then using the structures to educate the workers about what can be done to deal with the issues. And under the heading of Action, they examine ways of mobilizing members and potential members in that workplace to take collective action.

Jane Thompson, an English adult educator, has used anger to motivate learning. In the 1980s, while working out of the University of Southampton, she organized a "Second Chance for Women" course and helped establish the Southampton Women's Education Centre where women could learn "free from male control" (Thompson, 1988). For the Second Chance course, Thompson recruited only working-class women. The course met one day a week over a year. The participants studied themes in the morning and organized workshops in the afternoon. The study of themes—such as women and health, employment and the economy, and the politics of welfare—was rigorous and involved extensive reading, discussion and debate. The workshops were equally demanding but more practical, and included a writing workshop, an oral "herstory group" and a radio workshop. The starting point was always the women's own experience, which they often expressed in scarifying accounts of domestic and other kinds of violence, private and public sexism, and bureaucratic indifference, arrogance and injustice. Early on Thompson acknowledged the place of anger in her work, and welcomed it. "These are angry statements from women usually encouraged to keep quiet . . ." and, in a phrase which captures elements of both her educational philosophy and method, she adds that the anger was "focused with the precision that has the power to clarify and liberate us from our delusion" (1983, 165).

Thompson continued to use anger focused with precision at Ruskin College in Oxford during the 1990s in courses she conducted for women who came from working-class, trade union and community activist contexts. And more recently she used the same approach for women in courses organized by the General Federation of Trade Unions, and for The Women's Group, which met at the Rosemount Resource Centre in Derry in Northern Ireland. In her writing Thompson examines concepts of knowledge. In part her project is to reclaim knowledge for women, that is, to include women and the concerns, rights and achievements of women in our accumulated knowledge (Thompson, 1983). But she is concerned with generating "really useful knowledge" in the place of "useful knowledge" and in doing so she challenges the conventional forms of knowledge discovery, analysis and theory formulation (Thompson, 1988; 1997). She describes positivist and dialectical forms of analysis as limiting (Thompson, 2000, 92). She attacks the idea that knowledge from experience and struggle in everyday life "can only be legitimised when accorded the status of theory" (2000, 94). And she affirms the individual, passionate and personal statements that she helps women articulate as equally, if not more, legitimate ways of knowing. She sees hope (in the face of the political shift to the right) in "creative anger," "disaffection" and "oppositional culture" (2000, 61) and acknowledges that she has set out in her educational work to encourage "true rebellion" (Thompson, 1988, 199–200) and "irreverence, imagination and subversion" (Thompson, 2000, 94). In the concluding chapter of a book which can be seen—in part at least—as a critical review of thirty years' work as an activist educator, Thompson reaffirms her use of anger. She argues that the buzzwords of the New Left such as "inclusion" and "exclusion" may breed confusion, and goes on:

It would be more appropriate to begin from a sense of outrage that—
in the midst of relative affluence, enhanced opportunities and
increased expectations—the "price worth paying" still seems to depend on one third of the population being managed or contained on
the fringes of the good life, in ways that hold them individually
responsible for remedying their own situation [Thompson, 2000,
182].

Defining the Enemy

When people are angry, they are often angry *at* someone. They see
that person or those persons as the enemy, and we can inspire rebelliousness by helping people examine and more clearly define that
enemy.

In an earlier book (Newman, 1994) I argued that a lot of adult
education is simply too nice, too self-centered, or too concerned
with maintaining the status quo. Liberal adult education in the
form of evening courses in pottery or literature is concerned with a
genteel kind of personal enrichment. Courses and workshops on
self-esteem, public speaking, empathy, relationships, communication skills, conflict resolution and the like are concerned with people's individual concerns, therapy and personal growth. Vocational
courses, human resource development programs and industrial
training—now often subsumed under the sometimes vacuous rubric
of "organizational learning"—are concerned with helping people
advance in their personal careers, or with training people to meet
the objectives of an enterprise or corporation. And higher education is increasingly being urged (or, in Australia, pressured) by
government to more directly serve the interests of business and
the state.

But if we are to engage in learning in order to act on and change
our social or political world, then we need to examine who is trying
to lay our futures out for us, who is telling us what we should and
should not do, who is holding us back, and who is preventing us

from acting effectively in our own and in others' interests. We need to do our learning by identifying and naming the wielders of power, analyzing the kinds of power they hold and, where we deem that power to be malign, examining the ways they use it. Effective learning will be done by defining the enemy.

I argued for this approach as an antidote to the learner-centered focus of much of the adult learning theory from the 1960s on, and as an antidote to the idea—fostered by writers on experiential and transformative learning in the 1980s and 1990s—that learners can start best by looking at themselves. In the process of learning by defining the enemy, we look outside ourselves and try to understand the struggles confronting us. We scrutinize our enemies. We examine their weaknesses and their strengths, the value systems according to which they operate, their histories and their current activities and, as far as possible, their intentions. Only then do we study ourselves. And we do not look at ourselves in some semispiritual belief that by knowing ourselves we will know others, nor according to some pathology model of education whereby we search for and own up to supposed weaknesses. We examine ourselves with the pragmatic purpose of equipping ourselves to defy our enemies.

4

DEFIANCE, CHOICE AND CONSCIOUSNESS

Instilling Purpose

Rebelliousness is more a state of mind than of action. And it is a state of mind that can lack focus. During May 1968 in France the established left-wing parties and unions never wholeheartedly fell in with the students and young people in the streets. Many seasoned political thinkers were skeptical because of the lack of articulated policy and organizational structure behind the rioting, and because of what my friend Bruno describes as the party atmosphere of it all. Slogans such as "It is forbidden to forbid," "All power to the imagination" and "Be realistic: demand the impossible" may have expressed a glorious rebelliousness but they did not inspire confidence. "For some," McMillan comments (1992, 182), "May 1968 was not a revolutionary situation but a psychodrama." And a number of the hard-line left-wingers in the Communist Party of France (PCF) and the Workers Confederation (CGT) turned away from this exuberant self-indulgence in contempt.

Defiance is more thoughtful than rebelliousness. We normally defy somebody identifiable—our parents, our teachers, our bosses or our government—and the actions we take to express that defiance are commonly calculated ones. If we are to turn rebelliousness into defiance, we need to instill purpose into it. We may be rebellious by nature, culture or inclination, but we have to choose to be defiant.

Choice

One of my favorite quotes is this passage by the South African philosopher Rick Turner:

> Human beings can choose. They are not sucked into the future by stimuli to which they have to respond in specific ways. Rather human beings are continually making choices. They can stand back and look at alternatives. Theoretically they can choose about anything. They can choose whether to live or to die; they can choose celibacy or promiscuity, voluntary poverty or the pursuit of wealth, ice cream or jelly [1980, 8].

This is one of those passages which, when I put it up on a screen in a classroom and read it out aloud, gives me prickles on the back of my neck.

Turner's straightforward prose has depth, conveyed through both the style and the substance. His opening sentence is succinct, brooks no dispute and has the hint of an imperative. The word "stimuli" in the second sentence mocks the use of pseudoscientific language in the human sciences. The use of the phrase "they can choose" three times in the last two sentences echoes the opening sentence and gives the passage a rhythm and unity. And the last sentence has a cadence to it, dropping away and lingering in the softness and ordinariness of the final phrase, making this reader at least go on thinking after the full stop has been reached.

Turner studied in France in the early 1960s, and the influences of two major French philosophers are there. Jean-Paul Sartre's twin assertions inform the whole paragraph. We have absolute freedom, and therefore absolute responsibility for our choice of values. There is something of Sartre's idea of "the vertigo of possibility" in Turner's statement that we "can choose about anything." The future is an empty (and daunting) space which we can fill in any way we want. There is something of Camus's idea of the absurd in Turner's juxtaposition in his final sentence of such ludicrously different concepts as celibacy and jelly. There is no external guide to help us give relative meaning to either but we will do so nonetheless. There is something of Sartre's contention that an object or concept achieves value as a result of our choosing it, rather than our choosing it because it has value. And in offering us the choice of whether to live or to die, Turner is echoing Camus's examination of suicide, a choice both he and Camus suggest is open to all of us (Sartre, 1984; Camus, 1975).

The passage I have quoted appears in a book Turner wrote in the early 1970s called *The Eye of the Needle*. In the book he condemns the South African apartheid government of the time and calls on black and white South Africans to think and act their way out of the racist regime. The book is calm, passionate, logical and inspired by turns. Turner uses conventional forms of philosophical discourse, argument *via negativa*, crushing irony, anger and the philosopher's appeal to common sense. He dreams, imagining a utopian South Africa as an ideal to strive for. And he is savagely realistic in his revision of the history of white settlement. He is grim because his subjects of oppression, violence and death are grim, and at times he is wildly funny, as he is in his description of a typical afternoon tea party of middle class whites.

Turner followed the events of May 1968 in France (Morphet, 1980), and therefore, I imagine, the intellectual ferment that followed. Douglas Kellner (2001, xviii) points out that Baudrillard, Lyotard, Derrida, Foucault and other French theorists "associated with postmodern theory" were all participants in May 1968, and certainly Michel Foucault had already published extensively by the time Turner began writing *The Eye of the Needle*. Superficially Turner's book has something of the irreverence, variety of forms of discourse and "playfulness of text" associated with some postmodern writing. But the book is "ultramodern" in purpose and content. It displays a commitment to social justice and calls for resolute and rational political action. Turner is arguing that those people opposing the apartheid regime can stand back and look at alternatives, that despite all the political constraints imposed upon them they can still act, and that they have it in their power to resist domination and to struggle for liberation. Turner's book is a hymn to choice.

Central to Turner's ideas is the existentialists' linking of being with choice. Human beings, Turner says (1980, 8), "are continually making choices." These choices may be fatuous and insignificant, they may be profoundly moral or they may be about the question of being itself. But making choices means continually assessing, restating or reworking our relationship with the world around us. It is part of being truly alive. By continually making choices—to go on reading, to stop reading, to sit, to stand, to listen, to argue, to go on living or to commit suicide—we continue to be aware. When we let ourselves be "sucked into the future" (Turner, 1980, 8), when we let ourselves be swept forward by events, when we let others make choices for us, when we let ourselves be objects of social history, then we become only partly conscious.

Consciousness

There seem to be different kinds of consciousness. There is a meditative kind, which has about it a gentleness and involves "a stilling of the mind's activity" and "a turning from the outer world to the inner" (Neville, 1989, 231). Meditators try to achieve this kind of consciousness by blocking out external influences. They can do this in a number of ways, including "gentle speculation on an idea, the deeply felt contemplation of an image, autogenic training, focus on a phrase or mantra, repose in a state of deep quiet without thoughts or images, [and] guided and spontaneous fantasies" (Neville, 1989, 235). Some of these forms of meditation are associated with physical stillness and others with gentle movement.

There is a contemplative consciousness. This too is a goal of some meditators, but here they do not try to block out external influences. Instead, they seek to replace the "conceptualising, typifying mind" with a powerful "noting" consciousness (McIntyre,

1996). The mind becomes intensely receptive, but it is a contemplative rather than active engagement with the outside world. Meditators try to achieve this kind of consciousness through stillness, and through forms of breathing combined with mental exercises to increase concentration on situation and context.

There is a critical consciousness, in which we examine the values, assumptions, ideals and ideologies which constrain the way we think, feel and act (Mezirow, 1991). This is the consciousness we experience when we foreground and appraise the psychological and cultural factors which make us "tick," when we examine the history of our thinking in order to change it. An adult educator will help learners achieve this kind of consciousness so that they can examine and, where they deem it necessary, change their assumptions and values and so adopt new ways of thinking, feeling and acting. This kind of consciousness, therefore, is seen as necessary to engage in transformative learning. It is a consciousness which involves analysis.

Meditative and contemplative kinds of consciousness involve stillness, perhaps even a sense of repose. Critical consciousness requires us to "step back" and assume the role of a monitor, and so involves a sense of detachment. All three kinds involve retreating from everyday life, either into a protected space or a physical retreat, or into a classroom where part of the adult educator's job will be to provide a safe environment conducive to transformative learning.

Sartre (1984, 347–348) examines two more kinds of consciousness in his example of the man peering through a keyhole. They differ from the three kinds described above in that the conscious being is less in control. In Sartre's example, the man is motivated by "jealousy, curiosity or vice." His consciousness is projected into the room on the other side of the door. He is unaware of himself, and for the moment his whole being is determined by what he expects to see on the other side of the door. Sartre argues that in this moment there is no self to inhabit the man's consciousness. The man *is* the jealousy (or curiosity or vice), and the jealousy is the fact that there is a sight to be seen behind the door. But there are footsteps in the corridor and the man is suddenly aware that he is being observed. His consciousness is now intensely on his own side of the door. He sees himself because somebody else sees him. Sartre argues that the man now exists as *himself* but that he *is* without *knowing* it. I see this as the kind of vivid consciousness, that instantaneous sense of existence, which we experience when we are suddenly caught in the glare of headlights as we walk at night on a country road. At that moment we *are*, pure and simple. Sartre is an existentialist, and in his example the man's shame is the objective fact from which the meaning of the situation flows. After all, who knows whether the other person actually saw the man or what she or he made of the situation? So it is shame, Sartre argues, which reveals to the man "the Other's look" and himself "at the end of that look." In an ontological as well as a literal sense the man is not alone. His being flows into the Other, and meaning is given to his world though this Other.

Both kinds of consciousness have great intensity. One kind is projected outside ourselves, focused on an expectation and constructed on desire (in Sartre's example, the desire of the man to know what is happening on the other side of the door). The other is a form of intense self-perception, located in the present and premised on our existential relationship with the social world (in Sartre's example, the presence of someone else in the corridor). But in both these kinds of consciousness there is a lack of vigorous action. They involve an intense projection into or presence in the physical, social and emotional worlds, but do not imply an active engagement with those worlds. The man acts in kneeling down to look through the keyhole but beyond that is influenced or affected by events outside him, and is a passive figure.

For me, the most complete kind of consciousness is a proactive one. It is the consciousness I "saw" in those opening batsmen. Proactive consciousness is the aliveness we feel when we are assertively engaging with reality, when we are taking action, when we are continuously making choices. It is the consciousness Turner urged upon the antiapartheid activists in South Africa. It is the consciousness which combines reflection and action and is described by Marxists as *praxis*. It is the consciousness we experience when we defy other people and other forces and take full control of our moment. It is the consciousness to be found in the continual expression of will.

From time to time, while waiting for the bowler to return to his mark, one of those opening batsmen in the Australian cricket team will squat down on his haunches, place his hands together on top of the handle of his upright bat, turn his head to look up the pitch towards the bowler's end, and become momentarily motionless. Proactive consciousness does not reject other forms of consciousness. It sublates them. At such times we will block out extraneous external influences. We will note. We will analyze. We will project. Caught in the glare of our opponent's gaze, we will *be*. And in the best of these moments, even in the heat of intense action, because it is we who have made the choices and so have knowingly engaged with the future, we will experience a sense of repose.

One Man's Expression of Will

It may not be a good time to discuss suicide. At the time of writing our newspapers are full of it. Suicide bombers attack markets, police stations and army checkpoints in Iraq. They attack restaurants and buses in Israel. They attack residential compounds in Saudi Arabia. They attack hotels in Jordan. These are acts of unconscionable cruelty and we rightly see these suicide bombers as fanatics, sucked into a literally dead-end future by misplaced faith or perverted ideology. It is tempting to go one step further and dismiss them as mad, and to define their madness by the very fact that they do commit suicide. This is often what we do when reacting to the suicide of someone we know. We try to explain it by saying the friend was depressed, upset or temporarily deranged. After all, we say to ourselves, no sane person would willingly, really willingly, take her or his own life.

But Camus declared (1975, 11) in the opening sentence of *The Myth of Sisyphus*, "there is but one truly serious philosophical problem and that is suicide." In doing so he deemed suicide an act over which we can have control. He made it possible to envisage suicide, in certain cases at least, as a sane and legitimate expression of our freedom to choose.

I want to celebrate the death, a number of years ago now, of a friend and colleague. Billy chose me as his peer reviewer at our workplace. This meant that we met on a regular basis, talked about Billy's job, and plotted out strategies for him to adopt over the next two or three months in order to improve his performance in the job and increase the satisfaction he derived from it. Neither of us made very much of our formal encounters but I enjoyed and valued them. We laughed a lot. And our conversations often strayed from matters directly related to work, so I knew that Billy's partner was seriously ill and that a lot of Billy's time at home was spent in the role of carer. As well as our peer review encounters, I met Billy in the normal course of work and so I quickly learned when his partner died. The death had been a long time coming and, when I expressed my sympathy, Billy was calm and resigned.

A few months later, on a Sunday morning, Billy committed suicide. So it goes.

I had encountered Billy in the corridor and met him for a peer review session in the months preceding his death. He had been his slightly cheeky self in the casual encounters, and in the meeting he had railed for a while, as he often did, against the organization's bureaucracy. There had been nothing out of the ordinary and he and I had talked of strategies that stretched into the future, past the date of his death.

After Billy's death I talked with another colleague who had been a close, personal friend of his (and who helped me gain permission from Billy's mother to write about him). She had seen nothing to indicate the decision Billy had made, but said that when she could not raise him on the phone on the Monday, she knew what he had done. She had gone to his house, knocked on the door and then climbed though a window to find Billy's body in bed.

Billy's death had been carefully organized. He had taken a large dose of morphine, which he had kept from his partner's illness. He had arranged himself neatly in bed. His room and house were tidy. Over the days which followed it became clear that Billy had taken several weeks to organize his financial affairs so there would be as little trouble as possible for his family and friends. And we learned that he had traveled to an outer suburb of Sydney on the Saturday to mow the lawn of an aunt, a chore which he had performed regularly.

Billy was in apparent good health but he was HIV positive and he had told his friend that he did not want to go through the experience of contracting full-blown AIDS. He was Aboriginal and in our encounters he had sometimes expressed a profound dismay at the way white Australia had treated and still treated his people. At his funeral, attended by several hundred Aboriginal and non-Aboriginal people, there was a sense of loss but I detected no despair. As far as anyone could tell, there had been no madness in Billy's death. No loss of control. No being dragged down into some terrible pit. After a long conversation a couple of years later, his friend and I both felt that Billy's death was the final choice of a continual expression of will, an act of defiance in the face of an unwanted future.

Writing is an odd activity. When I was planning to write about choice and consciousness, Billy popped into my mind, as he does from time to time, and I decided to use his death as an example. So I have written the account with a sense of purpose and yet, if this is not too much of a paradox, without quite understanding why. Billy made a choice, and Camus has given me license to talk about his death in dispassionate terms and not explain it away as some kind of aberration. The problem in all this is that Camus came out against suicide. He sees the absurdity of the human condition and asks if life is worth living. Yet he argues (1953, 14) for an acceptance of the absurd and says "the final conclusion of the absurdist process" is "the rejection of suicide and the persistence in that hopeless encounter between human questioning and the silence of the universe." We can give that hopeless encounter value, Camus argues, if we knowingly choose it and bring to it passion, revolt, and a commitment to liberty.

Breaking the Silence

The madcap range of Turner's passage about choice fits the eclectic, wide-ranging nature of adult education well. Some who see themselves as adult educators may be helping people deal in various ways with matters of life and death, as occupational health and safety trainers do, or the trainers of ambulance crews, or the facilitator of a cancer support group. Others may be helping people learn how to make ice cream and jelly, literally, in a cookery class. In any of these activities we can both teach and learn choice. We can help ourselves and others understand that we do have choices, we can critically examine the choices available, and we can help ourselves and others develop the capabilities and willingness to make choices which matter.

There is, however, a catch. It is true that within a limited context we continually make choices. But all too often we deny ourselves the opportunity to make choices which matter. We accept the status quo. Making a choice may mean change, and there are times when we see significant change as just too hard. So we stay in the same job although it provides little or no real satisfaction, or we let someone dominate us because to challenge that person might result in conflict, or we vote a government back in because we fear change in an uncertain world.

We often let other people, organizations or authorities make the choices for us. We give up a range of freedoms in exchange for services, a sense of belonging, or protection. So we let a restaurant dictate our style of dress so that we can eat there. We subscribe to the rules of a club in exchange for the fellowship it offers. We obey the laws of the state in exchange for the security the state provides us. Clearly there are times when we choose to make these concessions, but there will also be times when we go along with these limitations unthinkingly.

And we subjugate ourselves to a Gramscian hegemony. We accept as natural and normal and in need of no explanation states of affairs that are not natural, not normal and in need of lots of explanation. In Australia we let our government lock up the children of asylum seekers in detention centers for indefinite periods, despite the obvious inhumanity of it. We allow ourselves to be controlled by publicity, advertising and propaganda. We live our lives according to routines set by others, be they our peers, our employers, our leaders or those people who have somehow become recognized as experts. All too often we accept these kinds of control without thinking, let alone speaking to others. We fall silent.

Talking to Billy

To help ourselves and others make choices, we need to break the silence. We need to talk, and to get others talking. People, Paulo Freire says (1972b, 62), "are not built in silence, but in word, in work, in action-reflection." We can seize the opportunity in that cookery class to get people talking about choice, incidentally as it were. We can aim to get people examining ways of making choices as an added informal element in the otherwise reasonably formal curriculum of that occupational health and safety program. And we can set out single-mindedly to teach choice, as a discrete part of a program or as an educational program in itself.

If I harbor a doubt about Billy's death, it is that he may have made his choice in silence. I was in my late fifties and Billy was in his thirties when we became involved in the peer review system. Because of the age difference I felt I was in a mentor role to him. Perhaps by writing this I am engaging in the discussion we never had about his decision.

If Billy had wanted to talk, if he had asked me in that slightly kidding way he had of talking to me, "Hey Mike, what do you reckon about my idea to commit suicide, eh?", I like to think I would have given him a printout of this quote from Freire's *Cultural Action for Freedom*:

> The Right in its rigidity prefers the dead to the living; the static to the dynamic; the future as a repetition of the past rather than as a creative venture; pathological forms of love rather than real love; frigid schematization rather than the emotion of living; gregariousness rather than authentic living together; organization men rather than men who organize; imposed myths rather than incarnated values; directives rather than creative and communicative language; and slogans rather than challenges [Freire, 1972a, 72–73].

This is another of my favorite quotes. It is incandescent, angry, full of moral force and political commitment. Freire has no compunction in starkly listing sins set against virtues in a text which echoes the chanted liturgies of his Catholic background. He offers choices. The Right is evil and you can be good, he says. In the first part of the paragraph he lists what the Right would have us all become: "dead," trapped in routines and living empty, loveless lives. And in the latter part of the paragraph he lists how the Right would bring us under its control: through the encouragement of "yes men," the imposition of shallow fantasy and the corruption of language.

When Freire used the term "the Right" he was referring to the military dictators and ruling elites of Latin America in the 1960s who destroyed democracies, established power through violence and held on to it through murder. But the quote applies to anyone who would deny others choice. I like to think that I would have told Billy that Freire was saying to all of us, "The Right prefers the dead to the living, and I choose the living."

Part Three

CHOOSING AND TAKING CONTROL

5

TEACHING CHOICE

We can break the silence by using different kinds of talk. One of these is the language of everyday reasoning and commonsense logic, the kind of engagement between people we might more formally refer to as *rational discourse*. In this part of the book I want to look at how we can put rational discourse to use in our learning and teaching in order to help ourselves and others make effective personal and collective choices. If we can make effective choices, we can defy those in positions of influence or power who may try to make the choices for us.

An Intellectual Skill

We use commonsense logic to address a problem. We can examine the problem, weigh up various possible responses, and then make the response we think will best suit our purposes. Simply by breaking the process down in this way we can see that problem solving is a skill. And because we encounter problems every day of our lives, even if many of them are small ones, it seems reasonable to describe problem solving as an essential skill. Yet I do not remember ever being taught it. What is more, despite the emphasis on critical thinking in curricula and the proliferation of management literature on problem solving over the past two decades, apparently I am not alone. Edward Russo and Paul Schoemaker suggest that many of us are self-trained in decision making. They point to the paradox of people (in affluent countries) turning to expert trainers to learn a leisure activity like tennis and yet in the skill of decision making relying on intuition, repeated experience and general intelligence to see them through (Russo and Schoemaker, 2002, xiii). Scott Fogler and Steven LeBlanc (1995, 11) suggest that some people resist the idea of problem solving being a learned skill at all.

I did my serious learning about problem solving in the university of hard knocks. I lived and worked for a number of years in the United Kingdom, and for my final four years there was the warden (my official title) of a small adult education college housed in a five-storey Edwardian building in inner London. As warden I was responsible for a full-time staff of ten people, some one hundred and twenty part-time teachers and a program of credit and non-credit classes attended by something like two thousand students.

I had imagined that my major duties would be to manage and develop the college's educational program. However, in the period between my accepting the job and taking up the position the roof of the college building was badly damaged by fire. From the moment I took up my post I was caught up with insurance companies and loss adjusters, architects, heritage authorities and one of the few building firms which still had the specialist crafts to rebuild the roof and cupola. The college continued to function while the restoration progressed, and we were forever juggling rooms and teaching spaces. Somewhere towards the end of the work on the roof, a section of the ceiling in the boiler room in the basement fell away, revealing blue asbestos. During my tenure the UK passed through a period of galloping inflation, meaning that my colleagues and I spent an inordinate amount of time trying to cut costs and prevent a terminal blowout of the college's budget. There were two classical studies teachers who disliked each other intensely. Each would complain to me about the other and on one occasion they burst into my office unannounced, stood face to face in front of my desk, and engaged in a shouting match. A mathematics teacher failed to turn up for classes two days in a row and on the third evening a colleague and I went to her private address in Hampstead. After dithering for an hour or so outside her flat, we enlisted the help of a police constable, broke the door down and found her on the floor where she had lain for three days, alive but severely disabled by a stroke. During my time at the college I had to deal with three catering managers, each in his own way an amiable brigand. One provided a service so miserly that I seemed to spend all my time pleading with him to improve it. The next one canceled all our contracts with long-standing suppliers so that he could get kick-backs from the new ones. And the police arrived one evening to arrest the third one for receiving stolen electrical goods. Shortly before I was to leave the college we had another fire, this one delib-erately lit inside a piano in one of the music rehearsal rooms on the top floor. The fire was intense but the soundproofing tiles prevented it from spreading to the roof. I talked with the police but we never identified the arsonist.

At first I was taken aback by the sheer relentlessness with which the problems occurred and thought they must slacken off, but of course they did not, and I began to realize that most management is actually crisis-management. Constant, sometimes hectic, choice-making about often unanticipated problems is the norm.

My time at the college was bounded by fires, and another inci-dent there also involved the possibility of fire. I was beginning to learn the business of management, and in response to this incident I consciously went through a process of decision making, applying it as one would an intellectual skill.

Classes finished by 9:30 in the evening and the bar closed around 10:30. I was working in my office sometime after 10:30 and conscious that the building was virtually empty when one of the college members popped his head around my door and said I should look in the smaller of the two common rooms. The room was used for college council meetings and by a few chess players, but it was located at the end of a corridor beyond the larger com-mon room and was often unoccupied throughout the evening. The person who had spoken to me left. I finished the note I was writing and then walked down the corridor and into the room. A woman in her mid-twenties was sitting on a chair in the middle of the room, motionless, looking down at the floor. There were lighted candles on several of the tables. As I approached her, something crushed under my shoes and I saw that the room was decorated with lines of coffee powder and sugar. The pattern of brown and white lines extended all over the room, covering the tables as well as the floor. I said hello but received no response. I stood in front of the woman but she did not look up.

"Are you celebrating something?" I asked.

No response.

I pulled a chair out from one of the tables and sat down a little to one side of her so as not to confront her and noticed, under the table and quite near her, a large tin of lighter fluid.

We both sat silently in the glow of the candlelight, and I reviewed my options. I could reach down and try to get the lighter fluid, but would the woman stop me? I could go to the door, where I could look down the corridor and still see the woman if she made a move, but the building now felt very empty. I could leave the room, get back to my office and ring for help, but would the woman pour the fluid out and start a fire while I was out of the room? I could talk to her, but her manner and the state of the room suggested she was in some kind of deep distress, and I had no training in this. I could suddenly take hold of her and try to restrain her, but then what? Or I could sit there with her, see the night out and do whatever I had to do if she made a move for the lighter fluid. Mrs. Cooper, the lead cleaner would appear sometime between 6:00 and 7:00 the next morning. I opted for calculated inaction, settled into my chair and began to wait.

Sometime around 11:30 I heard movement in the corridor and went to the door. The catering manager had been doing a stock take in one of the storerooms, had seen my office lights on as he headed out of the building and was now looking for me. He took over in the common room while I rang the borough council emergency social worker line, failed to get anyone and finally rang the police. Two police constables arrived and, with admirable gentleness, coaxed the woman to leave the room and then agree, with a mute nod of her head, to let them take her to an emergency center. The woman proved to be an art student at the college, and I learned the next day that she had responded to emergency counseling and had been referred for treatment. A few days later an embarrassed art teacher tried to tell me what had happened between him and the student but, beyond reassuring myself that the woman was on the mend, I preferred not to know.

Teaching Problem Solving

I returned to Australia in the early 1980s, and a couple of years later took my job with the Australian Trade Union Training Authority (TUTA). TUTA provided a range of courses for union activists, but the staples were three- and four-day courses for job representatives (shop stewards). In these courses we provided some information on the industrial relations system and the trade union movement, but for the most part we taught a problem-solving model. Through the use of trigger films, discussion and role-plays, we would establish that the model could be used to address single- and multiple-issue problems, provide a format for both formal and informal meetings, and create a structure for reports, advocacy work and campaigning. Again and again I watched the course participants getting to grips with the model, practicing and extending it, taking it on as their own, and leaving the course eager to apply it.

The model was based on three questions: "What's wrong?" "What can we do?" and "What will we do?" When I was running a course I would sometimes introduce these questions by asking the participants to break into groups of three and remain absolutely silent. I then distributed a sheet of paper headed "What would you do?" and carrying a problem expressed in a few sentences. The problem might be:

> You are the union rep at an engineering works producing car gears. Until now you have clocked on at the gate. This morning you arrived to find time clocks installed inside the works at different sections of the line.

I would ask the participants to maintain their silence while they read the problem and then, on my say-so, begin discussing it. Released from the enforced silence, the participants immediately started talking. I would let the discussions run for ten or so minutes and then call the group back together to hear the various solutions suggested.

The problem is a hoary one, and part of union mythology, but it carries a symbolic force. If the clock is at the gates, the workers walk from the gates to their places on the line on the boss's time. They are already being paid. If the clock is on the line, then they walk from the gates on their own time.

After we had canvassed the various solutions I would ask the participants to think back to the moment when I had released them from their silence. Could they recall who spoke first and the exact words that the person had uttered? Always there would be several who had used the words *should* or *ought to*: "We ought to send some of the bigger blokes to the works manager and tell him to move those clocks back to the gate" or "We should get somebody down from the union office." This allowed me to make the point that we often address a problem by suggesting a solution. We try to answer the question "What will we do?" first.

> *"We ought to call everyone out!"*

It may seem natural to go straight for a solution, but in fact we are racing ahead of ourselves. Before we answer the question "What will we do?" we need to spend some time on the question "What can we do?"

> *"If we go out on strike we'll lose pay. Let's look at other things we can do. We can work to rule. We can hold a stop-work meeting. We can go out for twenty-four hours. We can notify our intention to strike and then try to negotiate extra pay to cover the extra work time."*

But we are still ahead of ourselves. We are considering options without actually thinking about the problem itself. So before answering "What will we do?" and "What can we do?" we need to consider the basic question: "What's wrong?"

> *"The boss has moved the clock and extended the working day by ten or fifteen minutes, but is that the real problem? Maybe management is actually testing the resolve of the union. Maybe management is trying to divide the workforce. Maybe they want to break the line up and outsource parts of the work to other firms and other contractors."*

I would write the three questions on the whiteboard and say that managing a problem-solving process is like riding a horse which has a tendency to bolt. We need to rein the horse right back so that we can see what the problem really is, keep reining it back while we examine the various options open to us, and only let the horse have its head once we have decided how we are going to work towards a solution.

A Model

The groups of three would review the process they had gone through and then, back in the full group, we would develop the questions into a model. The questions break down into several stages.

To answer the question "What's wrong?" we need to check that we have the full story, and fill in the gaps where we do not. We may have to consult experts and do some research ourselves. If we are working in a group, we will need to recite the details to be sure that everyone agrees with them. Once we are sure of the facts we will need to identify the issues flowing from the facts. What does each fact mean? If the manager is fairly new, does that mean he is inexperienced? Or that he is ignorant of normal industrial relations protocols? Or that he wants to prove to his superiors that he is a mover and a shaker? Or that he has been expressly brought in to take a hard line? And we need to decide which of these issues is important so that we do not end up addressing an issue of less importance and solving the wrong problem. Moving the clocks may seem the major issue, but the covert way in which the clocks were moved overnight may actually be more significant as an indication of a change in management culture.

So in our formal model we have a first stage: Define the problem. And this involves two substages: establish the FACTS, and clarify the ISSUES.

To answer the question "What can we do?" we need to examine the various forms of action we can take to address the various issues. Clearly we need to concentrate on the major issues, but if we have time it will be useful to examine what we can do to address the minor ones as well. Sometimes dealing with a minor issue quickly and effectively will change the climate or set the scene in a way that makes dealing with the major issues easier. When looking at options it can be useful to consider extremes. We can always do nothing and, in the case of the example above, at the other end of the spectrum we can call the whole workforce out on an indefinite strike. Once we have established the (often impracticable) extremes, we can then look at the various options between them.

In our formal model we have a second stage: canvass the OPTIONS.

To answer the question "What will we do?" we need to make a decision on the options most likely to solve the most pressing issues. Often the action decided on will be multifaceted. In the example above, the job representative may decide on three kinds of action as an immediate response: instruct the members to continue working for the day but not clock on, seek a meeting with the works manager to have the decision reversed, and ask the national union office to make inquiries to establish whether the manager's actions reflect a change in company policy. Once the action has been decided upon, then we need to decide on personnel, resources, timing and ways of monitoring the effectiveness of the action.

In our formal model we have a third stage: decide on ACTION. And the model as a whole can be summarized in the following four words: FACTS, ISSUES, OPTIONS and ACTION.

The literature on problem solving and decision making draws on different disciplines. Russo and Schoemaker (2002), from the fields of marketing and "behavior science", construct a decision-making model made up of the following components: decision framing, gathering intelligence, coming to conclusions and learning from experience. Peter Drucker (2001), writing from a business perspective, offers the following sequence of steps: classifying the problem, defining the problem, specifying the answer to the problem, deciding what is "right" (rather than what is acceptable) in order to meet the boundary conditions, building into the decision the action to carry it out, and testing the validity and effectiveness of the decision against the actual course of events. And Fogler and LeBlanc (1995), two academics from the field of engineering, offer a "heuristic": define the problem, generate solutions; decide the course of action, implement the solution, and evaluate the solution. There are obvious similarities in all these models but the TUTA model has the advantages of clarity and apparent simplicity. The model is depicted in Figure 2.

Figure 2

1. What's wrong?	
Define the problem	
	FACTS
	ISSUES
2. What will we do?	
Examine the	OPTIONS
3. What can we do?	
Decide on	ACTION

From Trade Union Training Australia Inc. (TUTA). Used by permission.

Extending the Model

People can be exhilarated when applying the model. It releases them from a state of inaction into action. It provides them with something orderly to do in the face of uncertainly and disorder. They have a procedure to follow. But the model has its limitations. It places an emphasis on identifiable, verifiable facts whereas on most occasions, when we have choices to make, there are people involved. And these people will have attitudes and emotions which cannot be identified or verified so easily.

When I took up a post at a university I did a number of consultancies for government departments, unions and community-based organizations, and in the course of these consultancies I ran a number of workshops on problem solving. I would take the participants through the processes described above, using a problem which was tailored to their context. We would debrief the exercise and construct the model on the whiteboard. For their first problem, I normally asked people to work in groups of three. Now I would ask them to form groups of five or six and I would hand out another problem. Here is a problem I used for a workshop with principals of community adult education centers:

A tutor was absent from his pottery class for three out of a period of seven weekly class meetings. He rang the branch coordinator the first and second times on the evening of the class to say he could not attend, but simply did not turn up on the third occasion. The class attendance kept up reasonably well. Following the tutor's third absence the coordinator found a replacement tutor. When the original tutor turned up to find his class being taught by someone else he flew into a rage, saying that he was still legally the tutor, and left.

The coordinator has asked you to sack the tutor. The tutor has written to you, complaining that the coordinator acted summarily in replacing him, gave him no warning, and refused to listen to his explanation. The tutor claims he had "family and domestic problems" which are now resolved. You asked the coordinator to consider taking the tutor back, but she said, "We cannot have tutors who don't show up." The tutor has talked of taking legal action.

The problem has facts to examine and issues to tease out from those facts, but it also involves a conflict between two people and so has the added complexities of personalities, different expectations of what is reasonable behavior, hurt pride and so on.

In this particular workshop I let the groups spend some time discussing the problem, then interrupted them and talked about the ideas of Roger Fisher and William Ury (1983) on position and interest. Fisher and Ury suggest that in disagreements people often take a stance or make demands which will not actually be of benefit to them. They adopt a position which is not in their interests. Sometimes they state their position so forcefully and publicly that they lock themselves into it. A solution has to be found which acknowledges their position but also serves their interests. Often, in practical terms, a solution is not difficult to find and the real challenge is to devise a way for the people involved to save face.

Having spent a few minutes on Fisher and Ury, I asked the groups to go back to the problem, look at the people involved, identify their positions, and speculate on what might really be in their interests. I reminded them that they should think about what might be in the principal's interests as well.

We completed the group discussions, reassembled as one group and compiled a consensus analysis on the whiteboard. It was decided that it was not in the interests of the branch coordinator to have an experienced tutor sacked, but it was in her interests to be seen maintaining good professional practice. A solution must not undermine her authority. The tutor's interests would not be served by suing the organization over a part-time job. It was in his interests to be employed at the center in the future, and perhaps all he wanted was an acknowledgment that he had been through a bad personal patch. From the principal's point of view it was important to maintain a harmonious center. Attendance had not really dropped in the pottery class, suggesting that there might be a stronger demand for pottery in the community than previously thought.

We then compiled a consensus solution. As the principal of the centre we would keep the class going with the replacement tutor and open an additional experimental class with the reemployed tutor in the next semester. We would organize a meeting between the branch coordinator and the tutor in which we would seek to clarify their various responsibilities and hopefully reestablish a civil relationship. We would ask the coordinator to work with all the pottery tutors to establish a protocol for informing her of a likely absence, and to set up a system of emergency replacement tutors amongst the potters in the area. And we would spend time ourselves with the coordinator and the pottery tutors reviewing how pottery could be taught around projects on which the students could continue working in the absence of a tutor, and establishing how the requirements of safety procedures, insurance and the like could be maintained in such circumstances.

We ended by reviewing the exercise and recognizing that we now had a problem-solving model with two starting points: FACTS and ISSUES, and POSITIONS and INTERESTS. Only after examining all four elements would we proceed to OPTIONS and then ACTION.

Extending the Model Further

Depending on the nature of the workshop, the participants and the time available, I might develop the model further through two more kinds of problem. I used a third kind of problem on a leadership course for people in the welfare sector. We had worked through versions of the first two problems in much the way I have described above. Participants in a course or workshop can take just so much small-group work, so in this case I distributed the problem to the full group, asked everyone to read it and then told two stories. This is the problem:

You are the regional director of a government department of community and youth affairs. Within your patch there is a grant-aided agency called Comhelp which has an elected management committee of ten people and a coordinator supervising eighteen community development, counseling, legal advice and administrative staff.

Ever since the last annual general meeting the coordinator has been uncooperative. Her reports to the committee have been brief to the point of being uncommunicative, and she has not passed on letters from your department concerning future policy matters. Now the chair of the committee has written to you, stating that all correspondence should be directed to him.

The coordinator did not attend the last committee meeting, saying she had "an organization to run and a community to serve." Last Wednesday the chair went into Comhelp's office and took all the account books. He called a special meeting of the committee, but the coordinator refused to attend.

Both the chair and the coordinator have asked you to take action against the other.

And these are the two stories. By now the participants were expecting me to provide another couple of words in capital letters to add to the model. The two words are encapsulated in the stories.

When I was a community education worker in London, the majority of the courses I organized took place in school buildings, and amongst the most bloody-minded people I have ever encountered were the caretakers of these buildings. With just one exception, they were surly and uncooperative. Sometimes I would arrive at a school and find the room I had booked was locked. I would then have to plead with the caretaker and put up with him ostentatiously taking his time to open it up. One evening at five minutes to 9:00, in a course which met regularly from 7:00 to 9:00, the caretaker came into the room and began stacking the metal chairs, making the completion of the evening session impossible. At another school the heating was sometimes just a little too low and

I would have to seek out the caretaker and ask him to turn it up. This kind of behavior was not exceptional. Colleagues in other adult education institutes in London had similar experiences, and most of us simply accepted that uncooperative caretakers were something we had to live with.

I was talking about this phenomenon to a friend who worked in the civil service as a criminologist. She laughed. It was no surprise, she said. Think about it. Caretakers lived on site and were effectively on duty for twenty-four hours a day. Schools were complex campuses, and the caretakers were responsible for the security and maintenance of the grounds, the buildings, and the fixtures, furniture and equipment in those buildings. They managed a team of cleaners who entered the school at 6:00 in the morning and, if the school was also used for adult education in the evenings, returned again at 4:00 in the afternoon. They oversaw deliveries to the school. They managed the plant that heated the building or buildings, and they maintained the school kitchens. In effect, they had to ensure the physical well-being of everyone on site, throughout the day and into the evening. Caretakers were people with very high levels of responsibility.

But look at the way people treated them, my friend said. Although they might have some title like "site manager," everyone thought of them as caretakers. They had low status, and they and their work often went unacknowledged. Indeed, if they did their jobs well and the site functioned without any problems, they were all but invisible. The only way for them to have the essential nature of their work recognized was to do their job poorly. By leaving a room locked, they made us come to them to get it unlocked. By stacking chairs in the back of the room just before nine, they let us know that it was they who had to put the place in order and lock the building up. And by letting the heating run for a while at a lower than normal temperature, they could demonstrate that it was they who provided the warm and comfortable environment we had taken for granted. School caretakers were a classic case of a combination of high responsibility and low status leading to bloody-mindedness.

Of course she was right. The exception amongst the caretakers I had encountered was referred to as school manager, attended staff meetings and sat with the teaching staff on stage at school events. In effect he was accorded, or had earned, a status similar to that of a deputy principal.

My second story comes from my time as warden of the adult education college in inner London. In practice I was the principal but, under the college's constitution, that title was given to an eminent person who acted as the college figurehead. For the time I was there, the principal was an elderly gentleman with a hyphenated name who had studied classics, risen to a very senior post in the civil service and retired to a mansion outside London. From there he motored in four or five times a year to chair the college council and to preside over an annual event called Founders' Day at which scholarships were awarded and medals of one sort or another were distributed. At Founders' Day he gave an address on the state of the institution, and on one occasion in particular he managed to give the impression that he and the college council had done all the work. I must admit to being tempted at the time to take a leaf out of the caretakers' book and do something bloody-minded to demonstrate that my colleagues and I actually ran the place.

That, however, is not the point of this story. There was a period of several months when the principal came into the college more often, appearing unexpectedly in my office in the evenings. On these occasions he would offer advice on the day-to-day running of the college, and occasionally join in when I was dealing with a member of the teaching staff or talking over something with the accountant or administrator. These were confusing moments because my colleagues did not know how to react to his advice, particularly if it differed from mine. And differences did occur because the principal did not come in regularly and so sometimes made his comments from a position of relative ignorance.

I could see that these interventions were not done out of malice or a lack of confidence in me, but they were hugely irritating nonetheless, and sometimes counterproductive. For example, I thought I had managed the two classical studies tutors well enough, but the principal chose to talk to one of them, causing the dispute to flare up again. I wondered what was going on.

I sought advice from a friend who was the director of a settlement whose governance was similar to that of the college, and together we decided that the situation of the principal was the inverse of the caretakers'. A formerly busy and respected person had been elected principal of this small but historically interesting adult education institution. At the council meetings and on Founders' Day he occupied a position of ostensible importance, but for the rest of the time he had very little to do. To justify his title he had begun to intervene. A combination of high status and low responsibility was producing interference.

My friend suggested I was contributing to this situation by not making use of the principal's evident willingness to be of help. I had been trying to solve the problem by reducing the flow of information to him and cutting him off even more from the day-to-day business of the college. Instead, we needed to find a way in which he could make a positive and fitting contribution. A solution lay in matching the principal's responsibilities more closely with his status, just as a solution to the bloody-mindedness of the school caretakers lay in matching their status more closely with their responsibilities. Together the principal and I looked for ways for him to play a more obvious role in the activities of the college. As a start we instituted a series of public lectures which he organized using his contacts in government, and which he chaired.

Having told the two stories, I asked the participants in the leadership course what they now made of the problem I had distributed. It was obvious that I had constructed the problem on the stories I had just told and so, after a general discussion which included a number of stories of their own, we added two more words to the model. Now there were three starting points: FACTS and ISSUES; POSITIONS and INTERESTS; and STATUS and RESPONSIBILITIES.

Extending the Model Even Further

Occasionally I have been able to take a group through to a fourth kind of problem. Some years ago I conducted a week-long residential course for the eighteen officials of a small union of some twenty-four thousand members. We worked through the three kinds of problems in the way I have described above, with the sessions spread over three days and interspersed with others dealing with different skills and different union issues.

I had another pair of words to add to the model but did not use a written problem. Instead, I introduced the session by talking about the distinction Chris Argyris and Donald Schön make between espoused theory and theory in use (Argyris and Schön, 1996, 13–14; Argyris, 1999, 96, 131). People and organizations tend to make pronouncements about how they or the organization or indeed the world should work. People will say what they believe in and what they hope to achieve. Organizations publish mission statements, set goals and promote particular images of themselves through advertising and public relations campaigns. Schön and Argyris call these public expressions of values "espoused theory." But often these same people or organizations go about their affairs based on slightly or even totally different sets of values. Argyris and Schön call these values implicit in actual practice "theory in use." In effect, they are pointing to the common phenomenon of people not doing what they say they are doing. So a teacher will say that she or he respects the views of the learners but will actually always use the lecture mode.

People, Argyris maintains (1999, 131), "consistently act inconsistently, unaware of the contradiction between their espoused theory and their theory in use, between the way they think they are acting and the way they really act." Sometimes we can find reasons for this apparent perversity. A government-funded employment agency may state in its publicity and reports that it is committed to finding people jobs and providing them with ongoing support.

However, because its funding is dependent upon the number of people on its books and not the number placed in employment, its main concern will be to get as many people as possible to pass though its front door.

Having introduced these ideas, I led a general discussion in which we swapped stories of people and organizations we had encountered where there had been a disparity between their stated objectives and their actual practice. In effect the participants themselves were providing case studies of this fourth kind of problem. I made the point that, when espoused theory and theory in use drift too far apart, an organization can become dysfunctional. Some organizations may actually cease to meet their original objectives. So a small agency set up to provide emergency temporary accommodation for young homeless people may find some years later that all its energies are going into raising money, maintaining an office and staff, and constructing some low-cost housing which at best will house a limited number of families on a semipermanent basis. The organization's focus has shifted from young people to families, and while the construction is in progress the organization is not providing accommodation for anyone.

I asked these union officials to talk amongst themselves and to consider how much energy they devoted to improving the conditions of their members, and how much energy they were obliged to spend maintaining membership numbers, dealing with the union's finances, meeting the union's requirements under its constitution, meeting the union's legal requirements as a registered industrial organization, maintaining the union's property, and guarding their position in the political landscape of the country.

I made the point that part of the analysis of any problem may involve looking at all the individuals and organizations involved and, one by one, comparing their stated objectives with their actual practice. We discussed what two words we would add to the model. We recognized that we were talking about explicitly stated values and about values implicit in practice. We could have used the

Figure 3

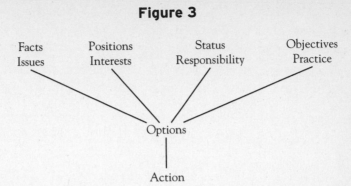

From Trade Union Training Australia Inc. (TUTA). Used by permission.

Argyris and Schön terms "espoused theory" and "theory in use" but in the end we opted for the words OBJECTIVES and PRACTICE. In the case of this union course, we ended up with a model on the whiteboard with four starting points: FACTS and ISSUES, POSITIONS and INTERESTS, STATUS and RESPONSIBILITIES, and OBJECTIVES and PRACTICE. The full model is depicted in Figure 3.

The problem-solving model provides us with a way of making up our own minds and resisting solutions imposed by others. It can help us analyze some of the forces, events and people around us. And it can also help us form an understanding of ourselves. We can simultaneously engage in and reflect on our processes of common-sense analysis. We can watch ourselves making choices and so develop a consciousness of ourselves as thoughtful, rational beings.

6

COLLECTIVE DECISION MAKING

Formal and Informal Meetings

The TUTA problem-solving model helps us understand the underlying agenda for most meetings. Meetings normally begin with a report (establishing the FACTS). The report may be a written one, perhaps circulated to participants before the meeting. Or it may simply be an oral statement or a series of comments. Whatever form it takes, the opening section of a meeting is normally concerned with describing the situation the meeting is going to make decisions about.

Following the report there is normally a period in which participants can ask questions. Some will ask questions simply to clarify the situation described in the report, but others will ask questions in order to tease out the implications (identifying and clarifying the ISSUES).

Then there is a debate about what to do (canvassing the OPTIONS). In informal meetings there will be a fairly freewheeling discussion in which suggestions can be made and discussed. If the mood is right and the discussion well managed, entirely new ideas can be generated. In informal meetings the options stage can be the most creative. In formal meetings options are likely to be canvassed in a much more focused, and limited, manner. There may well have been a creative discussion of the report but in order to move the meeting forward someone will formulate a motion, often actually writing it down, and then put it to the meeting. And there will be times when the motion has been formulated before the meeting and notice of it already given in writing. Once the motion has been put and seconded, debate is limited to speakers for and against the motion. Amendments to the motion can be made but, under formal meeting procedure, they cannot alter the motion substantially, so the debate remains restricted to the approval or rejection of a single line of action.

Finally there is a decision (deciding on ACTION). In informal meetings the decision will be by consensus. The debate will end when there is a general feeling that everyone present agrees with the proposed action or, at the very least, will go along with it. In formal meetings a decision is made by vote, and it is expected that those who have voted against the motion will abide by the decision. In our Western culture these two kinds of meeting are the normal ways in which groups make decisions, and so the problem-solving model becomes a codification of rational discourse. I have set out the two kinds of meeting against the problem-solving model in Figure 4.

Managing Meetings

Meetings do not always proceed as smoothly as the model suggests. Indeed, meetings can go off the rails or be sites for ferocious and destructive arguments. If we are to get our point of view across and

Figure 4

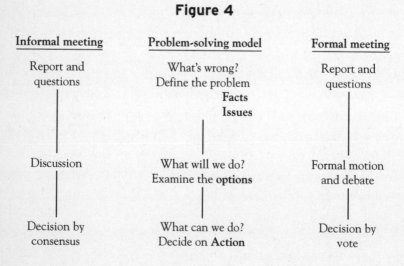

Informal meeting	Problem-solving model	Formal meeting
Report and questions	What's wrong? Define the problem **Facts** **Issues**	Report and questions
Discussion	What will we do? Examine the **options**	Formal motion and debate
Decision by consensus	What can we do? Decide on **Action**	Decision by vote

From Trade Union Training Australia Inc. (TUTA). Used by permission.

solve the problems we actually want to solve, then it is important to learn how to manage and even manipulate meetings.

When I run a workshop or a course on collective decision making I usually kick off by asking the participants to chat with the person next to them for a moment about horror meetings they have experienced. I then call the group to order and we share the stories. There are usually stories about difficult people. There are the ones who speak too much, or talk off the point, or criticize but never suggest a solution, or speak passionately on a subject but refuse to take any responsibility for implementing the decision.

There are usually stories of poor timing. A young enthusiast without any family commitments proposes an immediate and vigorous community action campaign at a meeting in the week before Christmas. A meeting is scheduled for the evening before a long weekend. A person sits silently through a discussion of a particular item until a decision has been made, and then wants to talk about it.

There are usually stories about the contexts in which meetings are held. A meeting between indigenous and nonindigenous people about joint land use, arranged after long and delicate negotiations and held next to an isolated sacred site, is washed out by a freak thunderstorm. A meeting is held in a room next to an increasingly rowdy party. Parents and municipal council officials, one of them very large, meet at a nursery school and have to sit on infant-sized chairs at infant-sized desks.

And there are stories about the conduct of the meetings themselves. The chairman gets lost in a morass of amendments and the whole process grinds to an embarrassed halt. A skilled spoiler raises points of order, dissents from the ruling of the chair, and moves procedural motions until everyone else simply gives up and she gets her way. Or an important vote is taken and it is only after people have dispersed that the organizers discover that a large number of them were not entitled to vote.

I try to make one- or two-word notes on the whiteboard for each story under the headings *participants, timing, environment* and *process*, and when the stories have been told I suggest that these four elements can be combined to produce the following definition:

> A meeting is a group of people (the *participants*) gathered together (*timing* and *environment*) to share information and make a decision about a problem affecting the group (*process*).

I ask how we can engage with each of the elements in order to effectively manage or manipulate a meeting. If I am working with people experienced in meetings, then the remainder of this session is simply one of drawing out techniques and ideas from the members of the group. If the group is less experienced in the madnesses and perfidies of meetings, then I may have to ask leading questions and provide more examples myself. There are videos available on meetings and on what can go right and wrong in them but I prefer to draw the ideas from the course participants themselves.

Participants

We can try to manage a meeting by getting as many of our supporters as possible to attend. If it is a public meeting, then we can try to stack it so that we can win any vote that is taken. If the meeting is limited to a defined membership but open to observers, then we can organize supporters to pack the back and the sides of the room. If the organizers of the meeting are unsure of its public or private status, then we should try to fill the room with our supporters before the organizers come to a decision. If the meeting is a closed one, we can still lobby people who have voting rights and who might support us if given a little encouragement, or who might come round to our way of thinking if given an opportunity to talk through their doubts.

It may make sense to hold a premeeting with our supporters and plan who will say what. In a large meeting it can help if we place our key speakers at strategic points in the room. A person from the other side of the room speaking in support of a previous speaker may have more impact than someone sitting next to that previous speaker. In any event, we should try never to go into a meeting alone, even if the meeting is with just one or two other people. It is always useful to have someone else there, if only to make approving noises and say "Well, that's right!" when we speak.

And we might identify the people most likely to oppose us, and allocate a "shadow" to each of them, to sit beside them and chat to them during the meeting. I have seen a speaker from the floor of a large meeting distracted by the person next to him whispering suggestions of something else to say, and I wondered at the time if the "helpful" whisperer had been placed there to do precisely that.

Timing

We can take account of the timing of meetings. Meetings usually mark out the cycle of an organization, and sometimes we can use the dynamic of these cycles. If we choose the right meeting at which to propose a project, the cycle may carry the project forward. So we may choose to suggest a new course in a university department at a meeting just after the middle of first semester when people are conscious of the courses which have enrolled well and those which have not, and when the initial tensions of getting the year under way have subsided but the end-of-semester period of marking is still a few weeks off. On the other hand, if we choose the wrong meeting then the cycle of the organization may work against the proposal. So a researcher in an enterprise proposes a brilliant but very expensive project at a meeting two weeks after the enterprise's budget has been approved and locked into place, and his project is thrown out. Worse, when he puts the idea up again at a more appropriate meeting, someone says, quite genuinely, "Haven't we heard this one before?" and his idea gets marked down as old hat.

The actual time and date of a meeting can affect the outcome. If we have control over the scheduling, then we can fix the meeting at a time that suits our supporters and perhaps inconveniences or discourages others. So we might schedule a meeting on the evening of the week when our most vociferous opponent plays competition squash. Or we might set the starting time of a meeting for a couple of hours after the end of the working day so that those who are not really committed will be tempted to go home. Or we might call a meeting off. People eager to oppose us this week may feel less impassioned next week. If we are not in charge of the scheduling, we can still try to influence the timing of a meeting, simply by talking to or petitioning the secretary or the chair.

And, once we are in the meeting, timing our own interventions can increase our influence over the outcomes. Sometimes we will want to set the parameters of the debate by speaking first. At other times we may try to have the last say. Often it will make sense to wait until a number of other people have spoken and we have an idea of the mood of the meeting. If there are several of us, then we can choose beforehand who will speak first, who will judge the mood and then speak, and who will try to close out the debate.

Environment

The environment of the meeting may be beyond our control. Many meetings are held in spaces already allocated such as boardrooms, conference rooms, council chambers and the like. However, if we have any say at all, we should try to select a location which favors us. This is a well-tried strategy in industrial relations. For a meeting between managers and union representatives, the managers may try to hold the meeting in one of their offices. This means they are on their own territory, can take phone calls and interrupt the flow of the meeting, demonstrate their magnanimity by offering refreshments, and call an end to the meeting at will, claiming they have other pressing business. But in a heavy industry context the union might argue that since the meeting is about some aspect of work on the shop floor, the meeting should be convened there, alongside the machine or the area of work in question. This is the union's territory, and it may be possible to increase the noise level or have a number of workers busy nearby in order to unsettle the white-collar members of the management group. By the same token, the staff of a childcare center might argue that none of them can get away from the center, and then organize a meeting with administrators from the central office in a space where they will be surrounded by the noise and continual movement of babies and toddlers. A toddler with sticky hands might be set loose to wander amongst the neatly creased trousers and business skirts.

There may be times when teleconferencing or the Internet may be a better choice, particularly if we are unsure of securing a suitable outcome. A virtual meeting is just that, and decisions may lack the substance of a decision sealed with a handshake. We may be able to say at a later date, "Look, had we actually got together, I think we would have sorted things out differently." I was involved in a teleconference which was torpedoed by one of the participants demanding a vote by secret ballot. The technology we were using made this impossible, the participant insisted and the meeting was postponed, giving him more time to lobby. E-mail can be treacherous territory. Three or four of us may be in correspondence over several days, copying e-mails to everyone else. In effect, we are in a virtual meeting and at some stage it may be necessary to clarify the situation in our own minds and modify our responses. It may be in our interests to alert the others to what is happening and "reassemble" as a real-time chat group, or not.

If the environment is already fixed, then we might consider how we can make it ours. We may be able to organize supporters to stand outside the building or pack the anterooms, and have them hold up placards or greet the participants as they enter the meeting. As we have already seen, we may be able to pack the meeting room itself. We might arrive with visual displays (and the necessary display stands) and festoon the room, claiming that we will want to refer to them during the meeting. Or we might connect up a laptop, arguing that we may want to make a presentation, and display our logo on the screen throughout the meeting. If we can get to the room first, we may be able to rearrange the furniture. Community workers meeting with administrators might remove the tables and arrange the chairs in a circle, an environment the administrators may not feel comfortable with, particularly if they have brought files and papers which they will have to juggle on their laps.

Process

The participant asking for the secret ballot in the teleconference was taking advantage of the environment but he was also manipulating the process. We can manage the process in a number of ways. For example, we may be able to influence the form a meeting takes. Organizations, even quite structured and large ones, do not always lay down precise rules for their meetings and, if this is the case, then we may be able ensure a result before the meeting really starts. If we have the numbers to win a vote, then at the moment the chair opens the meeting we can state firmly, "I believe that the matter we have to discuss is so important that we should use formal meeting procedure and debate a formal motion in order to arrive at a decision everyone will support." If the chair or the meeting agrees to follow formal procedure, we have already won. However, if we do not have the numbers, then at the moment the chair opens the meeting we can state firmly, "I believe that the matter we have to discuss is so important that we should adopt an informal procedure, discuss the matter freely and openly, and arrive at a consensus so that no one feels they are being forced into anything." If the meeting agrees, then we may still win by making sure our supporters are the most forceful and vociferous, even if they are in a minority. And if we feel the meeting is not going our way, we can remind the chair that the meeting agreed to strive for a consensus and that we should abandon the meeting if a consensus cannot be achieved.

Once a meeting is under way we may be able to control it by making it conform to the problem-solving model of facts, issues, options and action. If we are chairing the meeting, we can apply the model directly. We can ask: Well, what do we know about this particular problem? Can anyone give us a report? Are we sure those are all the details? Now what does all this mean? Can we put these issues in some kind of order? All right then, what can we do? Can we stick to the main issues for the moment? Can we make a decision now?

We may also be able to influence the meeting from the floor. Just like the chair in my previous example, we may be able to point out that there is a sequence of questions to address and, if the meeting is a small one, we may be able to ask the questions ourselves. But there may also be times when it would be impolitic to do this, or not in our interests to show our hand. In these cases we can try to control the process through the use of language. To someone using the language of solutions (*ought* and *should*) we can respond by using the language of options (*can* and *could*) or the language of fact (*is* and *are*). Sometimes a meeting may be so informal or spontaneous that there is no one person in charge of it, and there might even be resistance if someone did try to take charge. In that case, the use of language may be our only way of exercising control.

If we go back to the example of the group of workers angered by management unexpectedly moving the time clocks, to the comment "We should stop work straight away," we might reply "We could do that, but we can also go on working and just go slow." And to the comment "We ought to tell the works manager to bugger off," we might reply "The manager is fairly new." In all likelihood someone would respond to this last remark by saying, "What do you mean?" We might then be able to say something like "Well, the company is not normally this stupid. They put in a new manager. The first thing he does is move the clock." By using the language of fact, we might be able to pull the discussion back to the logical starting point and get the group to redefine the problem.

Effective Speaking

And, of course, one of the ways of influencing a meeting is by speaking effectively. To do so we need to prepare. And if we do not know what our position will be until we have heard the full story in the actual meeting, then we need to prepare a number of alternative speeches.

When teaching effective speaking I like to urge people to say everything three times. I tell them to follow the old adage:

Tell 'em what you're gonna tell 'em.
Then tell 'em.
Then tell 'em what you've told 'em.

And I like talking about the Town Hall in Sydney. The main auditorium is often used by organizations for their annual general meetings because it can accommodate several hundred people, and its acoustics are good. It does have a problem, however. The stage is set higher than one would normally expect, with the result that the executive committee or company board or church hierarchy sitting in a line onstage look a little like ducks in a shooting gallery.

Let us imagine the annual general meeting of a union. A member in the body of the hall catches the chair's eye, is given the nod and stands. His speech has a beautifully crafted beginning, in which he tells the audience what he is going to tell 'em: "My name is Harry Bloggs," he says, "and I am an ordinary member of this union. I am going to take about three minutes to tell you mob up there on that bloody stage what a mess you are making. And I am doing this because if you lot don't fix things, we will have to elect some comrades who will."

Harry moves on to the middle of his speech, in which he tells 'em. He has broken this part of his speech into three sections. "Let me start by looking at what you have done at a national level. You went for a 20 percent pay rise across the board and got us a measly three and a half percent. That's all I want to say about your magnificent achievements at national level."

By stating that he is talking about the union at a national level, Harry creates the expectation that he will talk about the union at other levels. He goes on: "Now let's see what you have done at a state level. Well, here in New South Wales, you went for a cost-of-living allowance, and we got absolutely nothing! And that is all I have got to say about you lot at a state level."

The logic of his speech takes Harry to a third section. This time he opens with a question, implicitly challenging the audience to add examples of their own: "And what about at a local level? When we had a dispute at my workplace, you sent an official along to help us. He was all gung-ho and told us to go out on a twenty-four-hour strike. But the first date he suggested was a public holiday! And that is all I have to say about you lot at a local level."

Harry ends his speech by telling his audience what he told 'em: "So, at the national level you have been pathetic. At the state level you have been useless. And at the local level you have been worse than useless. You mob are no better than a bunch of silly galahs, and I am foreshadowing a motion of no confidence in the lot of you!" Harry pauses very briefly and then says, "That is all I want to say for the moment, and I am sitting down now."

Most participants laugh at the story of Harry Bloggs. Clearly he is an exaggeration, but if they have any experience of meetings, they usually recognize aspects of Harry in people they have encountered. We talk about Harry for a while and then I ask the participants to form groups of three and for each person to prepare a three-minute talk to give to the other two, bearing Harry Bloggs in mind.

I argue that, like Harry, we should break any talk down into a beginning, a middle and an end. In the beginning we should establish our identity. This may involve stating our name, often effective even when everyone already knows it. We should state our authority for speaking. This may derive from a position we hold, or a qualification, or experience, or from the fact that we are, like Harry, a fully paid-up, rank-and-file member of the organization. We should say what we will talk about. People like to know what is coming. We should state how long we will take. People adjust their ways of paying attention according to the time they expect to be listening. And we should state our purpose and so reassure the audience that we are not talking just for the sake of talking. Harry makes it clear that he wants to spill the committee!

For the middle of the talk, we should make brief, preferably one-word, notes, arrange those notes into a logical order, and then speak a "paragraph" for each note. And because an audience cannot actually see what we are saying, we must, as Harry did, say when we are starting and when we are finishing every paragraph.

For the end, again like Harry, we should give a summary or a conclusion, and make a proposal or tell our audience what is going to happen next. Harry foreshadowed a motion of no confidence in the entire leadership of his union. And we should try to end in a way that makes our audience go on thinking. Even when people have been listening closely, if a speaker ends abruptly, they can be caught by surprise and wonder why there is a sudden silence. Harry wanted his audience to go on thinking about what he had said, and so he removed any potential element of surprise by telling them that he had stopped and that he was going to sit down.

In the exercise on effective speaking I suggest that after each participant in a group of three has spoken, the three of them debrief and decide what pointers they can pass on to the next speaker. Although each person is presenting her or his own speech, the exercise is a group activity and the aim should be to make the third speech the best one.

Cynic or Realist?

When I have talked about managing and manipulating meetings some people have looked pensive. Others have been shocked. On one occasion a young man accused me of having no scruples. I expressed regret at having distressed him but made no apology. I have seen too many people go into meetings without having established what they wanted to achieve, without having thought about how the meeting might proceed and without having prepared what they might say or do. On one occasion four of us went into a meeting with the intention of getting a proposal approved. One of our group was scheduled to put the proposal forward but another spoke up early before the meeting had time to absorb the details. He spoke enthusiastically but was disorganized in what he said. When we reached the right moment in the meeting, our case had already been made and what little more we said sounded like gratuitous repetition. When our proposal was voted down, the member of our group who had spoken walked out of the meeting, making it even more difficult for those of us left behind to recoup the situation. For him the justice of our cause was obvious, and he was unable to recognize that his ill-prepared and ill-timed intervention, and then his disrespectful departure, had contributed significantly to our failure.

Meetings are a mixture of ritual, ceremony and social artifice. We need to understand what is ritual and should be respected, what is ceremony and can be varied according to the circumstances, and what is artifice and can be deconstructed and reconstructed to meet our purposes. If this is a cynical position to adopt, then so be it.

I watched a television documentary on Nelson Mandela in which this apparently gentlest of men talked of the proponents of apartheid whom he was fighting back in the 1950s, and said with straightforward intensity that he had hated them. Hateful people— or at least people with hateful views—do exist and I would have no compunction in using any knowledge I had of meetings in order to combat them. If I felt people with hateful views were in a majority at a meeting of an organization I valued, I would do what I could to turn the mood of the meeting around. If I could not do that, then I would do what I could to prevent the meeting from arriving at a decision. And if I knew that I had the numbers, I would do everything I could to ensure that these people with their hateful views were resoundingly and publicly defeated.

7

TEACHING DIALOGUE

I admit to a perverse pleasure in outlining ways of manipulating meetings. I like having thought through some of the strategies I might use in decision-making forums to get my own way, and this in turn sits well with the idea of defying the futures someone else might want to lay out for me. But I also feel a sense of unease. I realize that, whenever we can, we should strive to make choices and solve problems in conditions free from duplicity, if only for the pragmatic reason that the decisions will be more honestly informed, better accepted and, in all likelihood, more effective. I also realize that if I get my own way, then, in a classic Sartrean sense, by exercising my freedom I am restricting the freedom of others. It seems reasonable, therefore, to look for a mode of collective decision making in which real consensus is achieved and no one feels her or his freedoms have been intolerably compromised. Perfect consensus is probably unachievable, but we can envisage it as an ideal to strive for.

Paula Allman proposes that we strive for consensus through dialogue. She contrasts dialogue with discussion and argues that what usually passes for discussion, even in educational settings, is actually the "sharing of monologues." People take turns telling others what they already know, and their monologues "often bear no relation to one another except that they address the same topic or question" (Allman, 2001, 175). If there is any debate, then it is about ideas already formulated and knowledge already acquired. While members of the group may take away knowledge and ideas new to them as individuals, the sum total is no greater than that already possessed by the members before the discussion took place.

No new knowledge has been created. In this kind of discussion there is usually a leader whose role is to ensure that all the members of the group have an equal opportunity to speak, and this can sometimes be interpreted as giving each member an equal amount of *time* to speak.

Dialogue, Allman argues, is radically different. Whether between two people or in a group, it is a creative exchange in which new understandings are generated. Previous ideas and knowledge may be injected, but they are offered as tools and not as ends in themselves. The objective is to *use* the knowledge or thinking of the members of the group and, when necessary, the expertise of others in order to help the group examine a theme or issue critically (Allman, 2001, 176). The ideas of group members become "objects of collective focus." The group examines why individual members think the way they do, explores together with each member the history and cultural origins of her or his thinking, and seeks to make use of that collective analysis. If this is done as a truly collective activity, then the group develops "trust, care, collaboration and commitment" in the place of "competition and individualism" (Allman, 1987, 223). Any artificial allocation of time would run counter to the spirit of genuine dialogue since it could prevent the group from spontaneously pursuing a particular line of inquiry or from taking a particular analysis as far as it would go. The result may well be that the group appears to give over a considerable amount of time to one person, helping that person explore her or his values, assumptions and ideologies and come to understand more clearly how she or he has made meaning of the world. But the objective of such a focus would be to expand the thinking and develop the knowledge of the group as a whole.

Allman finds theoretical explanations for dialogue in Freire's educational principles and practices, Marx's theory of consciousness and praxis, and Gramsci's ideas on hegemony and counterhegemony (Allman, 1987; Allman, 2001, 177–184). True dialogue can transform us by transforming our understanding of ourselves in relation to our social, cultural and political worlds. It can transform our conception of knowledge. It can alter our consciousness. We cease considering knowledge as "an object that can be possessed" and think of it as being "as open and dialectical as the movement and development of reality we must constantly and endlessly seek to comprehend" (Allman, 2001, 180). Dialogue, Allman argues (2001, 177), is a form of communication that involves continuous struggle to radically change our ways of knowing and being.

Ideal Speech Situation

When trying to facilitate dialogic learning, I make use of Allman's ideas in the design of exercises, and I make direct reference to her distinction between discussion and dialogue. I also find it useful to refer to some of Jürgen Habermas's ideas on communicative action, and in particular his ideas on utterance and "criticisable validity claims" (Habermas, 1984).

Habermas argues that whenever someone—the prime minister, a person giving someone directions in the street, a teacher, your partner—speaks to someone else with the intention of reaching an understanding, whether the speaker knows it or not, she or he is making a number of validity claims. These claims are to truth, rightness and truthfulness. That is, that what she or he is saying is true, that she or he has a right—an authority or a legitimate reason—for saying it and that she or he is sincere in saying it (Habermas, 1984: 99, 307). Habermas describes these claims as "criticisable" because they can be tested and met with a yes/no answer. So when someone speaks, we can ask whether the speaker is meeting these claims. To test for truth we can ask: Has the speaker included all relevant information? Has the speaker done everything to represent all information fully and correctly? Has the speaker revealed and accurately represented all sources? Do we as listeners accept and share the knowledge of the speaker? To test for rightness or legitimacy we can ask: Is the speaker in the appropriate role and context? Does the speaker have the agreement of those on whose behalf she or he is speaking? Is the speaker observing the required norms? Does the speaker occupy a position which entitles her or him to speak on these matters? To test for sincerity we can ask: Is the speaker being consistent in what she or he says? Has the speaker disclosed all interests, and all responsibilities to other parties? Has the speaker been open and frank about her or his motives for speaking, about her or his feelings, beliefs and values?

Habermas (1984, 100) argues that each of these criticisable validity claims can be judged against one of the three worlds we inhabit. So, in asking if the utterance is true, we are asking whether there is a fit between the utterance on the one hand, and the objective world on the other. In asking if the speaker has a right to make the utterance, we are asking if there is a fit with the social world. And, in asking if the utterance is sincere, we are asking if there is a fit with our subjective world.

Habermas posits "an ideal speech situation" in which everyone present seeks to redeem these validity claims. That is, each person makes every effort to say only what she or he believes to be true, to speak only when she or he has the right or the authority to speak, and to be sincere in everything she or he says. In an ideal speech situation, there is a consensus on the character of the communication rather than on its substance. This kind of consensus forms the basis of what Habermas calls "communicative action." Sometimes this form of consensus can be enough because it enables people with very different ways of thinking to coexist, and to make parallel choices instead of choices which compromise or negate those of others. Many of us know couples, for example, who have lived together for years in harmonious disagreement on quite significant issues of lifestyle, politics or religious belief. They do not hide their differences but manage them through continuous, open and honest communication.

Habermas does discuss two other "claims." These have to do with the intelligibility and aesthetic nature of the utterance (Habermas, 1984, 23). To test for intelligibility we would ask: Is the utterance comprehensible? Does it conform with good communicative practice? Can I understand it? And to test for the aesthetics of the utterance we would ask: Is the utterance pleasing? Does the utterance conform with values which I find agreeable? But in my teaching I tend to spend less time on these two claims. They are different. They depend on the subjective judgment of the listener. They cannot be tested and met with a definitive yes/no answer since one person may find an utterance intelligible or pleasing while another may not. And, most significantly, neither of the claims goes to the integrity of the person making the utterance.

Facilitating Dialogue

From time to time I have used a three- or four-stage exercise to discourage people from sharing monologues and to nudge them into dialogue. I was running a two-day workshop on organizing in the workplace for members from two associated political organizations. The participants were streetwise activists with strong opinions, and I was keen to avoid exchanges along predictable party lines. I delayed the start, suggesting we might wait for possible latecomers. Several discussions started up, and after a moment or two I joined in one of them myself. After ten minutes or so I called the group together, introduced the program for the day and asked the participants to form pairs, each person choosing someone she or he did not know. I asked the pairs to learn about each other by the time-honored methods of asking and telling. Again I let this run for a while, and then asked each pair to find another pair and to go on with the process of getting to know each other. However, I wanted them to observe a rule: they were to avoid using the word *I* and to try using the word *we* when talking to the other pair.

I let the groups of four talk for another five minutes, then interrupted them and talked about Allman's claim that most discussions were no more than the sharing of monologues. I asked them to think back to the spontaneous discussions before we made a formal start. Had they been engaged in the sharing of monologues? Now what about the exchanges in pairs? They had been asking questions and replying. Had any of the questions elicited something other than a monologue? Now what about the groups of four? Had using *we* changed the nature of the discussion? Was it a restriction? A challenge? A catalyst of any kind? Had it prevented the exchange of monologues?

I asked the groups of four to prepare to go back into discussion by moving away from the tables and positioning their chairs as best they could in a circle. I then placed a polystyrene cup on the floor in the center of each circle. I said that in discussions people relate to one another but that this time, instead of relating to one another, they were to examine how they "related" to the cup. They were to focus on the cup and what it might represent or mean. When they analyzed a response, they were to concentrate on that response and not on the person doing the responding. Of course, they could use the word *I*, but whenever possible they should go on making use of the word *we*.

For a while the discussions were hesitant, but they picked up and developed into exchanges about consumerism, fair trade in coffee, international trade in general, environmental issues, local politics . . . I let these discussions run for a while and then interrupted them and talked about the three validity claims. I suggested that they go back into their discussions, bearing the ideas of truth, rightness and truthfulness in mind. The discussions resumed, and I let them run for a while longer before drawing the exercise to a close. I debriefed by simply asking the whole group for their reactions. The mood was a cheerful one and I could intervene from time to time, openly testing various speakers' validity claims by asking questions like "Are you absolutely sure of that?" or "Are you in a position to say that?" or "Do you really mean that?"

I used this exercise in this particular workshop as part of the process of helping people get to know each other a little better and, after a coffee break, we moved on to organizing in the workplace. However, if I have half a day or a whole day or several meetings over a number of weeks in which to concentrate on dialogue and consensus, then I will use a more detailed form of this exercise, interspersed with papers and presentations. The exercise becomes three long exchanges, ideally in groups of about eight people. I open by talking about Allman's ideas on the sharing of monologues. I then place a simple object which we are likely to use in our everyday lives—a key, a pair of scissors, a diary—in the center of each group and ask the group to discuss it. I ask them to let the object mediate the exchanges. They can critically analyze the various responses to the object, that is, help each other tease out and appraise the underlying assumptions and values in their reactions to the object, but they must not criticize, in the sense of demeaning, attacking, or even disagreeing with, the people doing the responding. We debrief and, if the process is taking place over a number of weekly meetings, I usually distribute a reading by Allman (2001, 175–177). Somewhere in the debriefing I try to make the point that much sterile debate is locked into the present. "You are wrong. No, I am right. These are the reasons why you are wrong. These are the reasons why I am right." I suggest that a way out of this kind of dead-end exchange is to examine the biographical, social and cultural backgrounds of the ideas being put forward. "That is an interesting idea. Where did it come from? What experiences, events and influences caused us to construct or take up the idea? Do these explanations hold good now?"

In the next phase, I introduce ideas on dialogue, drawing on Freire and Allman and using articles or quotations from their writings. I tell them that Allman uses the phrases "objects of thought" and "objects of interest" when talking about the focus of a dialogic exchange (Allman, 1987, 2001). I then ask the groups of eight to reconvene. This time, instead of a utilitarian object, I place a piece of paper in the circle with a problem or challenge written on it. I ask the participants to treat the problem as an object of thought, to help each other explore their responses, and to try to generate new ways of thinking. (In an exercise I ran shortly after a gunman killed thirty-five people at Port Arthur in Tasmania I wrote on the paper: "Port Arthur.") We debrief the second phase, discussing how we can examine assumptions, values, ideals and ideologies in a way that accepts both the emotion and allows for creative exchange.

Somewhere in the debriefing I try to mention that Allman (2001, 179–180), taking a leaf from Gramsci's prison notebooks, acknowledges the place of passion in her vision of dialogue.

In the third phase I talk about Habermas's concept of the ideal speech situation. When it is possible, I provide readings in advance in the form of an excerpt from Habermas himself (Habermas, 1984, 99) and commentaries on Habermas by people like Welton (1995) and Dallmayr (1996). I ask the groups of eight to reconvene. I tell them that I am symbolically placing an idea in the center of the circle as an object of interest. I ask them to conduct a collective inquiry mediated by the idea, to make every effort to redeem the three validity claims in every utterance they make, and to try to generate new ideas and new knowledge. An idea I have "placed" in the center of the groups in the past is "Quality is an absolute. When it is there in an object, an activity or an idea, we can always recognize it."

The debriefing of this third phase also becomes a debriefing of the whole exercise. I try to draw from the group the conclusions that, if we use dialogue, we are likely to form authentic understandings of the problems confronting us. That if we try to achieve an ideal speech situation, then we will make choices about those problems in a climate of trust and commitment. And that this kind of collective decision making is more likely to result in effective, communicative action.

8

CONFLICT, NEGOTIATION AND POWER

Conflict

All but the smallest and most isolated societies are pluralistic. They are made up of an array of groups of people defined by multiple loyalties, beliefs, pursuits and relationships. There are countless cases of cooperation, of course, but there are countless conflicts of interest as well. Some of the conflicts will be minor ones, resolved by a glance, a gesture, a quick conversation or through a multitude of established rituals like those which take place between a salesperson and a customer in a shop. But society is also constructed on major conflicts of interest occurring in multiple configurations within and between a vast variety of structured, semistructured and informal groupings of people. These conflicts are managed by continual and often complex negotiation. It could be argued that negotiation, like problem solving, is an essential skill.

Negotiation differs from collective decision making. In collective decision making everyone involved has some common bond. People may have widely differing viewpoints and the arguments may be fierce but they will all be members of the same organization, parents of children in the same school, people with the same interests or needs, or people with the same oppressor. There will be a commonality which brings them together, and which requires them to make choices that relate to them all. Whether by informal or formal meeting or by dialogue, the aim is to arrive at an agreement. The consensus may reflect a genuine harmony or be threadbare, but the decision is accepted, grudgingly or otherwise, by all. If individuals cannot abide by the decision, then they will probably abandon any idea that they have interests in common with the others involved, and leave.

If collective decision making is a process of achieving a consensus, then negotiation is a process of trying to reach a "nonconsensual agreement." The various parties will always share certain features and interests—they may come from the same culture and speak the same language, for example—but there will also be significant differences. In negotiation one or more of the parties involved will have to concede and, even when concessions are made by everyone involved, there are still likely to be comparative winners and serious losers. Negotiation is a response to conflict and is just one of several ways, along with mediation, coercion and violence, of dealing with that conflict.

Power

Negotiation can only take place when all the parties have some kind of power. If one of the parties has no power, it must comply. If there is an imbalance, then the weaker parties will enter the negotiation reluctantly, try to limit the matters negotiated, and perhaps even stall or spoil the process. If the balance is fairly even, then genuine negotiations are possible. They may be tough but they are likely to get somewhere.

Before we enter into a negotiation, therefore, we need to do some thinking about the power of the different parties involved. But arriving at an accurate understanding of relative power is not so straightforward. One party might have considerable power of one particular kind while another might have an array of different kinds. When we go into a negotiation we will be bringing different needs, interests and demands to the table, and we will be pitting different forms and combinations of power against each other.

I like to begin the process of teaching negotiation with a discussion of power. I ask the participants to think on their own for a moment of someone they have some kind of power over, how they demonstrate that power, and where their power comes from. I give

them some time to do this, and then I ask them to think of someone who has power over *them*. I suggest they make a note and then
talk over their examples with one or two other people in the group.
In the full-group discussion which follows, and in subsequent discussions, instruction and debriefings, I hope to draw out and examine a number of definitions, and a number of ideas on applications
and sources of power.

Defining Power

Social theorists depict power in radically different ways. As we have
already seen, Weber (1968, 53) defined power in terms of being able
to carry out one's own will despite resistance. Understood in this
way power is a tool we wield to make people comply with our
wishes. In this depiction we tend to think of power as vested in an
individual, or in a group or organization pursuing a single-minded
objective in much the same way an individual does. And we see
power in hierarchical terms, with people at the top using their
power to influence, control and dominate those with less power
below them. Power is a force to be borne down on people.

Hannah Arendt (1986, 64), on the other hand, sees power as
deriving from people's ability to act in concert. Power in this case is
not the property of an individual. If it has been vested in an individual, then that is only because the individual has been empowered by a number of people to act in their name. In this form, power
is less a force to be used and more a resource to be drawn upon. It is
shared and is delegated upwards. We can still interpret this kind of
power in hierarchical terms, but it may be more difficult to locate it
accurately since it can be disguised, existing as potential rather than
actual power. People drawing upon this kind of power may seem at
first glance to be less powerful than they really are.

We can see these two kinds of power at play in the industrial relations arena. Management makes use of power according to Weber's
definition. It acts much as an individual does, expressing a unified
will. It seeks to make the workers comply with that will. And it

claims an authority, something called *management prerogative*, to justify doing so. The unions, on the other hand, derive their power from the people they represent, and so make use of a power conforming more to Arendt's definition. Their power depends on the support they have and can be estimated in terms of the size and solidarity of the union's membership.

Weber used the definition above as a starting point only. He argued that in modern societies power has shifted from individuals with identifiable positions, capacities and prestige to impersonal administrative systems applying abstract rules. But he still saw power as a form of domination. Postmodern theorists have depicted power as more diffuse, and have understood the way it "flows" differently. Taking their lead from Foucault (1978, 1980), they depict power as decentered, pluralistic, ubiquitous and non-hierarchical. Power is expressed in a myriad of locations, events and ever-changing relations and groupings of people, rather than being centrally located in large apparently stable structures such as the state or the legal system or a corporation. The large structures and organizations exist, but they come afterwards as a means of describing and bringing some order to these myriad expressions of power. Power is neither vested in anyone nor anyone's property. The forces that influence and control us can be found, for example, in the family, and in the values that come with the family, as much as in our political leaders.

In many depictions power is seen as a force of control, and therefore of limitation and oppression. But Foucault argues that power is also productive. It produces what we can do. We turn to it in order to make sense of ourselves. And so, in the way power may "make" a large structure or organization, power makes us. This leads Foucault to look differently at the relationship between power and knowledge. It is a truism to say that knowledge is power, yet if we make sense of ourselves by turning to various bodies of knowledge, then we are the objects of interest in those bodies of knowledge. *They* define *us*, and so effectively exercise power over us. This is particularly true, Foucault maintains, of the bodies of knowledge known as the "human sciences," which may ostensibly describe and analyze us but actually dictate who we are and prescribe what we do (Foucault, 1978, 1980; Danaher, Schirato and Webb, 2000).

Foucault's ideas on power are expressed in a discourse drawing freely from art, literature and the human sciences. At times and in a manner common to other French thinkers, Foucault writes in an elated or inspirational style very different from the traditional English modes of rational argument (Merquior, 1991, 11–12). However, as happens with postmodern discourse, its freedom from the strictures of conventional rationality can prompt us into alternative ways of thinking. In effect Foucault turns the modernist ideas of power on their head. He gives us license to analyze the powers of parties to a negotiation in terms of ebbs and flows and multiple and dispersed relationships, and to reflect that some of their claims to power may be more mirage than reality. An apparently all-powerful government may try to legislate changes in national character, only to discover that this particular kind of power is dispersed across literally millions of individuals, families and social groupings. In much the same way, parties to a negotiation may assume they have a particular kind of power only because they have never tried using it. And again, one of the parties may assume they have power over the others because they are privy to particular knowledge. But by referring back to that knowledge, and in effect defining themselves by it, they may actually limit the way they interpret the issues to be negotiated, prevent themselves from looking for original and creative solutions and so restrict their avenues for action.

A Caveat

Ideas like these, and the exhilarating style in which they are often expressed, can make postmodern discourse on power seductive. But the ideas can also be illusory. Postmodern discourse provides plenty of exciting "theory," but it is often theory which offers little or no guide for practice. An enthusiastic advocate of "postmodern education" for example, was stymied by the question "But where can I find a postmodern educator?" for the simple reason that no such animal exists.

Postmodern ideas can provide us with alternative ways of analyzing our world, but we need constantly to remind ourselves that the world remains in the grips of modernist ideologies such as capitalism and patriarchy and even premodern ideologies such as religious fundamentalism. The power of these ideologies is strong and pervasive, and we must not abandon modernist theory and its associated modernist practice as we seek to deal with them, and with the ideologues who promote them. When talking about the applications of power, therefore, I return to a more modernist, critical analysis.

The Ways and Means of Power

We can apply power in a number of ways, and I like to categorize these applications in terms of Habermas's "tripartitions" (Habermas, 1972; Dallmayr, 1996, 85–87), locating them respectively in the objective, social and subjective worlds. So, in the objective world, we can apply power by instrumental means. We build dams, plow fields and crush grapes. And just as we use instrumental means to engage with the physical environment, so we use them to control people, much as if they too were physical objects. So we push people around, lock them up and make them comply with our wishes through force or the threat of force. Elsewhere when outlining this kind of categorization of the applications power, I used the term *physical force* instead of *instrumental means* (Newman, 1999, 60–62). But the term *physical force* does not so easily accommodate those less obviously physical yet completely instrumental modes of applying power and gaining control over other people, such as electronic surveillance and all the organization, commerce, manipulation and mobilization taking place on the Internet. But there are losses as well as gains in my change of terminology. We talk of "virtual worlds" and "virtual reality" as if they were nowhere and did not really exist, but of course these worlds are physically present, there in graphic form in front of our eyes on a screen and, despite the illusions, subject to the laws of cause and effect.

We can see both benign and malign applications of instrumental power. A government may encourage the construction of blocks of residential units and the conversion of office blocks to units to draw residents back into the business district and so reinvigorate the center of a city. Another government may use the police and the army to displace whole populations of villages or towns against their will. A firm may access a range of legitimate electronic databases in the interests of its clients. Another may amass information in order to intrude unsolicited into people's lives.

In the social world, we apply power through institutions. We can see this institutional control at work in government, the legal system, banks, schools, sports clubs and families, all those institutions which we have established to enable us to live our lives in a reasonably secure, civil, efficient and fulfilling way. As we have already seen, all of us submit voluntarily to various forms of institutional control in return for the benefits those institutions provide us. But sometimes this institutional power is used coercively. The government requires us to pay taxes and enforces this through legislation and, if necessary, prosecution through the courts. The banks make us keep up with our mortgage repayments through the unspoken threat of eviction, which we know from occasional well-publicized examples they are perfectly capable of carrying out. We can see from this example that instrumental power "folds over" into institutional power, since some institutions exercise their control through the menace of physical force as much as through the structures and processes of the institution.

In the subjective world, we apply power through ideas. We seek to establish an intellectual hegemony. We try to get the ideas, values and moral codes which benefit us accepted as mainstream, so much so that to question them would invite ridicule. Advertisers try to establish a particular brand as the standard one that everyone in her or his right mind would want to use. Politicians try to express ideologies and policies in catchwords which will lodge in the language, become common wisdom, and so simply not be challenged. Action, interest and pressure groups all struggle to have their stance become the correct one. So people at the big end of town eying off efficient and therefore potentially profitable state utilities will want everyone to accept that "privatization is the only way to go."

Again institutional power folds over into hegemonic power since values and patterns of thinking are instilled in populations by means of institutions such as government, schools, churches, the mass media and the leisure industry. And institutions in their turn exist as much by virtue of the policies, ideas and value systems they embody and promote as by their people, buildings, structures and processes.

Sources of Power

We can draw power from a number of sources. Bernard Mayer (1987) lists some of these. I have added some of my own to his list, and grouped the lot into sources of instrumental, institutional and hegemonic power. So, we can derive instrumental power from brute strength. We may simply be large and physically strong and so cut an imposing or menacing figure. We may have access to tools and equipment and be able to alter the environment. And we may have weapons. Large and wealthy countries can and do exercise power over weaker ones for exactly these reasons. We can derive instrumental power from our control over resources. Oil-producing countries, for example, derive their power from their capacity to manipulate supply. And we can derive instrumental power from specialized knowledge and skills, which we may use or withhold. Internet technicians, for example, can have huge potential power in an enterprise because they manage, and can therefore alter or disrupt, the flow of essential data.

We can derive institutional power from our formal position in the structure of an organization. Certain positions confer authority and the right to make decisions, as the title "manager" and an officer's rank in the army do. But we can also derive power from an unofficial position. Organizations have informal as well as formal structures, and some people will get power from their position as the longest-serving employee, or the most popular, or the most outspoken or as the member of a group of colleagues who, say, share an interest in fishing. We can derive institutional power from the customs and practices of an organization or community or society or culture. So doctors in a small town traditionally have an influence or authority that extends well beyond their medical remit. We can derive power from the law, as a parent or guardian does over the affairs of a minor, and we can seek power through the courts and tribunals of the land, as someone suing for damages may. We can derive power from our control of processes and procedures. As we have seen, people can gain influence and get their way by manipulating meetings. And we can derive power from our association with others who have power, as the people close to a leader might, and as political lobbyists constantly try to do.

We can derive hegemonic or counterhegemonic power, that is power in the realm of ideas, from our personal attributes. We can influence, change and perhaps even control the thinking of others through our self-assurance, determination and endurance. We can influence them through our articulateness, our command of information and our capacity to provide convincing solutions to problems. We can derive power from people's habits, introducing change in ways which seem least disruptive to their everyday lives, and getting them to resist change by appealing to their fear of the unknown. We can use the mantra of "We have always done it this way." We can derive power from people's assumptions and values, presenting arguments in ways which conform to their assumptions, or appeal to their values. We can derive power from established mores by arguing that our ideas and actions conform to tried-and-tested traditions.

And we can derive power from established moral codes by arguing that our ideas and actions are good.

Powerful People

It can make for an interesting roundup to ask participants in discussions of power to speculate on the sources from which a number of public figures get their power. I have used figures from politics, sport and industry. With one group we decided that the then leader of the federal opposition had little direct power in parliament, and that he derived his power from the support of the caucus, his own personal attributes and a desire in parts of the population for an alternative government. The effort he put into scoring points off the government when parliament was in session may have been a ritual necessity but that his real sources of power did not lie there. We decided that a leading sporting figure gained his power from his prowess at his chosen sport, his success as captain of a national team, his reticent public persona and the respect gained from the fact that he devoted money and time to support orphanages in India.

With another group I discussed the sources of power of the two key figures in a drawn-out industrial dispute on the Australian waterfront in 1998. One of the major stevedoring companies had locked out its workers and tried unsuccessfully to replace them with nonunion labor. At the company's Sydney port the workers had been escorted off the docks by security guards with dogs. We decided that the chief executive officer of the stevedoring company derived his power from his wealth, his position, his association with senior political figures and the perception he had fostered in the media that the union had too much control on the waterfront. The leader of the union derived his power from his personal attributes of calmness and determination, the commitment of the union's members, the fact that he had been elected to his position by those members, and the support of other unions. He also derived power from the moral codes of the country, which many saw as having been flouted when dogs were used against working people.

A Useful Precursor

Analyzing power is a useful precursor to any engagement, whether that engagement be collaborative or adversarial. It helps us understand ourselves, and the people we engage with. And it helps us choose the kinds of action we will take, in company with, or in opposition to, those people.

9

TEACHING NEGOTIATION

When we come to the actual process of negotiation I can draw on the experience of a number of very skilled educators. In TUTA, for example, we pooled and adapted definitions, ideas, processes and resources as we went along, and a good bit of what follows in this chapter comes out of this pragmatic, collective wisdom.

Consultation, Negotiation or Dispute

Once we have decided to engage, we need to decide whether the engagement will be consultation, negotiation or a dispute.

We can define negotiation as

the process whereby two or more parties with both common and conflicting interests come together to talk with a view to reaching an agreement.

There are two important features to this definition. The first is that the parties talk with a view to reaching an agreement. One party may lose out badly and another may make considerable gains, but everyone is intent on reaching an agreement, even if it is minimal, temporary and unstable. Indeed if any party comes to the table without intending to reach an agreement, then the process is not a negotiation but simply a moment of masquerade, a stratagem, a jab or a feint in the course of a dispute.

The unions working on a large site in the central business district of Sydney grew troubled by the deteriorating relations with the developers. Work had been progressing well, and the core of one of the towers had already risen above the surrounding city buildings. Now the developers seemed to be creating disputes and, when challenged, demanded changes in work practices. Negotiations started, but the developers kept stalling and changing tack until the negotiations broke down and all work ceased on the site. The unions were blamed for the breakdown, but it subsequently became known that the developers had been in financial difficulties and so in all likelihood had never intended to reach an agreement in the first place.

The second important feature in the definition of negotiation is that the parties involved have both common *and* conflicting interests. The common interests bring them to the table to talk, and the conflicting interests mean they have to go through the difficult, stressful and usually time-consuming process of negotiation when they get there. The situation is paradoxical. They cannot use collective decision-making processes because of the conflicts of interests, yet no matter how extensive their differences may be, they need each other's concurrence to achieve some significant objective.

That objective may be survival. The breakdown of a marriage may be complete, but both people may see access to their children as essential for their own emotional survival. However distressing the encounters are, they still need to achieve some kind of agreement with each other. In industrial relations, management needs the cooperation of the workforce to continue in business, and the workers need management to provide the work and pay their wages. Both have a common interest in production since production ensures their continued existence. But within the very activity about which they agree lies the source of their conflict since once production is ensured, both sides want an increased share of it. Management wants its share in terms of more profit, and the workers want theirs in terms of better wages and improved working conditions.

In modern workplaces the equation is never simple. Profit may be expressed in dividends, salary packages, capital investments and acquisitions for growth and diversification. Wages and conditions may take the form of pay, safety, services, superannuation and less quantifiable features such as education, opportunities for advancement and reduction of stress. The divisions between management and workers may be unclear. Four lawyers may work together, apparently as equals, but three may be partners while the fourth is a salaried employee. In a small IT company the informality of relationships may disguise and confuse the relationships between manager and employee. And in an example I came across recently, a small circus operating as an informal group of performers won a grant to appoint a business manager. The performers selected the manager who set in place formal business structures, and the performers then found themselves having to negotiate their conditions and salaries with the person they had appointed. Negotiation is rarely a tidy business.

From the definition of negotiation we can derive a definition for consultation as

> the process whereby two or more parties whose common interests outweigh any conflicting ones come together to talk with a view to sharing information and solving problems to their mutual advantage.

This echoes the definition of a meeting. All the parties are already essentially in agreement. They share the same philosophies and aims, and discussions will concentrate on how to work together to achieve those aims.

From the definition of negotiation we can also derive a definition of a dispute as

> a process in which parties whose conflicting interests outweigh any common ones engage with one another, each with a view to furthering its own interests or gaining ascendancy for its own viewpoint.

Here the parties have different philosophies and aims. Each party regards the other or others as a hindrance, and there is no desire to reach agreement.

Consultation, negotiation and disputes are worked through according to different "rules." Consultation is carried out through formal and informal meetings. There is normally an agenda agreed to by everyone. Rules of procedure or customs of practice are followed. Information is shared. And relations are friendly or at least civil. In negotiation the parties talk but do not necessarily share all the information they have. There are no set procedures. There are no rules. There is no hard-and-fast agenda, no chair and no set time. There will be sudden adjournments, breakdowns, and resumptions. There will be claims and counterclaims, moments of silence, heated exchanges and sudden shifts of focus. However, because both sides need each other they will keep at the negotiation until some kind of agreement is reached. This means that during the negotiations relations can become strained but that outside the actual negotiating room the parties remain civil to one another. Disputes, on the other hand, are worked out through direct, tough, sometimes ugly and sometimes terminal forms of confrontation. They can involve angry, damaging encounters or long-drawn-out stalemates in which one or more of the parties goes to the wall. It is because of the potential of disputes to cause irreversible harm that we often try to resolve them by appeal to a third party in the form of a mediator or the courts.

Getting Ready to Negotiate

If we decide we can enter into negotiation, then we can use a mnemonic of four *P*s and two *C*s to help us prepare for the actual encounter.

The first *P* is for *prepare*. Negotiation is possible because all parties have common and conflicting interests, and our first major task is to identify and understand in detail all those interests.

The second *P* is for *partialize*. I have taken this word from a book by Mark Anstey (1991, 130–132), who developed procedures for negotiation, mediation and conflict resolution amidst the anti-apartheid struggles in South Africa in the 1980s. He uses the word to denote the process of breaking problems down into their multiple parts.

The third *P* is for *plan*. This is the stage in which we set our objectives and formulate our demand, target and resistance point on each of the major issues. The demand is what we will ask for at the outset of the negotiations. The target is what we expect to get. And the resistance point is the lowest offer we will accept. A union representative in a small workplace might enter into negotiations for a pay rise across the board, setting her demand at $20 per week, her target at $16 and her resistance point at $12. She must choose her initial demand carefully, and be able to justify it with convincing arguments so that any move away from it can be interpreted as a desire to reach an agreement and not as a sign of a poor or overstated case. This will put the onus on the other side to make a move towards an agreement also. Her target needs to be strong but realistic. It must satisfy the people she represents and enable her to emerge from the negotiations with her relations with both the workforce and management uncompromised. And she must be confident of her resistance point. This is the point beyond which she will not be pushed, and she needs to have reassured herself beforehand that she will have the active support of her fellow workers if she calls off the negotiations.

The demand, target and resistance point above are expressed in straightforward dollar terms, but often they consist of "baskets" of different and interconnected claims. Let us imagine that a well-known photographer has been approached by the owners of an art gallery to record in detail the repairs and renovations which will be made to their heritage-listed building over the period of eighteen months. His demand might be a figure of, say, $50,000, the retention of the copyright of the photographs and an undertaking from the gallery owners to exhibit his photographs for a period of one month in their gallery within a year of the completion of the renovations. His target might be a figure of $40,000, copyright of the photos to go to the gallery owners but their permission to develop a photographic study for his own use of the skills of the craftspeople doing the heritage renovations, and a commitment to an exhibition of his photographs of the skills within two years of the gallery's reopening. His resistance point might simply be a figure of $35,000.

In fixing our resistance point we need to review those principles upon which we cannot compromise. A union must not compromise the safety of the workers it represents. An investigative journalist negotiating a story cannot compromise her or his sources. The photographer will not compromise his standing in his profession.

The fourth P is for *predict*. Once we have our own case prepared and planned we need to look at the kinds of case the other parties are going to argue. We need to spend time thinking through how they might analyze the problem or challenge, what objectives they might set, what their demands, targets and resistance points are likely to be, and how they might justify them. In effect we need to go through the same process we did for ourselves, trying as far as is feasible to put ourselves into our opponents' shoes. In the case of the union representative seeking the pay rise, she might anticipate that management's demand is likely to be a $5 increase, their target $10 and their resistance $15. The demands, targets and resistance points for both sides are represented in Figure 5.

If the resistance points overlap, then agreement is likely in the overlap area, in this case somewhere between $12 and $15.

Figure 5

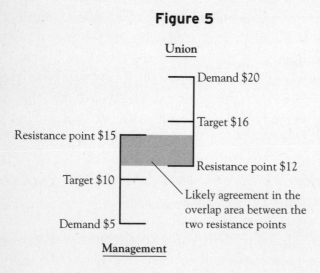

From Trade Union Training Australia Inc. (TUTA). Used by permission.

The first C is for *coordinate*. If we are negotiating in a team, then we need to allocate roles. Key roles are those of lead speaker, backup speaker and note-taker. The lead speaker is just that, the person who puts the demand and justifies it, and who does most of the arguing. The backup speaker intervenes from time to time to add to an argument, or to offer a predetermined concession, or to distract the other side for a moment in order to allow the lead speaker time to pause and reorganize her or his thoughts. The note-taker records each offer, shift in position or concession made by the other parties. This is a vital role because it enables the two speakers to refer back accurately to what the other side has said and so lock any concessions or offers into place.

The second C is for *control*. If there are enough people on the negotiating team, then one member should be given the authority to call for adjournments. This team member watches for any loss of control, lack of coordination between the speakers or departures from agreed tactics. Negotiators can get caught up in the tension and excitement of the process and easily lose perspective, and they must agree beforehand that this team member's authority to call for adjournments is absolute. And it is useful to have yet another member of the team whose job is to evaluate the progress of the negotiation, to sum up during each of the adjournments, and to suggest changes and improvements to the tactics. Even in a negotiating team of no more than two people, it is useful to acknowledge and, where possible, allocate these different coordinating and controlling roles.

At the Negotiating Table

We can teach people what to do before a negotiation but, because there are no rules, it is less easy to teach people what to do in the negotiation itself. Every negotiation will be different. Some will be short, others drawn-out. Some will be about one issue, others about multiple issues. Some will be about minor matters, others about life and death. Negotiators will differ. Some will speak quietly, making the others lean forward to hear them. Others will shout and thump the table. Some will be logical, others purposely erratic in their arguments. Some will be cool, calm and collected, others petulant. Some will be conciliatory, others menacing.

There are few actual practices to teach but there are guidelines to be borne in mind and possible patterns to follow. When I worked as a trade union trainer we "taught" negotiation by putting the course participants through a series of negotiation role plays. These allowed the participants to experience negotiation for themselves and to develop their own negotiating styles. The exercises were organized so that there was a move from single- to multi-issue negotiation, and so that the participants had an opportunity to play different roles and take different sides. In one particular four-day course, the final negotiation took up a full day, with an hour and a half allowed for the teams to meet and prepare, up to three hours for the actual negotiation, and at least another hour and a half given over to the debriefing. For a residential course running from Sunday to Friday, I designed a scenario which required the participants to go through a series of negotiations leading up to a major negotiation on Thursday, followed by a debriefing on Thursday evening and Friday morning.

The training rooms we used had large whiteboards and ample wall space on which to hang large sheets of newsprint. Towards the end of the process the room would be festooned with the common practices and guidelines we had come up with during the various debriefings:

Make sure that the other side has the authority to commit to any agreement you reach.

Never go into a negotiation alone.

Listen.

Get the other side talking first, and listen.

After listening, adjourn.

When you do talk, be able to justify what you say.

Never reveal your bottom line. If you do, the other parties will push you to it.

Do not try to score points. This is not a game. The negotiator scoring the points may be losing the negotiation.

Use adjournments to rest, reflect, evaluate your progress and do more research and planning.

Adjourn if the negotiation takes a turn you did not anticipate during your preparation.

Adjourn if you are not making progress.

Adjourn if there is any lack of coordination in your own ranks.

Always adjourn before accepting an offer.

Make strategic use of the simple issues. Settle them quickly and establish a climate of trust.

Make strategic use of the simple issues. Force the other side to fight for them.

Never give anything away without getting something in return.

Use your power. Apply sanctions, withhold resources, organize a news story, apply moral pressure, call a twenty-four-hour strike . . .

Compromise on details, never on principles.

Never declare a negotiation complete until you have a statement signed by all the parties.

Phases

When there was sufficient time, we would videotape a negotiation exercise and play back parts of it during the debriefing. Although there is no standard agenda, many negotiations do move through a number of phases, and sometimes we used the video to get the participants to identify and discuss these phases. Sometimes we could see that these different phases were marked out by different forms and styles of language.

Normally there is an *opening* phase in which the parties assemble at the negotiating table. There will be greetings and introductions, small talk if some of the people know each other, and a period of settling down in which people get their papers in order, pour themselves a glass of water and the like. During this phase the legitimacy of some of the people present may be challenged, and their presence may have to be justified. Also, apparently minor matters may be decided which can have an effect on the negotiation, such as seating and the timing of refreshment breaks. (I watched an experienced negotiator manage to adjust the seating slightly so that a member of the other party was sitting more to the negotiator's side of the room, subtly disrupting the way the members of the other party related to each other.) On the surface or in reality, however, the matters dealt with in this opening phase will be uncontroversial and consequently the language used will be informal in style. Sentences will sometimes be unfinished. There will be questions asked as a matter of form and not requiring an answer. "Do you two know . . . ?" "Of course, you've met one another. Where was it?" "All right, I reckon we should . . . "

This phase is important. If the negotiation is going to progress, certain civilities have to be established. It is also an opportunity for the negotiators to get a sense of the levels of confidence and commitment of the other parties.

The opening phase gives way to a *demand* phase. This is the beginning of the negotiation proper when each party makes its demands. This is a period of disputation in which the wills of the different parties are tested by demand and counterdemand. The demands may be restated several times in different ways, and a number of different arguments may be put forward to justify each one, but no one moves from their original position. In this phase the language used is direct. The sentences will be short, complete and for the most part in the form of statements:

"The company is making money. We want a pay increase now."
"You know we can't do that. It's just not on!"

"The manuscript's finished."
"It's too long."

"A child needs his father."
"But you're a drunk."

This demand phase often ends in an adjournment. Having heard the arguments, the negotiators are in a better position to decide whether to continue to negotiate or not.

If the negotiations do not break down in the demand phase, then they move into a *speculation* phase. This can be long and drawn-out. Possible outcomes are proposed without commitments being made. The language is couched in the conditional and the sentences are often rambling and incomplete. There are constant disclaimers:

"Of course, I can promise nothing at this stage, but if you were to move a little on that business of the overtime allowance, we might be able to think again about one or two of the other matters . . . "

"If you increased the royalties, maybe we could talk about first right of refusal on my next book . . . "

"I am not sure whether there is anyone available, but let's just say for the moment that we could find someone suitable to be present during the first few visits . . . "

Adjournments are called to consider these different proposals. The negotiators will return to the table with slight adjustments to the last proposal and then go into adjournment again. Each side is testing the flexibility of the others, seeing how far they can be pushed and trying to sense where their targets and resistance points are.

When the different parties feel they have examined the possible solutions and gained a feeling of what the others will bear, the negotiations move into the *ultimatum* phase. Final positions are spelled out. The details, and therefore the language in which they are expressed, are precise.

"We will pay a 4 percent increase, applicable from the signing of a formal agreement, in return for your commitment to move to semi-autonomous work groups over a period of one year. We will pay another 4 percent increase at the end of the year, subject to the work changes meeting the requirements set down in the consultants' document."

"The increase must be 5 percent now and 6 percent in a year's time. We agree to the conditions in the consultants' document but want the training for all our members to be accredited and transferable."

"We will not vary our royalties, but we will fund your travel and accommodation for three conferences—one in Europe, one in North America, and one in Australasia—in order to promote the book."

"I want the accommodation to extend for a week following each conference."

"Access to the children every second weekend, the program for the weekend to be discussed three days in advance with the allocated social worker, and the situation reviewed in one year's time."

"We want a written commitment now that if the conditions are met, the children can start living with their father for one week out of every four from the beginning of the second year."

If the ultimatums are reasonably close, then the negotiations move into a *closing* phase. In a series of rapid mini-negotiations the final differences are settled and the practical details worked out. The language is businesslike but relaxed and often interspersed with apparently unrelated conversation as the parties put the heat and unpleasantness of the negotiation behind them and establish or repair the relationships needed to make the new arrangements work.

Using Language

Negotiations are complex and untidy, so knowing that there are common phases can help us keep track of where we are in the process. And knowing that these phases are sometimes marked out by different styles and forms of language may help us not just understand the process but influence it. For example, we might have grown tired of the other parties simply reiterating their demands, and want to move into the speculation stage. We could suggest that we move on, but we might want to do it more subtly. In this case we could loosen up our expression a little and begin employing phrases more suited to the speculative phase, and so draw the other parties into the next phase without them being fully aware of it.

But there might also be times when we would like to slow a negotiation down and delay the move from the demand to the speculation phase until we felt sure we had a better measure of the teams on the other side of the table. In this case we might continue using the more precise forms of expression of the demand phase and refuse to respond to the looser more exploratory language of the other parties.

And we might be able to use our understanding of the phases to anticipate moves by the other parties. The other party might still be making proposals and so operating in the speculative phase but their language might be tightening up, giving away their intention to make a move to the ultimatum phase. If we thought it would be to our advantage to state our definitive offer first, we could move into the ultimatum phase ahead of them.

Negotiation is about reaching an agreement, but we should never forget that the other parties are our opponents. They, like us, will be trying to win. Language is the medium by which much of the negotiation will be conducted, but it can also be a device, a tool, and a weapon.

10

NEGOTIATION, CONSCIOUSNESS AND REFLECTION

We negotiate in order to solve problems, but the resolutions are usually only temporary because the underlying conflicts of interest remain. Often the agreements are fragile, established so that all parties can get on with their activities, jobs, businesses and lives until the conflicts of interest grow too great again and further negotiations are needed. Localized cease-fires were negotiated in the First World War so that the wounded lying in no-man's-land between the trenches could be attended to and the dead buried, but after a lull, the fighting resumed. The management and unions in an enterprise may reach an agreement so that work can be resumed but the agreement will have a limited lifetime written into it on the understanding that conflict will emerge again. A divorced couple will negotiate a change in the arrangements for access to their children because of changes in the ages and interests of the children, but there may be little change in the former couple's relationship.

A lot of negotiations, then, tinker at the edges. They can be intense, even harrowing experiences. They can help people make decisions and choices. They can help people put dysfunctional situations temporarily right. But they do not radically alter those situations. Indeed, by adjusting matters and taking the pressure off, many negotiations actually contribute to the maintenance of the status quo.

In making these comments I do not want to trivialize the pragmatic forms of negotiation. But, as I did with collective decision making, I want to take the discussion further. I want to look at how we can use and teach negotiation in ways that might transcend both common and conflicting interests, bring about significant changes in the people involved, and disrupt and alter the status quo.

Metaxis

By playing back the videotapes of their negotiation exercises, my colleagues and I were able to help course participants examine their own actions, identify the phases through which their negotiations had passed and listen for changes in the language they had used. When I used video to debrief an initial exercise and then put the participants into a second exercise, some were able to experience a kind of "dual" consciousness. Negotiations, even in the form of role plays in a training room, do suck people in. Often the participants would engage in the second exercise with the same sense of immediacy they had displayed in the first one but, because they had debriefed and analyzed the first exercise, they were also observing themselves. In discussions after the second exercise some said they had been able to hold the two kinds of consciousness in balance, and to work within them simultaneously.

Some years later I encountered Kate Collier's examination of metaxis. Collier (1998, 1999, 2005) writes on the use of role play in adult education. She points out that a lot of theorizing on role play draws on the discipline of humanist psychology, and suggests that this may be a mistake. She argues that in adopting a role, participants act, and so it makes sense to turn to theater and the arts, both for a theoretical understanding of role play and for guidelines for practice.

Collier takes a number of theatrical concepts and applies them to role play. All of them, of course, apply to negotiation role play. In theater a defined physical space, conventionally the stage, is established and everything placed within the boundaries of that space takes on a significance. The people who enter and the events that take place there become symbols. In theater there is an interaction between reality and illusion, between the concrete and the abstract. A sword can be both a weapon and a symbol of struggle. In theater the playwright and the performers choose events or segments of life because of their significance. They edit out the trivial or unexceptional features and so rework, streamline and intensify "real life." And in theater what happens is intensely in the present. Novels recount past events. They depict "realities" which are finished. In theatre the audience is watching what is happening *now*. And this "now" is unfinished, creating a tension which propels the events forward.

Collier argues that good educational role play, just as good theatre, operates in a designated space where people, objects and events take on symbolic significance. It too can combine the concrete with the abstract. It too can concentrate on the significant features of an event. It too can deal intensely with the present. And it too can present the incomplete and so create a tension which propels events forward.

But if we are to develop role play of quality, Collier argues, then we need to examine not just how we can draw on theatrical practice but how we can emulate a theatrical aesthetic. Here the parallels between theater and role play are less obvious. Aesthetics requires an audience. It is the people in the audience who are moved, excited, disturbed, delighted, purged of emotion or driven to action. It is they who judge the work of art good or valuable or beautiful. It is in their reaction that we affirm the work's dramatic quality. For the actors, the playwright, the director and everyone else involved in mounting the theatrical event, the reaction of the audience is the objective, and in a sense the only, reality.

Since there is no audience in an educational role-play, Collier turns to the actor's experience of metaxis in order to resolve this problem. Metaxis at its most basic is a survival mechanism. It is the sense the actor has of being both in a role and still her or himself, of being "not me and me" at the same time. If actors gave themselves over completely to their roles, they would become mad. Indeed, some actors attest to the stress involved in some kinds of actor training when they are encouraged to delve deeply into character, to improvise from within that character, and so behave rather than

act. But when an actor learns to exist simultaneously in the everyday realities of the self and in the fictional world of the character,
metaxis becomes much more than a survival mechanism. It becomes an acute and nurtured form of dual awareness in which a
rational, watchful consciousness sits comfortably beside the engaged
and passionate consciousness. And the actor uses the rational consciousness to monitor the engaged one, and so makes aesthetic
judgments and imposes standards on her or his performance.

Collier argues that drawing upon theater and the arts to inform
practice in experiential adult education is not just useful but can be
essential. If the different realities of the everyday and the imaginative are not emphasized, then a "seepage" between the two worlds
can occur. In games and simulations where such distinctions are not
always made, participants can take on roles and act in ways that
have consequences for relationships outside the educational activity. A work team may play a game during a weekend workshop
which encourages boorish behavior and then, on returning to their
workplace on the following Monday, find the civil and productive
relationships they have established over years badly damaged.

Instead of playing down the dramatic aspects of role play,
Collier maintains that we should emphasize them. We should high-
light the theatrical concepts of space and time, symbolic representation and significance so that the participants can experience a
state of metaxis and understand that they are taking part in a fictional enactment that is both different from, yet related to, the real
world. If this is done, then each participant becomes audience
to her or his own actions and "the drama aesthetic is complete"
(Collier, 2005, 177). The learning will not be just about the substance of the role play but about the experience of being. In the
process of using one kind of consciousness to monitor another,
the participants may achieve a heightened level of self-reflection.
The learning can become transformative, and the participants can
change.

The negotiation role plays I have designed and run are a far cry
from experiential exercises of the Rogerian kind. They are not con-

cerned with personal growth but with the development and practice of a political or industrial skill. Nonetheless, they can present participants with intense existential encounters in which choices must be made, their own futures pursued and the futures of others defied. With Collier's ideas in mind, we can design, conduct and debrief a sequence of exercises not just to help participants develop their skills in preparing for and engaging in negotiation but also to help them understand metaxis. We can help them acknowledge the experience of a dual consciousness and then encourage them to make use of it. We can get them to practice being both detached and engaged, critical and creative, considered and spontaneous, and thoughtful and rebellious.

In negotiation we must learn to operate outside the rules. With Collier's interpretation of metaxis in mind we can help the participants in a negotiation role play make the running, and we can help them watch themselves making that running. We can help them learn how to both live within and take control of their moment.

Identity and Self

Metaxis is a form of *dual* consciousness. In effect we are asking the participants to be two selves simultaneously. In the debriefings we may also be able to postulate, as some postmodern theorists do, that the self can be seen as multiple and variable rather than singular and whole.

I like this uncompromising summary by Zigmunt Bauman of the postmodern view of things:

> Postmodernity is marked by a view of the human world as irreducibly and irrevocably pluralistic, split into a multitude of sovereign units and sites of authority, with no horizontal or vertical order, either in actuality or potency [Bauman, 1992, 35].

Adult educators Robin Usher, Ian Bryant and Rennie Johnston apply Bauman's pluralism to identity and self, and argue that

The unified, coherent and sovereign self of modernity, the firm ground for the fixing of identity, becomes a multiple and discontinuous self, traversed by multiple meanings and with shifting identity [Usher, Bryant, and Johnston, 1997, 10].

In the course of our teaching and training we can raise the idea of a person being made up of an indefinite number of different, matching, opposing, intersecting and separate concepts of self. We might ask the participants to list the kinds of role they currently have: course participant, working person, parent, neighbor, amateur tennis player, member of a political party and so on. We can then ask them to talk about the different personae they can inhabit in each of those roles. So for course participant they might list some of the following: engaged participant, dispassionate participant, reflective learner, deductive learner and so on. We can depict the person as engaging in a constant revision of her or his concept of self in the face of the "irreducibly and irrevocably pluralistic" world (Bauman, 1992, 35), rather like a busy actor having to choose and take on new roles in a succession of plays, television series and films. We can depict the person as a collage of selves in which, at different times and in different conditions, different parts of the collage predominate. And we can depict the person as ceasing to have any predominant self at all and becoming a flock of Others. In all these interpretations, stability and continuity are gone. The person is variable, changing and open to continual definition and redefinition.

The idea of "a multiple and discontinuous self" (Usher, Bryant, and Johnston, 1997, 10) is useful in understanding some relationships and how those relationships have been negotiated. The manager of a workplace and the union representative in that workplace may be implacable enemies during a strike but redefine themselves as colleagues after the strike is over, using the fact that they are both supporters of the same football club to mediate the process. A married couple may be sexual partners, parents to their children, professionals in different fields and adherents to completely different religious faiths, and construct their relationship through physical passion, love for their children and vigorous, uncompromising debate over spiritual issues.

A long-lasting and loving relationship has to be continually redefined and renegotiated. If we see the people involved as two collections of selves, then the relationship will be brokered by certain of these selves, while other selves are kept silent and still others ignored or even suppressed. A committed feminist may continue to live with and love a partner who, by his gender and elements of his behavior, can be identified with the patriarchy. And she will do this because their relationship has been established between their private, affective selves and not between her more public self and his more conventionally gendered one.

Negotiating a Relationship

We can design exercises to explore the implications of these ideas about identity and self. If we have established a frank and trusting climate in the workshop or course, then we can set up an exercise in which the participants simulate the negotiating of a long-term relationship. We need to be sure of ourselves and of the participants because the negotiations deal with difficult and challenging issues such as sexuality, freedoms, limitations, finances, responsibilities, expectations, possible futures and possible future setbacks.

The last time I dared do this was with a group of activists from the Victorian Independent Education Union (VIEU). I distributed the pages of the "proviso" scene from William Congreve's play *The Way of the World* in which Mirabell and Mrs. Millamant negotiate their marriage. This is one of those moments in English literature full of wry humor and underlying seriousness. Mirabell and Millamant are in love so there is no tension about the outcome in terms of affection. But they are people bound by pressures of society, fashion, property and money, and so they use "the methods of formal debate and cross-examination" (Griffith, 1995) to agree to a set of conditions. The play was first performed in 1670 but most of the conditions are very modern:

Millamant: I can't do it, 'tis more than impossible. Positively,
Mirabell, I'll lie abed in the morning as long as I please.
Mirabell: Then I'll get up in the morning as early as I please.
Millamant: Ah, idle creature, get up when you will—and d'ye
hear, I won't be called names after I am married; positively
I won't be called names.
Mirabell: Names!
Millamant: Ay, as wife, spouse, my dear, joy, jewel, love, sweet-
heart, and the rest of that nauseous cant in which men and
their wives are so fulsomely familiar. I shall never bear that.
Good Mirabell, don't let us be familiar or fond, nor kiss
before folks. . . [Congreve, 1995, 68-69].

Further on, Mrs. Millamant establishes her right to equality and
respect in their relationship. This is superbly done. She opens with
a feint, claiming the demands are unimportant, then moves
through a list of "provisos" which build from a number of minor
ones to a demand for complete and inviolable independence. And
to soften (or disguise) the effects of this final demand she rounds off
with a touch of gentle irony and the conciliatory use of the word
dwindle:

Mirabell: Have you any more conditions to offer? Hitherto your
demands are pretty reasonable.
Millamant: Trifles. As liberty to pay and receive visits to and from
whom I please, to write and receive letters without interro-
gatories or wry faces on your part. To wear what I please
and choose conversation with regard only to my own taste;
to have no obligation upon me to converse with wits that
I don't like, because they are your acquaintance, or to be
intimate with fools, because they may be your relations.
Come to dinner when I please, dine in my own dressing
room when I'm out of humour, without giving a reason.
To have my closet inviolate; to be sole empress of my tea-
table, which you must never presume to approach without

first asking leave. And last, wherever I am, you shall always knock at the door before you come in. These articles subscribed, if I continue to endure you a little longer, I may by degrees dwindle into a wife [Congreve, 1995, 69].

Further on there are understated references to "endeavours" to do with "breeding," allowing the actors opportunities for banter and coquetry. The negotiations end with these words:

Millamant: I hate your odious provisos.
Mirabell: Then we are agreed. Shall I kiss your hand upon the contract [Congreve, 1995, 71]?

I let the participants read the passage and talk a little about it, and then asked them to prepare and then negotiate the conditions they would want in order to establish a successful long-term relationship. These are the instructions I gave out:

You are to work in groups of four. Each group represents a seasoned VIEU rep. You are going to meet and negotiate with another seasoned VIEU rep, represented by another four people. This is the scenario. Do not take it too seriously.

Both of you are so committed to the union that you really do not have much time left for the slow dance involved in forming a permanent relationship, and so you live alone. You work in different schools but have got to know each other around the traps over the past few years. You rarely go to the theatre but you did want to see a production of Congreve's *The Way of the World,* so simply went to the theatre on the off chance. You saw each other in the queue, bought seats next to each other, had a drink at interval and went to dinner after the performance. During the course of the dinner, like the no-nonsense people you are, you decided to set up house together. You recalled with amusement how Mirabell and Mrs. Millamant had negotiated their relationship in the play, and you agreed to meet in two days' time and work out the conditions upon which you would live together. As pragmatic trade unionists you have agreed that any matters of intimacy will be left until the more practical matters of everyday living together have been discussed and agreed upon.

Debriefings always differ but at some stage in this exercise I try to get the group to explore how meaningful it was to think of the person as a collection of selves. I ask which selves they chose to broker various parts of the agreement and which selves they kept silent. And I encourage them to discuss how they might use the ideas of multiple selves in real-life negotiations, both in the ways they present themselves and in the ways they interpret the people across the negotiating table.

Before closing, however, I issue my standard warning against assuming that postmodern interpretations carry some kind of universal truth. The ideas of the multiple and discontinuous self or the self as a collection of others might be useful in some analyses but we need to remind ourselves that in the world of agreements, for example, the concept of individual responsibility prevails. The person who signs a contract is seen as single and whole. Indeed, in many aspects of our lives we will hold others responsible for their actions as single, whole and unique individuals, and we will assume that they hold the same expectations of us. To do otherwise would invite madness.

Rational Self-Reflection

If we use structured exercises to introduce learners to metaxis, we are asking them to be conscious of their own consciousness, and in the debriefings we may be able to discuss some of the different kinds of self-reflection we can use to do this.

We can make use of a form of self-reflection in which we identify the assumptions, prejudices, beliefs and habits of mind we have taken on over the years and which now govern the way we react to people and events, take on roles, and form relationships. This is the kind of ordered reflection we engage in when we take time out to understand what makes us tick. In his earlier writing on transformative learning Mezirow (1981, 10) uses the phrase "the structure of psycho-cultural assumptions," and when talking about his ideas I have asked the participants to imagine a pile of cardboard boxes of different sizes glued together into a large and higgledy-piggledy construction on the floor in the center of the seminar room. I say the boxes represent different assumptions of mine and their size and position in the structure affect the degree to which they influence the way I think, feel and act. One of the boxes represents the racial prejudice from my culture and childhood in a small community in the 1940s and 1950s. Another box represents my assumption, based on witnessing my brother's serious illness when he was eight, that life is none too certain. And another represents a belief, drummed into me by my mother, that no one person is inherently better than another. I argue that Mezirow's theory of perspective transformation means that we can take a long, hard look at this pile of boxes, take it apart and reassemble it. In my case this might mean actually recognizing that the racial prejudice box is there, pulling the bloody thing out of the structure and relocating it in a much less influential position. My proposal that I relocate the racial prejudice box can lead to an argument over whether we can throw a box away altogether. If I intervene, it is normally to argue that we can become aware of our cultures and our psychological histories and take decisive action to control or counter their effects on us but, like it or not, we cannot deny or discard them.

We can make use of a form of self-reflection to examine the criteria we both consciously and subconsciously apply when making choices and decisions. Stephen Brookfield (1990, 1995) has written about using critical-incident analysis and criteria-analysis exercises to help people engage in this kind of reflection. In essence these exercises require people to choose a significant incident in their lives, to describe it and, in response to different forms of questioning or analysis, to form an understanding of why they judged it significant. We can ask participants to nominate incidents about which they felt satisfied and incidents about which they felt dissatisfied, incidents which caused pleasure and incidents which caused discomfort or difficulty, successful professional incidents and unsuccessful ones, and so on. Often these exercises are conducted in groups of three, with each person sharing her or his story in turn and the other two asking questions to help analyze it. The aim is to help each of the participants identify the values that underpin her or his actions and, in the company of two other people, subject those values to critical scrutiny.

And we can use a form of self-reflection as a kind of monitoring process for our current actions. Schön (1983, 1987) examines the interplay of theory and practice in the working lives of successful professionals. He is interested in practitioners who can think on their feet and adapt their practice accordingly. He describes the phenomenon as reflection "in-and-on" action. By reflecting on our practice, we foreground the theory which was formerly implicit in that practice, evaluate and refine it, and reapply it consciously. Reflection becomes a habitual act, part of our makeup, a process by which we evaluate and refine both our theory and our practice in a kind of continuously evolving loop.

These three forms of reflection complement each other. Mezirow concerns himself more with reflection on our long-term cultural and psychological histories, Brookfield more with reflection on critical incidents at precise moments in our more recent past, and Schön more with reflection on our current and evolving practice. But all three are writing about self-reflection of an essentially critical kind, in which we study how we interact with our professional, relational and cultural worlds.

We can also use a form of self-reflection informed by humanist psychology and more concerned with our affective lives. Boud and Walker (1991) write about using reflection to turn experience into learning, giving prominence to "feelings" in each stage of the "reflective process." They depict experience as a cluster of behavior, ideas and feelings, and they propose reflecting on this experience in three steps. The first step involves returning to the experience. The second involves attending to feelings by utilizing the positive ones and, where possible, removing the obstructing ones. And the third step involves reevaluating the experience. They state that the outcomes from this reflection will be affective as well as cognitive, adding that in any given situation it will be difficult to distinguish between the two.

Phenomenological Reflection

Mezirow, Brookfield, Schön, and Boud and Walker propose rationalist forms of self-reflection. All of them suggest there are orderly procedures, even steps, we can follow. And all see self-reflection as a process of making judgments in order to improve ourselves and our relationships.

But self-reflection need not necessarily involve judgment, nor be driven by some imperative to improve. When discussing reflection I like to mention two other forms which are less rationalist than the ones described above, and more private. Both are concerned with coming to understand oneself and one's world a little better and may result in insight. Change, even significant change, may come about but that is not the primary motive.

The first of these two forms of self-reflection makes use of some of the principles and processes of phenomenology. In this form of reflection we try to go behind our preconceptions and values when we examine an object, a person, an idea, a relationship, an event or ourselves, and achieve a preinterpretive state. We examine the "phenomenon" not as we feel about it or react to it but as it *is*. Edmund Husserl saw phenomenology as a response to weaknesses in the Cartesian view of reality. Instead of returning to the pure ego or thinking substance as the absolute foundation for the development of "science," Husserl proposed we return to the apprehension of phenomena. We were to "bracket" the values we had derived directly from our natural immersion in the world, and "straightforwardly," "intuitively," perceive a phenomenon, establishing ourselves as "disinterested onlooker" of both the phenomenon and the perception of the phenomenon (Husserl, 1995, 35).

Peter Willis has written a phenomenological study of adult education and argues that in this form of inquiry the mind does not "seize upon the object" to analyze and subdue it. The consciousness is active "but the act of thinking is different: it is an act of reception which holds the thinking mind back from closure and returns again and again to behold the object" (Willis, 2002, 173).

Willis identifies a conundrum to do with language and our apprehension of reality. We encounter our world though language, and in this process our ideas, beliefs and interpretations become embedded in the language we create. So when we try to make sense of new experiences we almost inevitably name them according to pre-existing values. In phenomenological inquiry we try to achieve a *prelanguage* state. We "hold the phenomenon in our gaze and drink it in, waiting for it almost to name itself in our consciousness," and we resist the temptation to locate it on existing "conceptual grids" or in existing "grand theories" (Willis, 2002, 174).

In Willis's study the phenomena are episodes from his professional life as an adult educator, and he uses a number of methods to apprehend them. He dwells on each episode, then uses "stem sentences" in order to visit and revisit it. "What I discover in adult education practice in this episode is . . . " "I recognise adult education practice in this episode as . . . " (Willis, 2002, 119). And he describes what presents itself from each episode in terms of "four existential coordinates": a bodily experience, a temporal experience, a spatial experience and a socially embedded experience. So he writes, "Adult education practice as a *bodily* experience in this university teaching episode is about being weighed down with boxes full of papers and readers and handouts. Bodily movements are quick and energetic, the voice loud, optimistic, even joyful and always challenging. The eyes scan the room" (117). From these attempts at a preinterpretive apprehension of the phenomenon, Willis moves through a form of thematic identification to a commentary full of untrammeled ideas and insights about each episode. He writes, for example, "As a phenomenon, adult education practice . . . has a constant element of judicial and prudent dealing, compromising, clarification, etc., like the sound of the drone in bagpipe music that permanently colours whatever melody is being played" (121).

Pondering

Finally, I want to mention a form of self-reflection in which the focus is blurred and there is no imperative to achieve anything or arrive anywhere. This form of reflection is the time-honored activity of pondering. We find time to relax, to sit, to stroll, to wind our physical activity down and let our thoughts take us wherever they will. This kind of reflection in repose can be magical. Our consciousness drifts, and from time to time we can happen upon an insight. Sometimes, in agreeable solitude, with our guard down, we will think, and learn, profoundly.

Encouraging Reflection

Clearly we cannot canvass all of these forms of reflection in the course of debriefing a single negotiation exercise. But over a number of days in a residential context or during a semester-long course, we just might. And for those of us doing the facilitating, thinking through some of the different kinds of self-reflection may help us ask the right questions, make the right prompts and create the right contexts.

Once, when working with a group of about seventy trade union activists at a residential college, I finished a morning session twenty minutes or so before the normal break for lunch. We had been dealing with questions of recruiting, and the participants had been practicing various forms of presentation and informal negotiation. There had been lots of talk, so I closed by asking them when they had last spent time with a member of their union but not talked. I suggested they pair up with someone else in the room, leave the room together and spend the next fifteen minutes, in the building, in the gardens outside, in each other's company, aware of the other's presence but completely silent.

11

DISRUPTIVE NEGOTIATION

Many negotiations may tinker around the edges, but some can bring about significant personal change. And there are some which can bring about social and political change. Sally MacKinnon (1998, 2003, 2004), an activist educator within the Australian environmental movement, examines these kinds of negotiation. In her case studies the parties involved have serious conflicts of interest. They do not deny them. They transcend them. And they emerge from the negotiations having changed the very form and nature of the conflicts themselves. MacKinnon (2004, 56) sees this kind of negotiation as part of "transformative practice," which she defines as those "collaborative processes such as negotiation which disrupt, challenge or overturn the status quo." She contrasts transformative practice with other processes such as win-win negotiation, alternative dispute resolution and community consultation, all of which may make use of collaborative dialogue but are actually concerned with maintaining or reinforcing the status quo. I like the distinctions MacKinnon draws but believe that in using the word *transformative* she is in danger of associating her kind of negotiation too closely with the idea of personal transformation. To reinforce the distinction she herself makes, I have used the word *disruptive* in the title of this chapter.

MacKinnon (2004) describes and analyzes an agreement reached in early 1996 between graziers, indigenous people, and environmentalists over land use in the Cape York peninsula, an extensive region of cattle properties, scrubland and pristine rain forest in the far north of the state of Queensland in Australia. She interviewed a number of the people directly involved in reaching the agreement and wrote an extensive study of negotiation, using the agreement as the major case example.

MacKinnon presents herself as "an ideological researcher" and promotes negotiation as a tool to be used in struggle. She was attracted to the Cape York agreement because it was a landmark agreement and also because of the deep divisions between the different groups involved. "Make no mistake," she says, "there were times when the . . . parties were enemies" (MacKinnon, 2004, 267). Graziers, Aboriginal people and Greens had been in conflict in the region for the past twenty years. MacKinnon quotes one of the Cattlemen's Union representatives as saying that in the lead-up to the negotiations he had been genuinely fearful that there would be "bloodshed and mayhem in the Cape."

The Cape York agreement brought about potentially profound changes in the way people coexisted, and in how they used and preserved the country. Newspapers at the time hailed the agreement as an international precedent for indigenous rights and as a significant achievement in the reconciliation between Aboriginal and non-Aboriginal Australians. Without government intervention or presence, the representatives of the three groups had thrashed out mutually acceptable ways of guaranteeing access to land, preserving culturally significant sites, protecting high-quality ecosystems, and working towards economic security.

MacKinnon recounts how the different parties to the negotiation were given time to tell their stories. The graziers could talk of their individual and collective struggles to establish and maintain their industry and their establishment of the Cattlemen's Union, in some respects modeled on an industrial union, to put their case through advocacy and direct action. The Aboriginal representatives could talk of the history of dispossession and the long struggle for land rights. The environmentalists could talk of their concerns for the health of the planet and of the long slow battle to achieve recognition of their cause by governments, bureaucracies and the general public.

Misunderstandings were acknowledged. The environmentalists came to understand more clearly that their push to have parts of the Cape declared national parks would exclude not just developers, despoilers and polluters but also the traditional indigenous users of the land. Pressures were explained. The graziers could talk of the serious strains placed on them by the downturn in the international beef trade. And the gains and losses were described. The Aboriginal representatives could talk of their success at the federal level in gaining native-title legislation, followed by their dispiriting loss of control to new bureaucracies and state governments of different political colors.

In the language of critical theory (Rasmussen, 1996, 12), the participants in the negotiations began changing their thinking by understanding the history of their thinking. They came to understand how they had made meaning and how others had made meaning for them. They began to collectively construct new knowledge. In the place of prejudice and given wisdoms they established a culture of exchange and critique. They did not abandon their conflicting interests but they established a consensus on the way they might express and manage them. Their negotiations became an exercise in critical, communicative action.

The agreement also brought about radical changes in people involved. A number of the negotiators said that during the negotiations they ceased reacting to stereotypes, abandoned preconceived notions, and began engaging in more open encounters. These encounters led them to review themselves, their relationships with each other, and their relationships with the constituencies they were representing. As the negotiations progressed, the negotiators came to understand that no one was going to leave the Cape. They had to achieve a positive outcome, or everyone would suffer. This meant that they had to go back to their constituents, try to share something of what was happening in the negotiations, and "sell" the agreement they were slowly thrashing out. Instead of taking orders from their constituents, now they had to confront them. MacKinnon describes the dynamics of the negotiations changing from "outside in" to "inside out." To use Mezirow's phrase, the participants had been through a "perspective transformation," (Mezirow, 1981, 1991) and now they were faced with the challenge of helping their constituents go through a perspective transformation as well.

The Cape York negotiations, therefore, were transformative in both personal and political terms. MacKinnon provides a detailed analysis of the lead-up to the negotiations, the negotiations themselves, and their aftermath (in which forces outside the three parties' control—the election of new state and federal governments, and the formation of a rival graziers' organization—stalled the agreement's implementation). And she identifies a range of features that contributed to making the negotiations transformative.

The negotiations were proactive. Former confrontations between the parties had been in reaction to events. These negotiations were an initiative taken by "grassroots stakeholders." The negotiations demonstrated "good faith." The parties focused on solutions that could be implemented, the fundamental needs of each party were deemed non-negotiable, and points of irreconcilable difference were put to one side. A facilitator was used to maintain this focus but he could not be described as neutral in the conventional sense since he was openly committed to brokering an effective model for future negotiations for land-use and reconciliation. The negotiations involved emotional engagement. People expressed their anger, their fears and their anguish. The negotiations involved intellectual engagement. All the parties mounted carefully researched arguments and counterarguments. The negotiations addressed power issues among the parties and between the parties and various outside bodies. Lawyers were not used and government representatives were not invited. And, as is evident in all of the above, the negotiations involved and made use of profound learning. Old frames of reference were challenged, and new ones were formed.

Changes in Perception

MacKinnon has given us a rich and complex story to tell. And we can use it to track the changes in perception that the parties to a negotiation go through.

At the outset the parties are likely to perceive their adversaries as others or strangers. Sartre writes of the "Other" in a phenomenological mode. His study begins with these words:

> I am in a public park. Not far away there is a lawn and along the edge of the lawn there are benches. A man passes by those benches. I see the man . . . [Sartre, 1984, 341].

Until he sees the passer-by, Sartre tells us, the lawn, the benches, all the objects in the environment around him are in a temporal-spatial relation to him. In a sense they are there *for him*. If he thinks of the passer-by as a thing, a puppet for example, then the passer-by is simply one object amongst others, in this case an object beside the bench, a certain distance away from Sartre, exercising a certain pressure on the ground, and so on. As an object, the passer-by has little effect on the environment and could be taken away without seriously changing the relations of the other objects around him. But, Sartre says, if he perceives the passer-by as a person, then what was Sartre's space becomes the other person's space. The distance of objects in the environment no longer unfolds starting from Sartre but from the other person. "Instead of a grouping *toward me* of the objects, there is now an orientation which *flees from me*" (Sartre, 1984, 342). The Other has replaced Sartre as the central referential point in the park. It is as if the world is flowing away from Sartre through "a kind of drain hole in the middle of its being" (Sartre, 1984, 343). This realization that the Other can turn him into a powerless "thing" and drain his environment away from him so suddenly and so entirely makes Sartre's universe "disintegrate."

Sartre's description has a poignant relevance for the relationships between the indigenous people and the graziers in the Cape York negotiations. Until 1967 the indigenous people in Australia were denied citizenship in their own land. They were wards of the state, could not vote, were under the control of government administrators, puppetlike, and had no claims over the lands they had been deprived of by white settlement. As such they constituted little or no threat to the graziers using the land in the Cape and, insofar as they were acknowledged at all, would have been seen as little more than objects in the Sartrean sense. Even after 1967 they were regarded as having no claim to land. Because Aboriginal people were apparently nomadic at the time of white settlement, the legal fiction of *terra nullius* was maintained: for legal purposes, Australia was deemed to have been uninhabited when the white settlers arrived. It was only after a High Court decision in 1992 and legislation in 1994 that the concept of native title was acknowledged and Aboriginal communities could make claims for crown land with which they had maintained a continued association. In Sartrean terms, at this point the graziers noticed the indigenous communities, seeing them not as objects but as subjects. The graziers were obliged to reinterpret their world in relationship to the indigenous communities, to see the environment no longer necessarily in a temporal and spatial relationship to themselves but oriented towards, related to, there *for* the Aboriginal people. They could no longer fully objectify the indigenous people in the Cape, and they sensed that they in their turn were being objectified and so experienced a loss of freedom. The indigenous people became the Other, draining the graziers' world away from them.

Just as Sartre can gaze at the Other in the park, the Other can gaze at him. Sartre argues that in understanding the "permanent possibility" of being seen by the Other we experience shame. He is talking about shame, not in the mundane sense of shame because of some single action but about "shame of *self* . . . the *recognition* of the fact that I *am* indeed the object which the Other is looking at and judging" (Sartre, 1984, 350). As we become the object of the Other's gaze, so we too are forced to pass judgment on ourselves as objects, and we feel shame. MacKinnon quotes various people involved in the Cape York negotiations who describe their first encounters with representatives of the other parties. Again there are echoes of Sartre's ideas. In the lead-up to the negotiations, a leader of the Aboriginal people who was to become a key negotiator attended a meeting of the Cattlemen's Union. The encounter took place at a homestead on a large cattle station, with people arriving in four-wheel-drive vehicles and by light aircraft. The representative from the Aboriginal land council was flown in and he describes walking from the airstrip to the house and into the fearful, suspicious, anxious gaze of the graziers. The Cattlemen's Union's representative in his interview describes how he had asked the graziers present to give the Aboriginal leader a hearing, to behave well. It was he who had feared mayhem and bloodshed on the Cape. But there was no discourtesy or trouble. The graziers listened quietly, thoughtfully, attentively to the Aboriginal leader. Reading between the lines one can sense the effect of the Aboriginal representative's gaze on the graziers. One can sense the altering of the graziers' perception of their world. One can even, perhaps, sense their shame.

Sartre argues that the recognition of the Other's freedom to behave as a subject impinges on, destabilizes and limits our own freedom to act as subjects ourselves. The destabilization can be considerable. Because we do not know the Other but experience such a sense of loss towards her or him, the Other's freedom can seem "infinite" (Sartre, 1984, 362). The Aboriginal leader's attendance at that meeting of the Cattlemen's Union was a significant moment in the move towards negotiation. The Cattlemen's Union members saw that there were Others on the Cape. They were confronted by the indigenous people's freedom to act, and so were confronted by the limitations to their own freedom. The Aboriginal leader is an impressive figure, articulate, strong, quietly charismatic, an educated and experienced activist. For a terrible moment in that first encounter his freedom, his power to influence the graziers' world and take it away from them, may well have seemed infinite. In that moment of shock many of the graziers must have realized that in order to survive they would have to take the Aboriginal people into account.

We can see the starting point in the Cape York negotiations as an encounter of Others, but we can also see it as an encounter between strangers. Bauman (1990) and Segal (1999) explain the concept of "the stranger" by drawing a distinction between strangers and enemies. Strangers are the more threatening. Enemies accept the same terms of reference as we do and, although they oppose us, are from the same world. A stranger, however, is from another world, unknown, and we cannot anticipate that she or he will behave in any prescribed way. Bauman (1990, 143, 145, 146) describes enemies as "flawed friends" but strangers as "undecidables" who "bring the outside into the inside, and poison the comfort of order with suspicion and chaos." Segal (1999, 76) describes a stranger as someone who does not share the same "horizon of intelligibility," and at the outset this certainly was the case for the environmentalists. To the Cattlemen's Union and the indigenous people the environmentalists were outsiders. They were not even resident in the Cape and they were driven by an interest not just in the cape but in all environments everywhere.

MacKinnon gives an account of the way the conditions for the Cape York negotiations were established, how it was decided to exclude government, legal representatives and other third parties, how a facilitator was selected and how he laid down procedures. We can interpret all this as a process in which common boundaries were established and strangers were changed into enemies—"flawed friends"—who at the very least could meet in order to express and test their enmity.

Enemies can become allies. In the course of negotiations the parties may state their enmity forcefully, but they will also explore the areas of common interest that brought them to the table in the first place. In these areas they can agree to cooperate or, at the very least, not to work against each other. The agreement will be a pragmatic affair, a deal struck by each of the parties in order to promote its own interests. For this reason alliances are impermanent. Allies understand that as soon as their continued association does not meet their own interests, they will withdraw and the alliance will be broken. Where the common interests are several, the parties may be able to form an open-ended and wide-ranging alliance. Where there is a single but strong point of common interest, then a successful alliance is still possible but it will be established for a limited time and in order to achieve a clearly prescribed objective. Allies do not abandon their enmity but put parts of it on hold.

Allies can become comrades. An agreement to cooperate may put the parties side by side in a struggle against other forces. Now they will not just associate with each other, they will have to work creatively together. Ironically, it is in the encounter with a common enemy that these enemies-turned-allies may develop trust. In the heat of a struggle, unanticipated events will occur and rapid, spontaneous responses will have to be made. Allies will no longer be able to plan carefully, watching each other and weighing up their self-interest at every step. They will have to take risks and some of those risks will be with each other. If the parties measure up to the trust put in them in the heat of the moment, a shared history will be constructed and such histories are difficult to ignore. In a new situation, something other than the common interests of the various parties now comes into consideration. Loyalties have been formed.

As they engage to promote the common interests of their respective parties some of these new comrades will form a liking for one another. These people may form other interests altogether, take to meeting away from the joint areas of concern of the respective parties, and become friends.

Perceptions and Phases

These changes in perceptions, from Other or stranger to enemy, ally, comrade and friend, can match the phases negotiations pass through. In the opening phase of a negotiation, the parties may encounter each other as Other or stranger. The phase will be marked by uncertainty, anxiety, and even fear and shame, and the apparently inconsequential chat will be an attempt to counter the unknown. In the demand stage, the parties express their enmity. They make their demands in uncompromising fashion, emphasizing their differences. In the speculation phase, they seek out areas where they can become allies. In the ultimatum phase, they establish the conditions of the alliance and lock it into place. In the closing phase, they set up the conditions which just might lead on to comradeship and even friendship.

From MacKinnon's account I judge that the Cape York negotiations passed through a number of these phases and that the participants experienced a number of these changes in perception. I have indicated as much above but I would go further and suggest, again reading between the lines, that some of the participants moved beyond the status of ally. Once they found themselves agreeing on the significance of what they were doing they became comrades, engaged in a common struggle to communicate the value of their negotiations beyond the confines of the immediate group of negotiators. They were in it together. This shift extended into the postnegotiation period, when negotiators from the different parties found themselves supporting each other against adverse reactions from the state and federal governments and from dissenters in their constituent communities. There is even a sense in the quotes MacKinnon reproduces from her interviews that when the key players confounded the expectations of many, began really working together, and mapped out another kind of future, some of them became friends.

Enemies turned into allies and even friends, old frames of reference abandoned and new ones adopted, and new ways of living together agreed upon: MacKinnon tells a story of negotiation at its disruptive best.

Part Four

INSIGHT
AND ACTION

12

NONRATIONAL DISCOURSE AND INSIGHT

The problem-solving model using facts, issues, options and action can be represented as a flowchart, and this scientist element lingers in the extensions of the model and in formal and informal meetings constructed on the model. Dialogic forms of decision making may depart from the model but they still require ordered self-reflection and discussion. Negotiation may have no rules but the process can be broken down into phases which we can consciously manage. And transformative or disruptive negotiation in its turn can be seen as a progression through a sequence of relationships and states of self-perception which are open to analysis and management. These activities all involve, indeed require, the application of commonsense logic and discourse of a rational kind. Explicit or implicit in all of them are the instrumentalist ideas of cause and effect and of the person as object. If I pull this lever, that packet will drop. If I do this or say that, people are likely to react in ways I can anticipate.

Of course, human encounters cannot always be explained in terms of cause and effect, nor are human beings always predictable. We can be headstrong, independent, original and irrational. We can be perverse subjects rather than quiescent objects. We can be rebellious and defiant. But we may not even need to be that. We can disrupt another person's orderly universe simply by being there. Problems arise, challenges come about and choices have to be made because subjects encounter each other, because subjects clash and because people as subjects have differences in desires, outlooks, ideologies, values, assumptions, predilections and cultures. These kinds of problem cannot always be solved through rational discourse and so, in this part of the book, I want to look at how we can help ourselves and others solve problems, make choices and defy unwanted futures by using other kinds of "talk." I want to look at how we can help ourselves and others break the silence by using *non*rational discourse.

Proximity, Talk and Nontalk

It is no accident that people travel long distances to attend meetings. Problems can cease to exist as the result of a touch on the elbow, the linking of an arm, a handshake or an embrace. Proximity can alter opinions, challenge or eradicate prejudices, and turn Others, strangers and enemies into allies and even friends. At these moments the "talk" is through physical presence. Words take second place.

Sometimes we need to foreground the talk, but the talk itself and not the substance will be important. People can appear to communicate and yet be unable to come to an understanding. The problem may be in the language itself. Two people can be using the same word, apparently in the same way and apparently with the same meaning. Yet for each of them the word carries associations which are subtly or even significantly different, and so an effective agreement eludes them. The only way to deal with this barrier to communication is to go on talking. And talking. Little by little the interpretations each person places on the word will come closer together so that, without either person being able to point to a particular moment when a breakthrough occurs, they will nonetheless begin to communicate more effectively. They will know each other better and differently. They will have made meaning collaboratively and will now be speaking the "same" language.

Or the problem may be in the mode, the genre, of the talk. One person may be using an informal mode of talking, the other a formal one. One may be "validating" what she or he says through anecdote and implication, the other through an ordered presentation of information and elaboration of issues. One may be talking in uncompromising statements about the here-and-now, while the other may be using the language of hypothesis.

This problem of different genres can occur in encounters between Aboriginal and non-Aboriginal Australians. Two men can meet. They dress in the same way, have the same accents and open their encounter with a discussion of the football team they both support. Yet when they come to discuss the business of their meeting, the management of a youth center, say, they may find themselves at odds. Cultural differences previously disguised by cultural similarities now come into play and influence the way they talk. The Aboriginal Australian may well leave the encounter convinced that he put his case clearly and explained all that was necessary to explain. Indeed, he may be frustrated at the other's apparent lack of response. The non-Aboriginal Australian may well leave the encounter failing to realize the force of feeling in the other's discourse or that he has been presented with a set of proposals. The solution may be to get to know the culture behind the talk. In the case of our two men, much more time may need to be spent on the football so that each can come to understand and appreciate the *way* the other talks, the way the other puts across ideas, the way the other resists or concedes, the way the other expresses feeling— in short, the way the other communicates.

And there will be times when we can solve a problem only by abandoning any pretense at orderly exchange and engaging in nonrational or even willfully "irrational" discourse. Again we will talk, but it will be talk filled with metaphors, flights of fancy, emotions, ambiguities and ironies. It will be talk which abandons the pursuit of Habermas's ideal speech situation and strives in its place for a "supertruth" of the kind we find in novels, plays, poetry, visual art and sometimes even dreams. In a novel or a play, events may be described which have never happened and yet we feel are "true." In a poem or a painting or a dream, what is imagined or depicted or "experienced" may be impossible yet makes absolute sense. "Talk" which strives for this kind of "truth" opens us up to insight.

Insight

Insight is an almost mystical, often seemingly accidental encounter with originality and creativity. In one way, insight is a supremely intellectual experience. It is a realization, a sudden knowing, an instantaneous understanding. Insight abruptly fills a gap in our knowledge, makes up for a lack in ourselves, or completes some kind of schema we had only half-sensed was there. We may engage in hard work, detailed research and laborious thinking in the period before an insight and be thrown into furious activity afterwards, but in the actual moment insight is fluid and effortless. In this way, then, insight is as much an emotion as an act of intellect. It is an elation flowing into satisfaction, or a horror flowing into resignation or resistance. And like much emotion, insight eschews logic. There is no gradual fitting together of the pieces one by one in order to reach a conclusion. There is just the conclusion. For this secular writer, insight is a moment when, for good or bad, we speak with the gods.

Insight can be depicted as a positive experience. It is sometimes called the "Aha!" experience and implies a rush of joy as we suddenly understand and transcend a situation or set of conditions which has held us back. There is a sense of emancipation in these descriptions. But as I have said above insight can involve horror as well as elation. One of the most striking accounts of insight I have read is in a work of fiction and is the terrible moment in Joseph Heller's amazing novel *Catch-22* when Yossarian discovers—uncovers—Snowden's secret.

Catch-22 is set in the Second World War. Yossarian is a bombardier and is tending a wounded gunner in his plane as it flies back from a bombing raid. The gunner, Snowden, has been hit by flak and is "freezing to death in a puddle of harsh yellow sunlight." Snowden keeps repeating "I'm cold, I'm cold," and Yossarian tries to comfort him with the words "There, there. There, there." At first Yossarian can see that Snowden is injured in the thigh but Snowden keeps pointing to his chest. Yossarian cuts open Snowden's flak jacket and sees that a piece of flak has shot into Snowden's side just under the armpit and "blasted all the way through, drawing whole mottled quarts of Snowden along with it through a gigantic hole in his ribs." Snowden's insides slither onto the floor and Yossarian screams. Heller then writes this paragraph:

> Yossarian was cold too and shivering uncontrollably. He felt goose pimples clacking all over him as he gazed down despondently at the grim secret Snowden had spilled all over the messy floor. It was easy to read the message in his entrails. Man was matter, that was Snowden's secret. Drop him out of a window and he'll fall. Set fire to him and he'll burn. Bury him and he'll rot, like other kinds of garbage. The spirit gone, man is garbage. That was Snowden's secret. Ripeness is all.
>
> "I'm cold," Snowden said. "I'm cold."
>
> "There, there," said Yossarian. "There, there" [Heller, 1964, 464].

Resulting in horror or elation, insight enables us to *understand* even if that understanding cannot be explained. And if we understand, then we will be better able to take control of our moment and defy the "the dark wind blowing from the future" (Camus, 1954, 53). In Heller's anarchic novel Yossarian, equipped with Snowden's secret, resolves to honor his own spirit, to flee and, by fleeing, to break out of his catch-22.

Teaching Insight?

If insight does not involve an orderly progression, a gradual fitting together of the pieces, then how to do we teach and learn it? How do we help ourselves and others understand what cannot be articulated or explained? How do we break free from our own catch-22?

The trouble is that once we try to tie such an experience down, we are in danger of destroying it. If I watch a magician, what do I want to appreciate? What do I want to truly understand? The joy and amazement at the trick? The atmosphere in the circus tent? The pleasure? Or do I want to learn about the sleight of hand and the hat with the false bottom because, if I learn how the magic works, of course it ceases to be magic.

I began reading a book by a number of psychologists on insight (Sternberg and Davidson, 1995) but quickly understood that they defined insight as the grasping of a solution and that each was trying to expose the sleight of hand or find the false bottom to that hat. I took their notion of completing a schema into my musings above, but not much else. These psychologists place insight within an existing schema rather than *outside* everything already known. They see insight as part of something, or as a coming together of parts, rather than a new and shocking understanding of the whole.

Understanding

My partner and I were staying with a cousin of hers in the far south of France, just in from the Mediterranean coastline and just north of the border with Spain. Her cousin lives in a hamlet of some fifteen or so houses perched on a slight promontory halfway up the side of a valley. From the balcony of his house, you look out over the upper reaches of the valley. There are steep hills covered with vines in the foreground and the Pyrenees rising massively in the near background. The vines are held in place on sloping terraces by a higgledy-piggledy arrangement of ancient stone walls creating strange and disordered patterns. When we were there the grapes had been harvested and the vines were tinged with the first colors of autumn. The valley side fell quickly away to the floor, where a small road ran alongside a stream between the foothills towards the mountains. We arrived late in the afternoon, and the three of us sat on the balcony in the mild evening looking at the valley as the light went from the sky.

The next morning we ate breakfast on the balcony, looking again at the valley, transformed now by the silver sunlight of that region. At about 10:00 I left the house for a walk. The day was growing hot and I turned by chance away from the hamlet onto an unsurfaced road which ran along the side of the hill and gradually upwards. Our cousin's house was just to my right, slightly below me now, shielded by a line of closely planted cypresses which also hid the lower part of the valley from view. It took only about fifteen paces to reach the end of the line of cypresses and two or three steps more for me to find myself suddenly, extraordinarily alone on the hillside, the hamlet behind me and out of sight, the heat, the intense silence, the immense space enveloping me, wrapping around me, taking sudden hold of me. The shock was physical, intellectual, emotional, even (and this is difficult for me to say) perhaps spiritual. I was not overcome by awe as you can be in front of a wonderful painting. I was not an observer. I was in this, part of it, *understanding* it.

13

FACILITATING INSIGHT

Reading those psychologists dispirited me and I worry that, if I keep trying to define insight with any precision, I will dispirit you. Better, perhaps, if I go on from here by describing how I have tried to facilitate insight. Better, for the moment at least, if I describe how I have tried to help myself and others converse with the gods.

Using Literature: A Novel

On the title page I use the byline "A book written in wartime." I began writing this book well after the armed forces of a number of countries, most prominent amongst them the United States, entered Afghanistan to pursue the terrorist organization al-Qaida and its leader, Osama bin Laden. The action was part of what quickly became known as the War on Terror. Eighteen months after the incursions into Afghanistan a force made up of U.S. and British troops and a small contingent of troops from Australia invaded Iraq.

The reasons given over time for the invasion of Iraq were various and the war itself changed in character. At the outset, the invading forces waged war against Iraqi armed forces and so seemed to be at war with the Iraqi regime of Saddam Hussein. Once these forces were defeated and Saddam Hussein captured, the invading or occupying forces seemed to be engaged in warfare against remnants of the defeated regime and, it was said, against foreign terrorists who had come into Iraq to join a resistance against the occupying forces. As time progressed local militias engaged the occupying forces and the war changed again. Now it seemed to be between the occupying forces and elements of the population.

About a year into the "Iraq adventure," an act of terrible barbarity took place which put the name of the Iraqi town Falluja into the headlines. Four male citizens of the United States, described as contractors, were attacked in their car and killed. The car and their bodies were burned, and the charred corpses of two of them were strung up from the superstructure of a bridge. Television coverage showed an apparently jubilant crowd of people surrounding the car and the charred corpses.

U.S. forces moved into Falluja to find and arrest the perpetrators. However, they met extensive resistance, and over several days of fighting a number of U.S. troops were killed or injured. The U.S. forces responded with increasing ferocity, attacking points of resistance using ground troops, helicopter gunships and warplanes. Houses and a mosque were bombed. It was reported that in a week's fighting 600 Iraqis were killed, many of them civilian men, women and children. The U.S. forces had responded to an act of barbarity with an even more terrible barbarity. Their actions seemed like an exercise in punishment or revenge, and the war was now being waged against civilians.

On a television news program I saw what seemed like ordinary houses blown to smithereens. The television coverage was from a distance and no information was given about the fate of anyone inside the completely pulverized houses. Listening to a smartly dressed spokesman for the U.S. forces describing how his forces had acted with restraint and precision was like listening to some refined kind of madness. There is no restraint in bombing houses into nonexistence. He sounded like a character from *Catch-22*.

To make sense of this act of barbarity—well, perhaps not to make sense of it but to try in some way to react to it—I turned to a writer who had been on the ground during one of the most savage bombing raids ever conducted. I reread Kurt Vonnegut's *Slaughterhouse-Five*.

Vonnegut, an American, had been a prisoner of war in the German city of Dresden in the last few months of the Second

World War when the allies bombed and destroyed most of the city and killed 130,000 civilians. Dresden had no armaments factories and few defenses against air attack. There appeared to be no strategic reason for the bombing, so the only explanations can be that the allies wanted to inflict huge casualties and so batter the surviving German civilian population into submission, or that the allies simply wanted to exact a terrible revenge. Vonnegut explains how the central character in his novel survived because he and other American prisoners of war and four of their German guards took refuge in a slaughterhouse meat locker. "There were sounds of giant footsteps above," Vonnegut writes. "Those were the sticks of high explosive bombs. The giants walked and walked" (Vonnegut, 1979, 118). The bombing was so intense that a firestorm was created. "Dresden was one big flame. The one flame ate everything organic, everything that would burn" (118). When the American prisoners of war emerged at noon the next day, "Dresden was like the moon now, nothing but minerals. The stones were hot. Everybody else in the neighborhood was dead. So it goes" (119).

Having experienced the bombing and seen the aftermath, Vonnegut might have been expected to write a dark and tormented book and in a sense he has. But it is wildly funny as well. The book defies categorization. It is part autobiography, part fiction constructed around real events, part fiction based on invention, and part fantasy or science fiction. Vonnegut appears as himself in the novel, and events such as the deaths of Robert Kennedy and Martin Luther King are recorded. The first chapter is mainly autobiographical. It deals with Vonnegut's visit to a friend who was with him in Dresden and recounts his decision to go ahead and write the book. Most but not all of the remainder of the book is about a fictional character called Billy Pilgrim. But the autobiographical and the fictional intersect from time to time when Vonnegut describes some event involving Billy and the other prisoners of war in Dresden and exclaims in the text "I was there," or when he recounts a visit he and his friend made to the reconstructed Dresden. Other parts of the novel were created in Vonnegut's fertile imagination. Some are credible and others utterly incredible. Billy becomes an op-tometrist, marries and leads a conventional suburban life. Billy becomes unstuck in time. He travels backwards and forwards and revisits experiences several times, so knows of his own death beforehand, is dead for a while, and is then swept back into an ear-lier part of his life again. Billy is kidnapped by aliens, transported to Tralfamadore, a planet millions of light years away, placed in a zoo and mated with a minor Hollywood film star called Montana Wildhack.

The novel is full of madness and meaning. The events in Dresden are rendered no more or less explicable or credible than the events on Tralfamadore. Billy's passage backwards and forwards in time disrupts the idea of the progress of history or the causal rela-tionships of events. Billy's and Montana's very ordinary activities, including urinating, making love and giving birth to a child, are subject to the gaze of onlooking Tralfamadorians and rendered uniquely extraordinary.

In the course of the novel Vonnegut examines a number of themes, amongst them death, time, justice and the freedom of will. Death is everywhere, banal, dramatic, tragic and, in Dresden, hor-rific in scale and character, and Vonnegut celebrates every death with the mantra "So it goes." At first the phrase seems to imply res-ignation. Death, after all, is natural. It happens. So it goes. But as the novel progresses the mantra takes on an irony, challenging the reader to continue accepting death so easily and pointing up the unacceptable nature of so many of the deaths described. Vonnegut dares describe being dead. "So Billy experiences death for a while. It is simply violet light and a hum. There isn't anybody else there. Not even Billy Pilgrim is there" (Vonnegut, 1979, 97).

Billy swings back into life again, back to events in 1945. In trav-eling backwards and forwards through time Billy experiences time as the Tralfamadorians see it. For them, when a person dies that per-son (there are five sexes on Tralfamadore) only appears to die but is still very much alive in the past. "It is just an illusion we have here on earth," says Billy Pilgrim, "that one moment follows another one, like beads on a string, and that once a moment is gone it is gone forever" (Vonnegut, 1979, 25). When Tralfamadorians see a corpse, all they think is "that the dead person is in a bad condition in that particular moment, but that same person is just fine in plenty of other moments" (25). Through the aliens' concept of time Vonnegut challenges our ways of understanding existence. He seems to belittle the single event yet gives it a place outside the flow of time, suggesting it can be experienced over and over. Through the ludicrousness of science fiction Vonnegut makes us less certain about the inexorable flow of history, and questions our relationship to it.

Billy Pilgrim witnesses and experiences gross injustices. He is abducted by aliens and asks, "Why me?" and is told that there is no why, and that we are all, abductors and abductees alike, like bugs caught in a blob of amber. He sees a fellow prisoner of war in the moonscape aftermath of the Dresden bombing, the poor old high school teacher Edward Derby, arrested for salvaging a teapot, accused of looting, tried and shot. A fellow prisoner of war inexplicably takes against Billy, falsely accuses him of contributing to another prisoner's death and arranges for Billy to be killed more than twenty years later. Billy sees the bodies of a number of girls who took refuge in a water tower during the bombing and were boiled to death.

Most important for me in this stunning, paradoxical novel is the discussion of free will. On his trip in the flying saucer to Tralfamadore Billy engages in a discussion with one of his abductors:

"You sound to me as though you do not believe in free will," said Billy Pilgrim.

"If I hadn't spent so much time studying Earthlings," said the Tralfamadorian, "I wouldn't have any idea what was meant by 'free will.' I've visited thirty-one inhabited planets in the universe, and I have studied reports on one hundred more. Only on Earth is there any talk of free will" [Vonnegut, 1979, 61].

Again Vonnegut plays with paradox. He appears to dismiss free will as a nonsense dreamed up by human beings in the face of overwhelming evidence to the contrary. After all, Billy has no control over his time travel. It just happens to him. The girls in the water tank had no control over their death. So it goes. Yet if we play Vonnegut's game for a moment and assume the Tralfamadorian exists and what it says is true, then belief in free will makes us unique in the universe. Belief in free will sets us apart from all other imaginable forms of intelligence. The belief in free will is what makes us fully human.

True, for the victims of the bombing, the girls in the water tank, free will does not exist. True, in extreme cases the existentialists' idea of choice becomes a purely philosophical concept. A man manacled and tortured in a military prison, a woman raped and infected with HIV, people living below subsistence level in a drought-stricken region of Africa can do little to change their circumstances. But those of us who have escaped such horrors can. Vonnegut makes this point at the outset of his novel by giving over the opening chapter to an account of how he made the decision to write the novel, and of how he decided to write a novel which could not be turned into another war film starring John Wayne. His first chapter is about deciding to take action in the best way he could. His first chapter is about choice.

The brutalities in Falluja came to a halt. The U.S. forces withdrew from the city and the Iraqis established a form of cease fire supervised by other Iraqis. Here in Australia the Iraqi city fell off the front pages for several weeks until U.S. warplanes fired two missiles into a house in Falluja, killing twenty-two people. The report in the *Sydney Morning Herald* went on to say that at least five children were among the dead. So it goes. Witnesses claim that the planes fired one missile and then, when people rushed into the ruins of the house to help the injured, fired another, killing and injuring the helpers. The robotlike coalition forces spokesman said that there was "significant intelligence" that members of a terrorist network were in the house, but of course since the missiles leveled the house we may never know. Catch-22.

Like Billy Pilgrim I am flung backwards and forwards in time between the barbarity of this air strike on a house in Falluja and the barbarity of the deaths of the four contractors and the revenge wreaked on the city by the U.S. forces a few weeks earlier. I am left wondering why the five children were killed. And I am swept back, as it were, to the barbarity of Seneca's Rome and then forward again to wonder whether the commanding officers of those warplanes saw it as normal to kill both their enemies and the progeny of their enemies. So it goes.

The girls in the water tower, the five children in that leveled house have no free will, but I do. It may seem strange to list myself as a survivor because all I did was watch an attack on television and then read about the second attack in a newspaper, but people are dead and I am not and so I have survived. And if Vonnegut tells me anything, then those of us who do survive can make the effort to be fully human. We can remember or imagine those dead people as living, respect them, make meaning from their lives, and choose to do something about their deaths. Graham Greene called Vonnegut "one of the best living American writers." I can in no way compare myself with Vonnegut but, if I understand anything from reading him, then perhaps I begin to understand why I am writing this book.

Using Literature: Three Sonnets

I went directly to Vonnegut's wonderful novel in search of some kind of understanding. But we can also use literature a little more obliquely in our quest for insight. At a recent postgraduate summer school at an Australian university I was asked to give a talk on writing doctoral theses, and I started by handing out copies of Shakespeare's eighteenth sonnet. I asked the group to read it and then argued that this particular sonnet, while being wonderfully and originally itself, nonetheless conformed to the rules and conditions of a "standard" Elizabethan sonnet. It was made up of fourteen lines arranged in three quatrains followed by a final rhyming couplet. The language was courtly. And the "argument" of the sonnet was presented in a way that echoed the traditional form of the Petrarchan sonnet from which the Elizabethan sonnet had derived. The first eight lines posed a question, and the final six lines provided an answer or closure. The poem conformed to the English variation of the sonnet by capping off the whole argument epigrammatically in a couplet:

> Shall I compare thee to a summer's day?
> Thou art more lovely and more temperate.
> Rough winds do shake the darling buds of May,
> And summer's lease hath all too short a date.
> Sometimes too hot the eye of heaven shines,
> And often is his gold complexion dimm'd;
> And every fair from fair sometimes declines,
> By chance or nature's changing course untrimm'd;
> But thy eternal summer shall not fade
> Nor lose possession of that fair thou ow'st;
> Nor shall Death brag thou wander'st in his shade,
> When in eternal lines to time thou grow'st;
> So long as men can breathe or eyes can see,
> So long lives this, and this gives life to thee.

I argued that just as the sonnet is an art form, so is the Ph.D. thesis. (I was talking to people working in the humanities and the social sciences.) There are conventions within which the student, like the sonneteer, is expected to operate yet produce original work. A "standard" Ph.D. thesis follows accepted patterns of argument. It has a title, which should encapsulate the question being researched and be expressed in no more than twelve or thirteen words. The thesis itself should fall into some five sections. The first is the introduction in which the student states the question in detail, explains how she or he arrived at the question, and then outlines how the question will be addressed in the rest of the thesis. The second section states what is known so far. This is often in the form of a literature review in which the student critically examines what has been published on the question and establishes where existing knowledge can be corrected or enhanced. The third section deals with method. In it the student outlines and justifies the kinds of research she or he will do in order to take knowledge about the question further. In the fourth section the student presents and analyzes the data gathered. And the fifth section is the conclusion in which the student discusses what new knowledge has been discovered or constructed. Depending on the question itself, this final section may include a discussion of what the student has learned in the process, proposals on how the new knowledge might be put to use, and a list of further research questions the thesis has uncovered.

The standard thesis observes certain conventions of language. The use of the first person should be kept to a minimum. There should be no colloquialisms, affective language or hyperbole. And the prose style should be formal and measured. The standard thesis should strive for objectivity. Even when using qualitative research methods, the student should make every attempt to remove his or her own biases from the research, doing this by using the same interview questions with the different people interviewed or employing phenomenological techniques when writing descriptions or accounts. And the standard thesis should validate the data through cross-referencing, multiple sources and techniques such as triangulation.

We talked for a while about the challenges of operating within these conventions, and then I distributed Gerard Manley Hopkins's poem called "The Windhover." In this poem the word order is wildly unconventional, the lines as they are laid out on the page have a (deceptively) disordered look to them, and sound takes over from sentence structure. Yet the form is still that of a sonnet. A rhyming pattern is strictly laid out and strictly observed. There are fourteen lines, if one counts only the lines beginning with a capital letter. And the pattern of argument is still that of a sonnet. The first eight lines glory in the description of the falcon, while the last six comment and conclude. And the last three lines have echoes of the Elizabethan epigrammatic ending in them:

> I caught this morning morning's minion, king-
>   dom of daylight's dauphin, dapple-dawn-drawn
>   Falcon, in his riding
>   Of the rolling level underneath him steady air, and
>   striding
> High there, how he hung upon the rein of a wimpling
>   wing
> In his ecstasy! Then off, off forth on swing,
>   As a skate's heel sweeps smooth on a bow-bend: the
>   hurl and gliding
>   Rebuffed the big wind. My heart in hiding
> Stirred for a bird, —the achieve of, the mastery of the
>   thing!
>
> Brute beauty and valour and act, oh, air, pride, plume,
>   here
>   Buckle! AND the fire that breaks from thee then, a
>   billion
> Times told lovelier, more dangerous, O my chevalier!
>
>   No wonder of it: shéer plód makes plough down
>   sillion
> Shine, and blue-bleak embers, ah my dear,
>   Fall, gall themselves, and gash gold-vermilion.

[Hopkins in Roberts, 1965, 49]

I made the point that some artists can work within the conventions of their art and also flout them, generating a creative energy as they break free from the constraints. Hopkins produces a dazzling, eccentric poem. Some of the thrill of it is in the way he breaks the rules, but he breaks the rules within reason since the poem remains recognizably a sonnet.

In something of the same way, I argued, some Ph.D. theses break the rules. The student demonstrates her or his understanding of the conventions but then departs from them. I gave examples of a student who abandoned formal research for a mixture of reflection on experience and analysis of literature, of another who matched formal interviews of practitioners in one country against a theoretical debate in another, of another who constructed her "research" around the very subjective accounts of just four people and of yet another whose literature review was a description, accompanied by photographs, of her personal library of books.

We talked about the benefits and dangers of flouting convention. And then I distributed a poem called "warty bliggens, the toad." This is from a collection by the New York newspaper columnist Don Marquis who wrote in the 1920s. The poems are ostensibly written by a cockroach called Archy, who types them out during the night on Marquis's typewriter by climbing onto the framework and diving onto the keys. Archy cannot operate the shift keys so the poems are written without capital letters or punctuation. I asked the group to read the poem.

> i met a toad
> the other day by the name
> of warty bliggens
> he was sitting under
> a toadstool
> feeling contented
> he explained that when the cosmos
> was created
> that toadstool was especially
> planned for his personal
> shelter from sun and rain
> thought out and prepared
> for him
> do not tell me

said warty bliggens
that there is not a purpose
in the universe
the thought is blasphemy
a little more
conversation revealed
that warty bliggens
considers himself to be
the center of the same
universe
the earth exists
to grow toadstools for him
to sit under
the sun to give him light
by day and the moon
and wheeling constellations
to make beautiful
the night for the sake of
warty bliggens
to what act of yours
do you impute
this interest on the part
of the creator
of the universe
i asked him
why is it that you
are so greatly favored
ask rather
said warty bliggens
what the universe
has done to deserve me
if I were a
human being I would
not laugh
too complacently

at poor warty bliggens
for similar
absurdities
have only too often
lodged in the crinkles
of the human cerebrum
archy

[Marquis, 1963, 47-48)]

I said that the poem was not a sonnet. It was not written in quatrains. There was no final rhyming couplet. It was what Marquis (or archy) called *free verse* and so did not conform to the number of lines, the meter, or any of the rhyming patterns of a sonnet. And the argument, the content, was ludicrous. But I also made the claim that the poem *could not have been written if the sonnet did not exist*.

I then talked about the thesis by Peter Willis (2002) whose phenomenological mode of inquiry I have already described in Chapter Ten. I talked about how Willis adopts the persona of the curator of an exhibition and writes as if he were welcoming a visitor to a gallery. In an anteroom he briefs the visitor about the exhibition, describing the theoretical bases upon which the exhibition has been assembled. He then takes the visitor through seven rooms, each room containing a number of "panels"—an account, a poem, a collection of metaphors, a range of completed "prompter" sentences, discussion and conclusions—depicting in different ways a significant event from his life as an adult educator. Towards the end of the thesis, the curator takes the visitor into in a debriefing room where he offers final thoughts and conclusions. The thesis is thought-provoking, funny, worrying, original, brilliant. It differs radically from any other thesis I have read yet could not have been written if the standard thesis did not exist.

The chair of the department which had run the summer school accosted me a day or two later. He thanked me for my contributions but said that he was fearful of being plagued by students proposing research theses more inspired by the warty bliggens poem than by the sonnets of Hopkins or Shakespeare.

Using Metaphor

I used the sonnet as a metaphor for the thesis. Metaphor is the process whereby we represent and illuminate one object of our thought by reference to another, different object of our thought. The reference is unconventional (Goatly, 1997, 6): we describe one object in terms of another which, at first glance, is unlike the first. "Life," we say, "is peaches and cream." "Life," someone else says, "is a bitch." "It is a tale," Shakespeare has one of his characters tell us, "told by an idiot. . . . " In a successful metaphor there is a relevance which may require imagination to see but which gives the metaphor an "accuracy." Sometimes that relevance is spelled out, as in the opening sentence of L.P. Hartley's novel *The Go-Between*: "The past is a foreign country: they do things differently there" (cited in Goatly, 1997, 9).

A metaphor need not always be in the form of an obvious reference or comparison. It can be expressed in a single verb, as when we say, "The evening dragged," or with a single adjective, as in "He told me a barefaced lie." It can be in a phrase such as "He will support you in fair weather or foul" or a clause such as "She tends to jump the gun." Metaphors involve imagination, travesty, untruth and deliberate error. There was no starting gun, of course. And they propel you from one place into another. If I write, "The thought that he had hurt her with his remarks hounded him for several days," then I take the reader from the sitting room, the pub, the workplace—places of social interaction—into the forest or the ravine or out onto open ground—places where hounds harass their prey.

I have heard a friend and colleague in the academy described as a "towering figure in his field." I find the metaphor accurate, and nicely ironic. The person referred to is small so the word *towering* places his undoubted renown in contrast to his actual physical stature. The word *figure* has a certain implication of haughty grandeur in it when used in expressions like "He cuts a fine figure," and this image again sits nicely against the reality of the self-effacing, agreeably grumpy man I know. There are metaphors within the metaphor. The word *towering* describes a person in terms of architecture. The word *field* refers to an academic discipline in terms of an enclosed space for farming or a defined and marked-out area for a battle or for sport. And there is a subtle implication in the use of the word *his*, suggesting that my friend dominates his academic discipline so completely that he owns it. Metaphors, even banal and apparently straightforward ones, are rarely a simple connection between two objects of thought. As in the case above, they will almost always occur in a context, will often carry several layers of meaning, and will usually be open to a number of interpretations.

Earlier on I described how a colleague and I kicked off a workshop with two images of a ship and then asked the workshop participants to develop their own metaphors. We were encouraging the participants to think about their organization, but I have found that exercises constructed around the creation and analysis of metaphors are also effective in helping people examine their individual or collective professional practice. How I introduce one of these exercises depends on the nature of the group. Sometimes I will talk about metaphors and metaphor analysis in the way I have done above. Sometimes I will tell a story, perhaps of the way my colleague and I used the metaphors of the ships, to indicate that metaphors can unlock feelings and promote discussion. Sometimes I will simply give an example. For most exercises I do not worry the participants with distinctions between similes and metaphors. I do not mind if they use the words "as" or "like" and make straightforward comparisons, but I am careful in the examples I myself give to integrate the image into the construction of the sentence. And I will try to find the time somewhere in the process to make the point that the metaphor allows for more mystery, more madness, more of the nonrational, more supertruth and therefore probably more insight than a simile.

My metaphor exercises usually have a number of stages. To begin, I ask the participants to work on their own and to write down a metaphor which describes themselves in their professional practice. Often I give examples. These might be "I am a soaring eagle, relentlessly looking for prey to swoop down upon" or "I am a tugboat captain, nudging a massive container vessel into port." Both these examples usually produce laughter, irrespective of the professional group the participants come from. In the second stage I ask the participants to form groups of three. One person reads out her or his metaphor and the other two ask questions and help to unpack it. I ask them to do this until all three metaphors have been unpacked. In the third stage I ask the participants to reassemble as a single group and we discuss what happened. I ask for reactions and, if people are happy to share them, examples of some of the metaphors discussed. I look for examples of new understandings of the work participants do and of themselves as people doing that work. Almost always there are metaphors which cause surprise and stimulate discussion. In one workshop a professional woman described herself as "a shadow walking on eggshells." I suggest that the choices of their metaphors and the way they unpacked them may have revealed some of the assumptions and values they bring to their work. Here I may have to probe a little but in my experience there are always participants who acknowledge that the exercise has made them see things differently.

In the fifth stage I ask participants to go back into their groups of three and to discuss their metaphors further. This can be the most productive period of the exercise. In the sixth stage I call for silence and ask the participants to review their original metaphors, to confirm them, revise them or replace them completely. And in the seventh and final stage I ask participants to share their reviewed metaphors with the other members of their small groups.

David Deshler (1990) argues that the revision of the metaphors is crucial. If, during the unpacking of a metaphor, a participant has recognized that her or his metaphor is limited or inappropriate or carries within it unsatisfactory values and assumptions, then that participant needs to be given an opportunity to develop another metaphor. It is in the formulation of the second metaphor that the transformative learning is applied, and the person and her or his practice can begin undergoing a change.

I have used variations of this exercise when working with adult educators, trade union activists, community workers, mediators and port managers. The port managers were from the four major commercial ports in New South Wales and they were attending a two-day seminar at a resort in the Blue Mountains. There were sixteen of them. They were the men (they were all men) ranked just under the most senior port managers who actually made the ports function, organized the entry and the departure of endless streams of container ships, cruise ships and pleasure craft, enabled the host of maritime industries which inhabit working ports to operate, and sought to ensure the safety and well-being of everyone. A good number were former seafarers. They displayed an energy verging on restlessness in the seminar room, and gave the impression that they would not suffer fools gladly.

A colleague and I had been asked to run the two-day seminar. The Maritime Services Board, which oversaw the ports in the state, was being restructured, and the stevedoring industry was undergoing radical technological change. Our job was to lead discussions on issues of work organization and industry development and then help the group develop a document carrying policy recommendations. I had drawn up an agenda for the two days and had made the mistake of writing the word *metaphor* next to a session to be held on the morning of the second day. The plan was to lead into three sessions, one before lunch and two more in the afternoon, in which the managers would formulate their recommendations. A metaphor exercise had seemed a good way to get people thinking imaginatively before four or five hours of hard and focused work. For one of the managers, however, the word *metaphor* smacked of irrelevant nonsense, the worst kind of thing some fool of an outside consultant might try to impose on them.

"I think we should move on to the policy document," he said when my colleague wrapped up the preceding session and I took over.

"That's fine by me," I said. "My idea was to do something that would lead into the policy document anyway."

"So why not just go straight into it?"

"We can do that if you want."

"What do you mean by metaphor?" someone asked.

"I want to get you to think up images of what you do now and what you would like to be doing in a perfect organization."

"Give us an example."

"Well," I said to the person who had spoken first, "tell me how you describe your job."

"It's bloody hard."

"What's a common image for a job that is bloody hard?"

"Pushing shit uphill."

There was some laughter.

I said, "That's a metaphor. Can I ask you a question?"

A nod.

"Whose shit is it?"

"Most of it is his," someone else said.

There was more laughter but my critic looked thoughtful.

"All right," said someone else. "Let's give it a go."

Over lunch, after a grueling first session on the policy document, one of the participants said to me that he had considered giving the metaphor session a miss. I am not so sure that he could have done so because a top executive from the Board (a woman this time) had been present for the whole morning, but I did take the comment to mean that he had found the exercise useful.

Using Role Play

Role play can be used to encourage insight. Indeed in some senses a role play is like an embodied metaphor. Even if the role play has a prosaic setting like an everyday workplace, it is an imagined workplace in which we give the participants the freedom to do things differently. We encourage them, however briefly, to live out a lie.

In TUTA we used a role play to get newly elected union del-
egates to practice taking part in a workplace meeting. It was
called "Alf Ayer," and this was the scenario we distributed to the
participants:

Situation
A lunchtime meeting of members called by the union to discuss
the dismissal of Alf Ayer.

Background
Alf was found to have company property valued at $16 in his
possession when leaving work. Alf admitted to the security officer
that it was his intention to use the material for his own purposes
and signed a statement to that effect. He was suspended from
duty without pay and, following a hearing by the company's
disciplinary tribunal, was dismissed two days ago. However, in
view of his service record of eighteen years and his otherwise
excellent employment record with the company, he was allowed
to resign. Alf has asked the union delegate to take his case to a
meeting of members.

I was talking one day to the trainer who had written the exercise and commented on how effective it always was. The trainer was
a former union official himself, gruff and not always given to chit-
chat. He stared at me for a moment, chewing on the beard just
below his bottom lip, and then said, "I named it after A. J. Ayer."

Alfred Jules ("Freddie") Ayer published a major philosophical
text in 1936 called *Language, Truth and Logic* and, although the
English do not accord their philosophers the star status the French
seem to do, nonetheless achieved something of the same stature in
the world of twentieth-century philosophy as Albert Camus. He
published a vast amount, including another influential work called
The Problem of Knowledge in 1956, spoke regularly on the British
Broadcasting Corporation and remained a significant figure in
English thought until his death in 1989. Ayer led a liberated social

life, juggling sexual partners and mixing with actors and singers, poets and politicians. When asked later on in his life about Camus, he said that he did not know much about Camus's writing but had been friends with him in Paris just after the Second World War when he and Camus were making love to twin sisters (Rogers, 1999, 312).

Ayer's thinking was very different from Camus'. Ayer acknowledged his debt to the logical positivists, and his writing has little of the literary character of the French philosophers he knew. His prose is straightforward, his argument ordered, his ideas uncompromising. The passion in his texts is one of disdain for those whose ideas he attacks and not one of elation, love, awe, distress or angst, and certainly not one of self-doubt. It would have been impossible for Ayer to have written a short story like *L'Hôte*, in which Camus (1957) places two strangers within his passionately loved Algerian land- and skyscape and describes with exquisite finesse the complex and unresolved moral challenges each presents for the other. Indeed, assuming those twin sisters thought alike, it seems very odd that one would decide to take on Ayer and the other Camus.

Ayer argues that philosophy's aim is to discuss language. It has essentially to do with definitions "in use," that is, definitions and the consequences of those definitions. The philosopher is not concerned with the physical properties of things but only with the way we speak about them (Ayer, 1971, 76, 80). Already this tells me how clever my colleague's exercise was. A lot of the discussion was always about whether Alf's action was "theft" or just "pilfering" or "common practice," or even part of the unwritten "conditions" of the job. Was it an immoral and unlawful act or just an unlawful act or, in everyday terms, not even unlawful? The discussion may not have appeared to be about definitions, but in the debriefing we could see that the language we used altered our perception of Alf's action and of the degree of responsibility he should take for his action. Arguing a case may not mean arguing the merits and demerits but rather defining the objects of our discussion, establishing a lexicography, in ways that carry consequences to our own advantage.

Ayer argues (1971) that all "genuine propositions" can be divided into two classes. They are either "analytic propositions" or "empirical hypotheses." An analytic proposition need not start from evidence. It concerns ideas. It is a statement, a way of describing objects or concepts, an organization of symbols or an equation as in mathematics or science and so is, in effect, a tautology. An example of an analytic proposition would be "A spanner is a mechanical tool." Ayer explains (1971, 41) that analytic propositions "do not make any assertion about the empirical world, but simply record our determination to use symbols in a certain fashion." We use one symbol and equate it with another symbol. This kind of proposition has a certainty about it but that certainty comes from its tautological nature. We are saying no more than that a tool is a tool. Ayer acknowledges that analytic propositions can still surprise us, in the way a newly formulated mathematical analysis can surprise and delight mathematicians, but he maintains these new analytic propositions remain tautologies. Until this moment we had simply not expressed the relationship of the symbols in this way. Ayer's ideas can make one deeply suspicious of any statement, particularly grand assertions made with all the weight of some authority and intended to carry the day. Do they say anything new? Or are they the expression of one symbol in terms of another? Are they only so much talk, taking us nowhere?

The other kind of genuine proposition is the empirical hypothesis. It concerns matters of fact and is empirical in that it derives from our "sense-experience." An example would be "A mechanic uses a spanner to loosen or tighten bolts." Ayer says (1971, 41) that an empirical hypothesis need not be "conclusively verifiable" but that "some possible sense-experience should be relevant to the determination of its truth or falsehood." He argues that such a proposition is verifiable "in the strong sense" if its truth can be "conclusively established in experience" but that it may be verifiable "in the weak sense, if it is possible for experience to render it probable" (Ayer, 1971, 50). So we can observe the mechanic using the spanner to loosen and tighten bolts or be pretty sure that if we did observe the mechanic at work that is what she or he would do. (Ayer modified his distinction between weak and strong verifications in later writing but I prefer the distinction as he originally made it.)

So all genuine propositions are either tautologies or can be verified by reference to the senses. Now here comes the cheeky bit. Young Freddie Ayer—he was only twenty-six when he burst so spectacularly upon the philosophical scene—goes on to maintain that all other propositions, be they metaphysical, moral, aesthetic or anything else, are "literally senseless." They cannot be verified and so are neither true nor false. Metaphysical arguments start from abstract ideas, that is, effectively from nowhere, and so cannot effectively arrive anywhere. They are utterances with no literal significance, even for the people making them. Aesthetic propositions are really no more that expressions of approval or disapproval. "This painting has great beauty" is the same as saying "This painting, hurray!" Moral propositions are really no more than expressions of feelings or commands. "Murder is bad" is the same as saying "Murder, ugh!" or "Do not commit murder." With precocious, even arrogant aplomb, Ayer rejects all knowledge of a transcendent kind. Thought is not an independent source of knowledge in some way more trustworthy than experience. And he relegates apparently significant concepts like "truth" and "falsehood" to the role of simple assertions or negations (Ayer, 1971, 117).

But even the propositions related to matters of fact are not all they seem. Ayer (1971, 55) calls them empirical "hypotheses" and argues that their function is to provide rules "for the anticipation of experience." Probability, he says, is all that can be forthcoming. It is irrational to expect certainty in any knowledge because no evidence can ever reach a point when experience might not go against it (Ayer, 1971, 121, 129).

Philosophers can be troubling people. At first sight Ayer seems to put a stop to discussion and debate. But as I read him he does the opposite by releasing us, when we are engaged in "literally senseless" discourse, from the need to try to observe the processes of empirical inquiry or analytical argument. Our moral conviction need be no less, even if it is neither a tautology nor verifiable by reference to sense-experience. Our emotional response to a piece of music can still be as strong. We can still gain intellectual stimulus from metaphysical discourse. Indeed, Ayer actually allows for exchange in a particular way. He argues that science and religion, for example, make propositions that do not stand in any logical relation to each other and so there can be no logical ground for antagonism between the two (Ayer, 1971, 155). Ayer himself may have lived vigorously in the secular world and regarded with contempt some who held the views he attacked. But it would seem to me that he is nonetheless arguing that a lively interest in others' views remains eminently possible if each party understands that the others may be using language differently. And Ayer allows me to understand and welcome insight as "literally senseless." Insight involves a leap free from tautological thinking and, as we have seen, can resemble a conclusion without the empirical evidence or preceding argument to go with it.

The author of the Alf Ayer exercise had written instruction sheets for various participants. These included instructions to the chair, the minute-taker and the person who would put a motion for an indefinite stoppage. But there were also instructions to encourage people to participate in the debate in different ways. So, for example, one participant received a sheet of paper with these instructions on it:

> You are the boss's secretary, and you feel the boss was justified in her actions. After all, it is essential that the company makes a profit and how can it achieve this if people are stealing from it all the time? You will speak against the motion.

Looking at the exercise all these years later I can now see that my colleague encouraged some of the participants to use analytical propositions in the debate by placing analytical propositions in their instructions. "The material taken was of small value." He encouraged others to talk in the language of empirical hypothesis. "Alf would be forced to endure an enormous financial burden due to the difficulty of getting new employment at his age." And he encouraged still others to engage in the "literally senseless" discourses of moral condemnation, loyalty and fear. "The bosses do not care about working people." I trained alongside this colleague on a number of occasions and now understand that the kind of discussion he encouraged in turn enabled us as trainers to debrief the exercise using questions like "But did saying that take the discussion anywhere?" or "Could you have proved what you said?" or "What you said was just one person's beliefs. Other people would have equally valid beliefs, wouldn't they?"

But perhaps I am making too much of this. After all, a lot of us have walked out of our offices or workshops with a couple of sheets of paper or a pen or a disk, or an offcut of cloth or wood or metal, or information or an idea or a process that did not actually belong to us. Perhaps the discussions were equally driven by guilt and self-justification. In any event, the Alf Ayer exercise worked. The participants entered enthusiastically into the role play, there were intense exchanges, and in the debriefing people expressed excitement at what they had learned. The exercise appeared to offer the opportunity for some at least to experience insights, about themselves, about what they believed, about how they argued, and in particular about how they used language.

Question to Question

Freire talks of inauthentic and authentic language. If the words we use have been put into our mouths by somebody else, if we speak somebody else's vision, our language is inauthentic. We are using "false" words. But if we use our own words, if we express a view of the world which we have formulated ourselves, then our language is authentic. We are using "true" words. While ever we use false words we will be objects of social history. We will be described and spoken for by someone else. But when we use true words we become subjects of our own destiny. We become people who play an active part in "writing" our own story. A role of the educator, therefore, is to help people abandon false words and begin using true words.

I have used a straightforward exercise as a lead-in to an examination of Freire's ideas on the use of language. I ask the participants to form pairs, and then take them through five stages. In the first stage, I ask them to go through a classic listening exercise. Each one is to speak to the other in turn for five minutes. The listener must give every indication that she or he is listening but must not actually speak. If the speaker falls silent before the time is up, then the two are to remain silent and sit out the remainder of the five minutes. I tell the pairs to decide who is to go first and that at the end of the first five minutes I will ask them to change roles. I set the exercise running. Often I let the time run on for another two minutes so that each speaker actually has seven minutes in which to speak without interruption.

We debrief the first exchange. People usually say how intense the experience was. Few ever say they had any trouble filling the time, and some make the point that having an attentive but absolutely silent listener was like having a vacuum they felt impelled to fill with their thoughts. Most agree that in life we rarely get five minutes in which to talk without interruption, and often the group will spend some time talking about why this should be. Participants often acknowledge that if we are not forced to remain silent, there is always the temptation to interrupt and turn the conversation towards ourselves with phrases like "The same thing happened to me" or "I think I can explain that." Already participants will sometimes attest to having insights into the processes of speaking and listening, and some may say that in the course of "filling the vacuum" they found themselves talking of matters they had not previously acknowledged, fully understood or even effectively "known."

In the second stage, I ask the participants to talk again in their pairs for five minutes and engage in a normal conversation. We debrief this second stage and talk about how "normal" their conversations actually were, and about the extent to which they had been influenced in the ways they spoke and listened by the experience of the first stage.

I introduce the third stage by suggesting that during the first two stages everyone must surely have had their curiosity aroused by something the other person had said. In this stage, then, they are to ask questions of the other person to learn more about whatever aroused their curiosity. I give them about ten minutes and say that there are no hard-and-fast rules but that each person should give the other ample time to ask questions. As a precaution I also say that anything said remains within the pair and that everyone has an absolute right to refuse to answer questions she or he feels might be intrusive.

We debrief this third stage, and in the course of the debriefing I also set the scene for the fourth stage. During the discussion I find an opportunity to make the point that we commonly use questions in order to learn. One person asks "How old are you?" and the other person replies "Thirty-eight." There are two points to be made about this very ordinary exchange. It is the questioner who does the learning. And the exchange follows the normal order of things in many conversations, and that is to move from question to answer. In this fourth stage, however, I want them to break the normal order of things and move from question to question and for the person answering the questions to do the learning. Again, the participants are to work in pairs. For the first five minutes one of them will be the questioner and the other the learner. In the second five minutes the roles will be reversed. And there is a rule: the questioner cannot make a statement. She or he can only ask questions and should consider the answers to those questions important only insofar as they lead to new and more interesting questions. The aim is to make the respondent learn from her or his responses. I warn them that the process is difficult, and that asking questions leading to more interesting questions is a skill which takes time to learn. If they have trouble thinking of a new question, then they are not to worry. They can take their time or even let the silence do the work in the way it did for some of them in the first stage. Again, every-one has the right refuse to answer and even to withdraw from the exercise altogether.

We debrief this fourth stage, and these are some of the ideas that I try to bring out in the discussion. Normally, when asked a question, we respond with a statement. Statements express certain-ties. They lock things into place. They bring us to a halt. We speak, as Ayer would have it, either in tautologies which take us nowhere, or in hypotheses which try to fix the future into place. Statements impose stability, perhaps even stasis or, at their most adventurous, provide patterns we hope to count on. But genuine questions (as opposed to rhetorical ones) are by their nature more fluid. The asker does not know the answer and so is uncertain. More, the asker brings his or her uncertainty into the relationship. If, then, we can use the answers simply as stepping-stones to another question, we deny the finality of those answers. If we go on asking questions, we shift the focus of both the asker and the responder from cer-tainty to challenge, from stasis to flux, from the expression of solu-tions to the formulation of problems.

Freire (1972b) called this "problematising." Life itself becomes fluid, a process of continually defining existence in terms of prob-lems to be acted upon. After Camus (1975), there is no absolute answer but we go on asking questions. And after Sartre (1984), we are confronted by a vertigo of possibility. We experience life as a relentless, vivifying series of choices to be made.

In the fifth and final stage, I ask the participants to talk again in their pairs before considering the session finished. My hope is that for some, at least, this final chat will be on a different plane.

Naming and Renaming

I have discussed Friere's ideas elsewhere (Newman, 1993, 1994, 1999), as many, many others have done, but I return to him because he had an extraordinary educational insight, encapsulated for me in just one sentence:

Once named, the world in its turn reappears to the namers as a problem and requires of them a new naming [Freire, 1972b, 61].

Freire sought to engage his learners critically with the social and
physical world around them, and he did this by getting them to
name the world for themselves in their own terms. In the programs
he developed in Brazil in the early 1960s, Freire got artists to
develop stylized line drawings depicting scenes close enough to the
experience of the learners to be familiar but different enough to
make the learners look hard at them and, prompted by the educator, discuss them. Freire's genius was in his realization that if the
drawings were well enough conceived and carried strong enough
themes in them, then a dynamic could be established in which the
learners would not just name elements in the drawings but go on
renaming them. Through this process their world would reappear
to them as a problem upon which they would be required to act. So
a Freiran educator, using a drawing of an alleyway in a shanty town,
might encourage a group of people to focus on the water lying in
the streets, and to rename it dirty water, then sewage, then a health
hazard to their children, then an example of bureaucratic indifference, then yet another example of the differences between the rich
and poor sectors of the city, then an example of injustice.

But we do not need to use line drawings. As I have already described, I might use a polystyrene cup and encourage a group to
rename it as a coffee cup, then a disposable coffee cup, then an object not so easily disposed of, then an environmental pollutant, and
then, perhaps, as an example of the victory of easy immediate solutions over genuine care for our future. Or I might use a photograph
of a bunch of flowers placed against a post on a roadside and encourage the learners to rename it as a wreath, a marker of the place
where someone was killed, a reminder of the dangers of the roads,
then perhaps as a small and poignant remonstration against our passive acceptance of the road toll, against our dependence on cars,
against ludicrously misplaced priorities.

But we might not need to go through the process of renaming so formally. I might have Freire's dynamic of renaming in mind when I say during a discussion, "Can you put that in another way?" I might design a scenario for a specific group which reflects back to them issues in their own organization and then, in the debriefing, try to set in motion Freire's dynamic so that the learners rename the issues as problems to be addressed and, if possible, solved. Or I might ask a group to write a song. I did this when participants in a residential course looked weary and there was an atmosphere of joylessness. They were union officials, and we had been dealing with difficult issues for three full days. Towards the end of that third day, in a session ostensibly about developing group cohesion, I gave them the task of writing the words for a song about the trade union movement, setting it to a simple tune, and then performing it. There were four groups, and the songs and the performances that went with them were wildly funny. The participants' vision of the movement was recast in song and satire and, if my assessment of the chaotic session is right, their world was renamed as a source of enjoyment as well as challenge.

There is something a little frightening about the process of naming and renaming. Once the cycle has begun, there may be no turning back. The world will of necessity be different. Educators using Freiran methods need to be politically aware and completely honest with their learners. Above all, they must be ready to proceed slowly. Learners can be taken over by the excitement and shock of their new understandings, and impelled into action. In contexts where there are few checks and balances precipitous action may invite harsh reprisals. If used unwisely, there is a danger that the process of renaming, rather than gracefully empowering people, may be a little like picking them up and hurling them, arms and legs flailing, into the full flow of social history, where they may sink.

Used carefully, however, naming and renaming can encourage insight, a new understanding of one's world, a new vision of things. The unchallenged and ordinary are revealed as problematic and extraordinary. The accepted can become suddenly, provocatively, unacceptable. A polystyrene cup becomes the point of attention, the mediating presence, a spur to action in a discussion of the careless, irreversible destruction of our environment. A photograph of a bunch of flowers leads to passionate exchanges about the way we callously trade people's lives every year for the privilege of owning a car. A song set to the tune of "Three Blind Mice" briefly entertains and distracts people during an intense residential course, and just possibly alters their view of the context in which they work and so alters the way they do that work.

Forum Theater

Literature, metaphor, role play, question-to-question and naming and renaming are all present in forum theater, a form of political theater developed by Augusto Boal. Since forum theater is interactive, no two pieces will ever be exactly the same, so what follows is a very generalized description of the process taken from Boal himself (1979, 139–142) and as I have seen it practiced in Australia.

A facilitator or a group of theater activists engages with a community of some kind and through research, informal interaction, discussion and workshops identifies a problem significant to that community. They devise a short play which depicts the problem but leaves it unresolved. The play is then performed before an audience made up of members of the community. Depending on the circumstances, the actors may be theater activists or members of the community, or a combination of both.

The performance follows a particular pattern. The whole event is moderated or supervised by a facilitator, or "Joker," who introduces the event, explains something of the process and purpose and then calls on the "actors" to perform. The play is performed once, all the way through. There may be some discussion at this point but it will normally be brief. The Joker then announces that the play will be performed again and invites members of the audience to interrupt the performance at points where they believe something could be done differently, or where they believe the events portrayed do not conform with the world they know. The play is restarted and, when someone calls out, the Joker calls a halt. The actors remain in place, and the Joker asks the person to explain why she or he interrupted. This often provokes a discussion involving other members of the audience, and the Joker may invite the actors to join in as well. The Joker then invites the person who stopped the play to replace the actor she or he felt could have done things differently, and the play is either restarted or taken up again from a point just before the interruption. The actors are required to accommodate the new arrival but also to make every effort to reach the same ending as they did in the first performance of the play. Further interruptions occur, more actors are replaced, the play is restarted or continued, and new or refined ways of addressing the problem are played out. The actors who have been replaced move to the side of the performance area but remain in sight of the audience and the new actors. Their replacements continue to work through the problem center stage. And the audience continues to intervene. In the performances of forum theater I have seen, the play has never been completed a second time. The debate between the original actors, their replacements and the audience has taken over, and the Joker has eventually directed the discussion away from the play and towards a search for real solutions to real problems.

Boal began developing his particular forms of political theater in the 1960s, working with the poor and oppressed in his native Brazil. But his ideas have spread wide and practitioners now make use of forms of forum theater in many different contexts.

I saw an evening of forum theater in Sydney developed by a group of car thieves. The project was funded by a large motorists' association which wanted to understand the phenomenon of juvenile car theft, and it was facilitated by a worker from an inner-city youth club. Through his existing networks the youth worker made contact with what he described to me as "the car-thieving community," and he gradually established a group of young people with reputations (and often convictions) for car theft. The group met over a number of months, talked about themselves, their lives, their gangs and car theft and, through a variety of exercises facilitated by the youth worker, gradually developed an evening of theater. Of course the process was not as orderly as this brief summary sounds. The composition of the group continually changed. There were moments of trust, but equally periods of suspicion and distrust. The youth worker sometimes intervened directly in the workshop process, directing rather than facilitating, and he called on the help of other people with experience of forum theater and cultural action to advise and participate in the workshops. However, an evening was finally developed made up of three parts, the final part of which was effectively devised by a number of young people with experience of car theft.

The performances took place in a theater in Parliament House in Sydney. An audience of some two hundred people attended, made up of lawyers, social workers, youth and community workers, police, magistrates, local politicians, at least one member of state parliament, some members of "the general public," executives from the motorists' association and a good number of young people, among them a number of car thieves. I was there too. It was a rare group to see together.

The evening began with a reasonably conventional piece of theater. A young man stands in front of back-projected images of cars and talks about how cars are sold as status symbols, as expressions of success, sexual appeal and power, about how they are designed to be attractive, luxurious and tempting, and about how their presence everywhere and their inaccessibility to young street kids can become both an affront and a challenge. The more expensive the car and the more sophisticated its security system, the greater the attraction and challenge. This scene flows into another. The young man is joined by several other young people. They are in a street, doing nothing much. They talk, spar with each other, trade genial insults. Two police officers approach them, attracted, ironically, by the young people's inactivity. Their initial approach is civil but is greeted with suspicion. The exchanges grow sharper.

The police officers become more aggressive, asking the young people to empty out their pockets. The officers take hold of one of the young people, empty out his pockets and discover a screwdriver. Suddenly there is open hostility, pushing and shoving, harassment. The moment passes, some kind of order is reestablished and the police leave. The anger is now expressed in a bitter discussion in which the young people decide to strike back by stealing a car and ramming it through a shop window. The audience is left with the prospect of serious crime, violence, possible injury and even death.

During the interval a piece of invisible theater took place in the foyer. An older woman accused a younger person of brushing against her and stealing her wallet. The young person denied the accusation but the older woman was loud and unforgiving. Other people joined in the argument. I suspected that the theft and the argument had been staged, and I imagine that most of the other people in the foyer did too, but I returned to my seat feeling edgy and ill-at-ease.

Back in the theater the youth worker took up position onstage but to one side. He said that he was adopting the role of the Joker in a piece of forum theater, explained a little about the process and called on his actors to start the play. The play was the part of the scene from the first half starting from just before the arrival of the police officers. The play was performed, and this time round the police seemed more aggressive and the kids more hostile. The Joker explained the process of intervention in more detail and then asked the actors to start the play again. A social worker stopped the play, replaced one of the actors and the play was restarted. Another member of the audience stopped the play, explained why and replaced another actor, and the dynamic of forum theater was established. The scene was never completed. The performance gave way to an animated discussion between members of the audience in their seats, members of the audience who had taken on roles and were standing onstage, and the actors who had been replaced and were standing to the other side of the Joker. The discussion was at times uncomfortable. The young people who had devised the play had strong opinions, a strong sense of injustice and a strong sense of ownership of the play. Some of the professionals in the audience were unhappy with the depiction of the two police officers, and some were angered by the young people's apparent refusal to take responsibility for their actions. But by the time the Joker brought the evening to a close there was a mood of frank exchange, and some of the more passionate discussion was now between different professionals.

I know from conversations with the youth worker after the event that he felt he had not allowed for sufficient follow-up to the actual evening of theater. He organized debriefing workshops with the participants, held discussions with the motorists' association and colleagues at the youth center and wrote a detailed report. But I do know that in subsequent projects he has been careful to use forum theater in the initial stages of a project and not in the final stages, nor as the whole project itself.

But it would be a pity to end this description with a criticism, even a self-criticism, of the youth worker. My memories are of the Joker's skill in facilitating the evening, and of his affection for the young people who had devised the play, his trust in them, the humility with which he accepted opinions from all parts of the auditorium and claimed no time for himself and, as evidenced in the kinds of question he directed back at the audience, his optimism and hope.

14

REVISITING INSIGHT

Confrontation

As happened in that auditorium at Parliament House in Sydney, forum theatre can unsettle people. When effectively done, it confronts people with unsatisfactory or unresolved versions of their world. In the short term, it can change them from passive onlookers to people literally involved in the scene being acted out. It can stimulate passionate debate. In the long term, it can stir people to change the roles they play in real life.

Boal (1979) acknowledges Freire in the title and the text (p. 120) of his most famous book, *Theatre of the Oppressed*, and the influences of Freire's ideas on forum theatre are obvious. Naming and renaming underlies the reworking of the performance. The Joker encourages debate in the dialogic mode. And the aim of the whole event is to problematize the world of the people involved. Freire's processes focus on language, and on discussion in the form of a study circle. Boal's processes are theatrical, involving the elements identified by Collier (2005): the use of space, the physicality and immediacy of performance, the editing out of the inessential, and the potential for experiencing metaxis. Both sets of processes can stimulate insight.

I want to take the risk and return to a discussion of insight. I want to start with Martin Heidegger's contention that rupture makes the familiar explicit. Steven Segal (1999) examines this contention and makes it clear that he is drawing extensively on what he describes as "Heiddeger's logic," but Segal is a philosopher in his own right and the interpretations are his. Segal argues that the word *familiar* refers to those aspects of our life which are so much a part of us, so familiar that we are unaware of them. It refers to the know-how we possess and call upon without even knowing we are doing so. The familiar is "the paradigm" in which everyday activities can be performed in a taken-for-granted way. An example of the familiar, then, would be the distances we stand from another person depending on whether the person is an intimate, a friend, a colleague or a stranger. Every culture has its own patterns of social distancing, which we observe without ever having been knowingly instructed. It is a know-how we simply do not realize we have until we find ourselves in another culture where the patterns are different (Segal, 1999, 75–76).

Rupture

Segal uses this idea of the person from another culture (the stranger whom Bauman sees as more disturbing than an enemy) as an example of rupture. In an encounter with a stranger, there are no rules we can fall back on. Our security is threatened. We suddenly have no know-how, and we cannot rely on everyday practices. Yet, paradoxically, at the moment when we cannot use these everyday practices, we become intensely aware of them. Similarly, Segal argues, we do not come across phenomena such as culture, tradition, heritage, religion and history in the course of living in our everyday world "but when there is a rupture of this world" (Segal, 1999, 77–78).

Rupture (or, in the case of equipment, breakdown) renders the things of our world explicit. Our first relationship with our world is not one of thought, but of engagement and activity. We come to know about hammering, value it and understand the meaning of it by using a hammer, not by thinking about the hammer, and it is only when it breaks that we take notice of the hammer itself and it becomes "an explicit object of our concern"(Segal, 1999, 81).

Rupture or radical change or dysfunction renders relationships explicit. We come to know other people by engaging with them in different ways and in different roles. We engage with our parents from the earliest age. We engage with others and develop friendships. We engage with others at school, then at work and in our various social groups and communities. We engage with a life partner. Often we will only come to understand fully the meaning and value of a relationship when there is a loss or breakdown of that relationship.

And rupture makes the self explicit. For the most part we are absorbed in our engagement in the world and it is only through rupture that we become aware of that absorption, that we move from that state of engagement to the state of awareness of that engagement. So we may give ourselves over so totally to our work that it is only when that work is disrupted in some way, by redundancy or accident or illness, say, that we can become aware of the extent to which we were absorbed in that work.

There are similarities between Heidegger's ideas of rupture and explicitness and Mezirow's ideas of disorienting dilemmas and perspective transformation. Mezirow, however, examines the processes of recognizing and, where necessary, altering assumptions and values (Mezirow, 1981, 1991). He is, in effect, limiting his concerns to an examination of psychologically and culturally acquired habits of mind and frames of reference, and is proposing a process of self-reflection made up of a number of ordered stages. Heidegger's idea of rupture making the familiar explicit has a suddenness, an explosiveness, that does not seem to have quite the same place for rational thought. It is an event and not a process, and has the smack of insight about it.

Explicitness

We can see the association of explicitness with insight in Segal's discussion of the distinction between "objects or subjects" and "the context in which objects or subjects are situated." While we are involved in objects and subjects, we take the context for granted. Explicitness

comes about when there is a movement from being attuned to objects and subjects to an attunement to the context in which the
objects and subjects are located. This movement, Segal says,

> is not the product of an act of volition but presupposes an existen-
> tial gestalt switch, a sudden and unexpected transformation in the
> focus of our attention [1999, 85].

Things happened when I walked out on that hillside in the far
south of France. I was struck, confronted, taken over, by the context. Background suddenly became all-enveloping foreground. I was
in the middle of a huge globe made up of sharp clear blue sky, the
mountains, the hills, the vines, the brown earth and stone walls,
and the roadway. I felt the heat. My feet were firmly planted on the
roadway but I felt a "pull" down into the floor of the valley and up
the hillside toward the mountains and the sky. There was no sound,
but it was as if there were a noise giving a texture and volume and
density to the entire space. I stood still for a time but it was, as the
hackneyed phrase has it, time itself which stood still. I had sat in
front of this view in the twilight of the evening before and during
breakfast that morning, and the various features of the view were
familiar to me. Now I had walked up the inclined road and beyond
the line of cypresses, abruptly losing contact with the house and the
hamlet below and behind me, and this rupture had made the view,
the context in its totality, shockingly explicit.

But I was both inside the globe and outside it, part of it and yet
not part of it. Standing there in that silvery sunlight I also became
viscerally, explicitly aware of my absorption in the context. In
Segal's language I was both attuned to the context and attuned to
my attunement to the context. I was conscious that I was standing
stock still. I felt a chill of excitement in all that heat and wondered
at it. I was aware of my Australianness in this very French context.
I watched myself marveling again at the patterns on the hillsides,
and understood that it was the imprecise but considerable age of
something so simple as those stone walls which fascinated me. I was

able, briefly, to be utterly absorbed in and by my environment, and to be aware of and to examine that absorption.

Reflection and Action

Segal closes his discussion by warning that rupture does not necessarily lead to critical reflection. He maintains that a response to the explicit can just as easily be defensiveness, and points to the role educators can play to ensure that positive, active learning takes place.

Forum theatre provides the rupture and makes the familiar world of the participants explicit. And it is up to the Joker to use dialogue, colored, as Freire (1972b, 62–65) would have it, with love, faith, hope, humility and trust, to help make the response to that explicitness, to that insight, one of critical reflection. It is this kind of reflection that will lead to action.

15

TEACHING ABOUT ACTION

Making the Right Choice

There is a special pleasure in seeing someone make the right decision. You can hear it in the gasps and then the applause of the audience at a tennis match. A player is presented with the choice of returning a ball with a top-spin forehand angled diagonally across the court from corner to corner, or floating the ball straight down the sideline so that it drops just inside the baseline at the other end. The player chooses the latter and wins the point. Skill, instinct, experience and mind combine to make the perfect choice.

I watched an experienced activist make an equally perfect choice. I was in Durban, South Africa, and my time there coincided with a music festival called Awesome Africa, held on an open field in the Shongweni Resources Reserve. Two stages had been erected and the crowd of several thousand stood or sat on the field, shifting attention from one stage to the other as the different acts took place. The day was an extraordinary mix of music performed by an extraordinary mix of musicians. There were African hip-hop groups, a very intellectual jazz band, a group classified in the program as "trance rockers and ravers," a kora player from Senegal, a folk singer, a group of three men performing a powerfully rhythmic form of chant called *kwaito*, and the Shembes, a religious community "from the Valley of a Thousand Hills."

Amongst the people I was with was Pitika Ntuli, a professor of fine arts, a poet, a leading figure in the world of South African arts, and a passionate advocate for the new South Africa. He was one of the festival organizers, but for most of the day he remained a member of the audience like the rest of us.

The members from the Shembe Church performed late in the afternoon. Two singers had just finished their performance, and there was a brief hiatus. I had rejoined a group of friends on the side of the field. People were standing, talking, queuing at the food stalls. There was a subdued buzz from the crowd. Suddenly the air was filled with blaring, difficult, beautiful noise. Onstage a group of men were blowing into horns. The horns were of different lengths and anywhere up to two meters long, slender, gradually opening to comparatively small bells, ancient in form. The blend of the notes was rich and unsettling. Behind the horns was the steady beat of a drum. I joined the crowd and moved in towards the stage, drawn forward by the sound.

From the back of the stage came a line of women dressed in purple. Each woman was holding what looked like a small shield in one hand and a staff in the other. They danced in perfect unison, moving very slowly, side on to the audience, holding their bodies in a slightly crouched position but with their heads erect, eyes fixed on the crowd, moving forwards, backwards, turning, every movement done with mesmeric intensity. They were, I began thinking, engaged not so much in a dance as in an act of worship. The intensity, the gravity, of what they were doing communicated itself to the crowd, and people watched, murmuring appreciation. This, it would seem, was a Christianity that had traveled the length of Africa from Ethiopia, taking on forms of Zulu ritual and owing nothing to Europe. And the depth and the power of the noise made me wonder whether the horns had their antecedents in the trumpets that had sounded millennia ago outside the walls of Jericho.

The women's dance came to an end but the horns continued. The women moved back and a line of men moved forward to replace them. The men wore trousers and multicolored shirts, with green and brown the dominant hues. They too held small symbolic shields and staffs, and they too moved in unison, bodies in the half-crouched position, side on, heads turned towards the audience, eyes intense. For a while their "dance" seemed the same as the women's, but suddenly, in absolute unison, they each lifted one knee high and stamped. The rapidity of this one action, the unexpectedness of it, the immediate return to slow motion, gave the stamp a startling impact. The crowd shouted out. The dance continued, punctuated by these moments of rapid stamping. I watched, trying to find the pattern and anticipate the next stamp, but failed. I watched for signals from the man in the center of the line, smaller than the rest and seemingly more intense. I saw none. But always, when the dancers stamped, they stamped in unison. The crowd's excitement grew. Some of the African women in the crowd began responding with high pitched ululations, and others—Africans, Coloureds, Indians, and Whites, to use the terms still officially current in South Africa—responded with shouts and cries and hoots of appreciation.

The "dance," the expression of worship, whatever it was, came to a close. The line of men withdrew. The horns fell silent. And onstage, taking hold of a microphone, was Pitika Ntuli.

"We are," he said "truly a rainbow people." There were shouts of approval. South Africans were "a people in the making." More shouts of approval. By joining in the festival the Shembes were making their contribution to "the African Renaissance." More shouts of approval. The Shembes, the other performers, and you the audience, he told us, were proof that it was possible to create a new South Africa "based on trust and love." The crowd roared, cheered, clapped, danced and filled the air with ululations. Ntuli stepped aside and, when the noise abated, the next act began on the other stage.

I returned to the group of friends. Sometime later Ntuli rejoined us. There is a grin commonly seen in South Africa and made familiar to the world by Archbishop Desmond Tutu. Pitika Ntuli was grinning that grin. He had not planned to address the crowd, but the opportunity presented itself and he took it. Skill, instinct, experience and intellect combined in an impeccable choice. The ball floated, dipped and raised a puff of chalk as it clipped the baseline.

Categories of Action

When I talk about action, I talk in threes. If I have a number of sessions or a number of weeks with one group of people, I will talk
about three categories of action, three sites of action, three domains
of action, three forms of control, three kinds of social movement
and three modes of learning. (I have used this concept of threes for
some time and so I need to acknowledge that other versions of
these ideas appear in my contributions to Foley, 1995; Crowther,
Galloway and Martin, 2005 and others.) Some of the threes corre-
late quite closely to Habermas's tripartitions but others do not, so I
cannot claim to be producing a neatly cross-referenced grid. I do
like the device of the threes, however, because it provides me with
a way of describing, categorizing and trying to understand what is in
reality a very untidy business.

Pitika Ntuli used one of the most common and conventional
forms of action. He spoke. But of course he spoke eloquently, using
phrases he knew would rally the crowd, and he did so in order to
reinforce in people's minds an image of the society he believed all
South Africans should work towards. I call Ntuli's action "conventional" because it is one in a category of legitimate actions we can
use to participate in the affairs of our communities, our society and
our state. The other two categories are *confrontational action* and *violent action*. In compiling these categories I am drawing on the ideas
of Ian McAllister (1992) and Russell Dalton (1996). Both these
writers talk of conventional and unconventional participation in
the affairs of state. McAllister breaks down the unconventional category into legal protest, semilegal protest and radical protest. I have
collapsed McAllister's and Dalton's different forms of participation
and protest into three categories, and used the more generic concept of action. *Participation* can imply an acceptance of the status
quo, and even an uncritical desire for inclusion in the affairs of the
already powerful. *Protest* is normally in response to someone else's
initiatives. I prefer the idea of action because it can encompass

protest and participation but also carries within it the sense of a vigorous striving for positive change. In action of this kind, we take the
initiative.

Conventional action, then, enables us to participate directly and
peaceably in the affairs of our community, society and state. It involves activities such as voting, taking part in election campaigns
as party members and campaign workers, making contact with
politicians and officials through e-mail, phone calls, letters and
meetings, pamphleteering, setting up Web sites and blogging, organizing petitions, lobbying, and engaging in consumer boycotts, lawful demonstrations and lawful strikes. In this kind of action the
people involved are intent on changing policy and procedures
within the existing structures, and not with altering the structures
themselves. Middle-class people might take to the streets to protest
government changes to the public education system, but they are
not challenging the existing order of which, in many other respects,
they are beneficiaries. Indeed, these kinds of modern demonstration are often carefully managed, with people being bussed to pre-
arranged meeting points and kept in order by marshals provided by
the protesting organizations themselves (Dalton, 1996, 68).

Confrontational action is what it says. It takes on those in control
more openly and directly, and is more "in your face." It will involve
activities designed to disrupt such as invading a meeting, blockad-
ing a road, holding demonstrations which have not been coordinated with the police, hacking into a corporate Web site, occupying
buildings, and going ahead with a strike that has been decreed
unlawful by the authorities. So environmental activists, for example, will picket a uranium mine, block an underwater outlet from a
chemical works and dump waste outside a company headquarters.
In many countries people involved in confrontational action
tread a fine line between action which will result in prosecution
and action which, although technically illegal, will not be prose-
cuted to the full extent of the law. Activists may occupy a building, not knowing whether the police will arrest or simply eject

them. Hackers do not know whether the site they have disrupted will simply be closed down or whether investigations will be put in place to track them down and prosecute them.

Violent action involves damage to property and injury to people. There are gradations of violent action. Some activists do not engage in violent action themselves but put themselves in situations where they may provoke or be subject to violence. Black civil rights activists in the early 1960s in the south of the United States occupied seats in diners or restaurants previously patronized only by whites, in effect challenging the owners, the other patrons and the authorities to react. Some activists engage in action not intending to initiate violence but ready to defend themselves vigorously if attacked. During that 1998 waterfront dispute in Australia, police were ordered to move in on strikers at one of the ports, only to find themselves suddenly surrounded by hundreds of the strikers' supporters. Some activists engage in action with the intention of escalating their action to a violent level if the opportunity presents itself. So workers in Seoul took to the streets dressed and equipped to do battle with the police or armed services. Some activists engage in violence against property. "Eco-guerillas" have damaged or destroyed fields of genetically modified crops. And, as is reported on a daily basis by our mass media, there are activists, organizations, authorities, politicians and even preachers who are ready to advocate or actively engage in violence against their fellow human beings.

Violent action is physically dangerous. In all but state-sponsored violence such as capital punishment and warfare, it involves flouting conventions, flagrantly breaking the law and confronting authorities who will offer little leniency if the activists are detained. And, most importantly, even in the "mildest" of forms, violent action involves stepping across crucially significant moral boundaries.

Sites of Action

Action, of necessity, takes place somewhere. The student riots in Paris in 1968 took place in the streets around the Sorbonne but

they were also situated within a complex social, political and economic context. As it turned out, the site of the students' action
within that context was much less central than many of them may
have imagined in the midst of the rioting. Sometimes the action
itself, or the group of people involved, will define the site of an
action, but there will also be times when we can make a conscious
effort to locate our action in a specific social, political or economic
context. The concepts of *the system*, *civil society* and *the lifeworld* can
help us do this.

The term *the system* can be used colloquially, but it is also used
in critical social theory with a specific meaning. Habermas (1984,
1987) describes the system as being the processes of exchange that
make up the economy, and the political and administrative controls
that make up the social structures within which we all live. It is this
combination of money and power which dictates much of our lives.
The system is sometimes used synonymously with *the state*. But the
system is a more comprehensive concept and includes transnational
corporations, international agreements, international trade groupings and monetary unions, multinational consortia, and other facets
of power and exchange such as the International Monetary Fund
and the World Bank which transcend individual countries and individual political structures. The system is an object of study and a
site for action. We can analyze it, its multiple manifestations and
the agencies and people who make it work. We can identify the
ways it affects people's lives. And we can decide on the kinds of
action which will make changes to the system itself and to the way
we exist within the system.

Civil society is a more localized idea, and refers to that pattern of
relationships and groupings we enter into as we seek to manage and
fulfill our lives. There are different emphases in the definitions
of civil society. Jodi Dean (1996, 221) argues that civil society
comprises "the institutionalised components" of our lives which
"preserve and renew cultural traditions, group solidarities, and individual and social identities." Eva Cox (1995, 18) describes civil
society in more straightforward terms as those familiar community

groupings with democratic, egalitarian and voluntary structures such as sporting clubs, craft groups, local environmental associations, some religious groups, play groups and neighborhood centers. To these she then adds groupings in relatively egalitarian workplaces, and the household. This "familiar" kind of civil society is to be found in an association as informal as an undertaking I might enter into with a neighbor that we look in on another elderly neighbor on alternate days of the week.

Cox's vision of civil society is constructed on trust. She distinguishes between financial, physical, human and social capital, and argues that, for the first three forms of capital, excessive expenditure will lead to their depletion. So if we spend money profligately, we will have less. If we chop down the forests without replacing them, we will degrade the environment. And if management exploits its employees, this will lead to burnout, ill health and the loss of the accumulated skills and knowledge those employees possess. However, in the case of social capital, excessive expenditure can have the opposite result. Social capital is the accumulation of trust. The more we spend, the more we amass. The more we base our relationships on trust, the more trusting all the parties become. My neighbor and I keep to our agreement and so become ready to trust each other in other matters as well. This vision of civil society becomes an alternative to the system. It is another and ideally more important arena in which to act out our personal, social and political lives. Accumulating social capital becomes the aim, and it is trust, not power and money, which binds "a truly civil society" together (Cox, 1995).

Frank Youngman (2000) depicts civil society in slightly "harder" terms. He sees it manifested in reasonably formalized organizations like professional associations, trade unions, employers' federations, religious bodies and social movements. Youngman adds two elements to Cox's essentially humanist version of civil society. Through his inclusion of employers' associations and trade unions he allows for direct intervention in the economy, and through his inclusion of social movements he allows for collective struggle for change.

In envisaging struggle, Youngman is hinting, perhaps, at Antonio Gramsci's even more structural and much less benign version of civil society. Writing in prison in the 1930s in an Italy under control of the fascists, Gramsci (1971) described civil society as being made up of organizations such as schools and universities, state bureaucracies and the church. He described these institutions as ramparts shoring up the state, and argued that activists needed to gain entry to these ramparts in order to disrupt, deter and alter the state's policies and practices. Since these organizations promulgated the ideas and authority of the state, this kind of action had the potential to bring about significant change.

No single interpretation of civil society need take precedence in our thinking. We can see civil society equally as a site for living out our cultural and social lives, for constructing trust, for engaging in collective action and for defying the less benign influences of a state.

The lifeworld is a more abstract concept. It denotes the almost infinite number of shared understandings upon which we build our lives and upon which we base our interactions with others. Habermas (1987, 131) talks of a "vast and incalculable web of presuppositions," the countless givens we draw on when we make meaning of events and when we judge people's actions and utterances. For the most part the lifeworld remains unexamined. But it is possible to take a segment of our lifeworld, bring it into the foreground and consciously examine it while the rest of the lifeworld remains unquestioned, continuing to provide the frameworks within which we think and the background against which we act. So the lifeworld can be both a subject for examination and a resource to draw upon in the course of making that examination.

Pitika Ntuli, when he addressed the audience at the music festival, used the shared lifeworld of the audience as a resource, an object of examination and a site in which and upon which to act. He made no direct reference to the forty years of oppressive apartheid government in South Africa which had ended only a few years earlier. But he could count upon a shared understanding and experience in his audience. He foregrounded the pain, sorrow, struggle and triumph by his references to the new South Africa and to the rainbow people, two phrases coined expressly to replace the discourse of apartheid. And he ended his brief intervention by affirming the ideas of trust and love and so sought to embed these as unquestioned values in the lifeworld of his audience.

Habermas (1987, 367–368) talks of the way in which the system is gradually imposing its values on the lifeworld. Competition is replacing cooperation in our ordinary daily lives, and administrative rules and regulations are increasingly dictating the way we conduct our communal living. The system is colonizing the lifeworld. Michael Welton (1995) sees "the defence of the lifeworld" against this colonization as a major mission for educators and activists alike, and argues that civil society is the site where this struggle can take place. It is by reinforcing civil society, by affirming all those associations constructed on trust, that we will defend our lifeworld from the depredations of the system.

As I watched the Shembes there were two young women close to me, one white, the other black. The black woman expressed her appreciation in high-pitched ululations. The white woman expressed her appreciation in the high-pitched squeals you hear at rock concerts. I do not know whether they had come to the festival together but they were side by side, expressing the same appreciation in culturally different ways, part of a crowd brought together by the festival and by this extraordinary performance. The festival was a joyous manifestation of civil society, and it was at this site that Ntuli chose to speak of trust and love.

Domains of Action

Ntuli made his exhortation as a spontaneous contribution to the campaign to construct a new society going on in many different ways and at many different sites across South Africa, and I would describe what he did as an example of social action. We often associate social action with, and distinguish it from, community action and political action. Sometimes we use the three terms as if they designated different kinds of action, but they are references to different *domains* of action, to the boundaries, the circumstances and the duration of the action rather than to the action itself.

Community action happens in the local domain. The people who come together to engage in the action are defined by that locality. They live in the same neighborhood or street, or are associated with the same school or park or hospital. The aims of the action are limited to that locality. The activists want to improve the lighting in the neighborhood, close off a street to heavy traffic, improve conditions at the school, put a sports field in the park or prevent the closure of emergency services at the hospital. Community action is normally concerned with one issue only and is often in reaction to a single or small number of events. Two accidents happen in the street in quick succession. The health authorities announce their intention to close the hospital emergency services in three months' time. People form groups and organizations but the groups and organizations usually function only for the duration of the action. Once the issue has been addressed and dealt with, they are disbanded or simply, and often abruptly, cease to exist.

Social action is not constrained by physical location. The domain of the action is the society or some aspect of the society the activists live in. The people engaged in the social action are defined perhaps by social class, or a common history of disadvantage, or a common experience, or a shared interest or belief. The aim of the action is to make changes to the social world the activists live in. So a group of activists want to combat racism, sexism or ageism, or to prevent the erosion of the social services, or to promote a civil society. Social action is normally related to one issue, but that issue may be a broadly defined one such as the protection of the environment or the improvement of the systems of justice. Social action can give rise to organizations, both formal and semiformal, and these may be long-lasting. Social action can also give rise to or take place within the context of social movements. Moments of gay social action in the 1970s grew into the gay and lesbian movement. Now within that movement there is social action to gain the right to have gay and lesbian marriages.

Political action normally takes place in and around the formal structures of a state and so is located within the system. Political activists seek to influence the political parties in government and other parties, institutions and organizations which play a role in or influence the governance of the state. People engaged in action in this domain are usually united by a set of common ideals. They may engage in a struggle over one issue, but it will be one within a set of issues which they consider important for the kind of world they want. Political action groups tend to have articulated policies, defined memberships and formal structures, and they are usually established with long-term struggles in mind.

In some discussions the divisions among the three domains become blurred and, because of this, the term *social action* subsumes the other two and becomes the generic term. However, the divisions remain significant. They can help us understand the development of a campaign. Community action can become social action which in its turn can become political action. A group of mothers in a depressed neighborhood of Mumbai come together to read to their children. Amongst them are a number whose reading skills are poor and so the group becomes concerned with adult literacy as well. With the help of the regional representatives of UNICEF, the group forms an organization and establishes a lending library of children's books and a program of adult literacy classes. Some of these women then begin promoting the model beyond their immediate neighborhood, establishing groups of women in other neighborhoods. Some of these groups of women feel sufficiently empowered to begin taking on the local authorities over the social and economic disadvantages they and their neighborhoods experience.

The divisions can help us understand how activist movements are shaped. For example, in several countries the Green movement is made up of a multitude of small community action groups concerned with local and often very diverse issues such as bush regeneration in a small suburban parkland, recycling glass, reducing the use of plastic bags in a country town, protecting a wetland or opposing the construction of a coastal tourist resort. There are social action organizations concerned with national issues such as the preservation of wildlife and wilderness areas or global issues such as the reversal of global warming and ocean pollution. And there is a registered political party with members elected to parliament who are concerned with pursuing a Green agenda across a spectrum of political affairs.

And the divisions can help us understand activist campaigns. The struggle for the recognition of gay and lesbian marriages, for example, is being played out in the community, social and political domains simultaneously. Members of the congregation of a local church whose priest has spoken out against gay and lesbian marriages wear rainbow sashes as a statement of their sexual preference and of their support for their cause. Gay and lesbian people in various kinds of semiformal and formal groupings organize festivals, hold demonstrations, write books, publish newspapers, newsletters and leaflets, run interactive sites on the Internet and conduct meetings, seminars and conferences to influence public opinion in favor of gay and lesbian marriages. And gay and lesbian organizations lobby government, put candidates up for election and work within political parties to have the legitimation of gay and lesbian marriages included in party policy.

Forms of Control

All of the examples I have just given of community, social and political action have been in pursuit of what I see as desirable outcomes. But there is no guarantee that people will engage in community, social or political action in accordance with my particular interests or for reasons I might deem benign. People can engage in community action to make their neighborhood exclusive rather than inclusive. People can engage in social action to oppose abortion and deny women their right of choice. And people can engage in political action to support a government taking part in an unjustified war.

Action occurs where there are differences of viewpoint and conflicts of interest, and will involve a struggle for power. The activists will resist the forms of control exercised by others over them and their affairs, and attempt to assert their own forms of control. Action will often involve a struggle both for and against the three forms of control I described in Chapter Eight: control by *instrumental* means, *institutional* control and control by *ideas*. So a group of activist-artists broke into a large unused warehouse in a district called *le Marais* in Paris, occupied it and established an artists' community. They used the warehouse as both a residence and studio space, and held impromptu exhibitions of paintings and installations. The owners of the warehouse tried to evict the artists but the artists barricaded themselves in. The owners went to the authorities, but the artists argued that the owners were deliberately letting the space deteriorate in order to redevelop it for residential rather than commercial use. At the same time both parties sought to win the hearts and minds of the surrounding residents, the artists arguing that their community contributed to the life of the neighborhood, and the owners arguing that the artists were living in unsanitary conditions and degrading the neighborhood. The story ends badly for the artists. In their attempts to open up the space to the locals, they were undiscriminating about whom they let in. The warehouse was taken over by a large number of people who held a riotous party lasting well into a second day and providing the authorities with the justification to call in the police, who evicted not just the partygoers but the artists as well. The struggle for control was won and lost.

Kinds of Social Movement

Although Pitika Ntuli acted alone when he took hold of the microphone, he was playing his part in a social movement made up of many people working in many different ways to construct a new

South Africa. Social movements are large, sometimes massive, groupings of people who join together to resist or bring about some kind of social, economic or political change. People form social movements to promote causes. They take sides. They recognize that there are enemies as well as friends, and they construct their movement on solidarity within the movement and solidarity with similar movements. Solidarity encompasses the idea of trust, but it is not the all-inclusive trust envisaged in a humanist civil society. Solidarity involves a commitment to an ideal, loyalty to people who share that commitment, and a willingness to unite in action against those who oppose the ideal.

Some social movements are structured, some semistructured and some so diffuse that they seem to have little or no structure at all. Amongst the structured social movements are the trade union movement, some of the churches and some political parties. *Structured* social movements have many of the elements of a conventional organization. They usually have a headquarters, recognized leaders who are elected or appointed and can act as spokespersons, and a cadre of officials or officers. They have a defined membership, and people can prove their membership by showing their "ticket" or by reference to some kind of ritualized initiation. Structured movements usually have a clearly articulated vision of the future expressed in policy documents or in hallowed texts of some kind. And they have agreed histories, traditions often celebrated at regular events, and revered former leaders who are given legendary status and often placed beyond criticism.

Semistructured social movements include the environmental movement, the women's movement, the peace movement and the gay, lesbian, bisexual and transgender movements. These movements tend to be made up of a network of bodies, some of which are formal organizations, a range of less formally organized associations, and scatters of informal groupings of people. There is no recognized headquarters and no single, universally acknowledged leadership but there are various congregations of power, around one of the more formal organizations, for example, or the editorial board of a journal, or a meeting place, or a particularly active group of people. In semistructured movements leaders emerge for the duration of particular campaigns but carry little authority after the campaign is over. There is no cadre of officials or officers but simply some people who are more active or involved than others. There is no defined membership but people *know* that they are members and can usually recognize others from the views they hold and the ways they act. Semistructured movements do not have a single policy document or a single hallowed text, but they do have large bodies of literature debating the issues that give their membership their sense of identity. They do not have a single vision of the future but they do want a future. So environmentalists will struggle for a habitable planet but will differ on how that habitable planet might be organized socially and politically. Semistructured social movements have stories of former campaigns rather than official histories, and they have fewer formalized traditions. Semistructured movements do have affectionately remembered figures who, as is the case with Simone de Beauvoir in the women's movement, are revered but whose ideas may also continue to be debated and revised.

There is, I believe, another kind of social movement which has no real structure. These *unstructured social movements* are more like webs with gaping holes in them and detached sections, so that there is no guarantee that one part will ever be in contact or even know of the existence of some of the other parts. Amongst these unstructured social movements I would include activists on the Internet, the international indigenous people's movement, performance artists and cultural activists, and the vast number of people concerned with combating the spread of HIV/AIDS and caring for people living with HIV/AIDS. These movements do not have a centralized structure or even many undisputed congregations of power. Membership is unclear. A person caring for an AIDS sufferer may not even know or consider that she or he is a member of a movement. And, unlike the structured and semistructured movements, unstructured movements have little or no agreed vision of a future. "Members" are more likely to be motivated by an intense emotion. The carer for a person with AIDS may be motivated by compassion, and his or her concern for the future may be related solely to ensuring the comfort of the sufferer. Performance artists find most of their satisfaction in the intensely present experience of performance. Members of the indigenous people's movement can be motivated by anger and an intense desire that the injustices to their people be acknowledged by the invading population.

Social movements can differ from place to place. I had the Australian experience in mind when describing the struggle against AIDS as an unstructured movement. However, in South Africa the struggle has a name—Treatment Action Campaign—and it is made up of a network of groupings and organizations employing clearly defined strategies, so would be better described as a semistructured social movement. Social movements can change over time. In Europe the unstructured working-class movements of the nineteenth century developed into the structured trade union movement and political parties of the left in the twentieth century. And social movements can display elements of all three kinds of movement. So the campaign against the detention of asylum seekers in Australia is made up of formally constituted organizations, a fluctuating network of activist groupings, and supporters and sympathizers spread through the population.

Modes of Learning

To complete my collection of threes, I talk about learning. Jack Mezirow (1981; 1991, 72–89), drawing upon Habermas's discussion (1972) of "knowledge constitutive interests," develops three "domains" of learning, which he originally designated as *instrumental* learning, learning for *interpersonal understanding* and learning for *perspective transformation*. These ideas have been taken up by other writers and the terms *instrumental learning, interpretive learning* and *critical learning* have become reasonably current. I used to use

Mezirow's term *domain* but now when I present these ideas I lay stress on the content and manner and so talk of them as *modes* rather than domains of learning.

We engage in *instrumental learning*, then, in order to deal with our environment. We learn to move and build things, to do a job, and to manage people when we think of them primarily as performing functions and so part of the objective world. We learn about cause and effect and how to solve problems by commonplace logic. In the world of academic disciplines, this mode of learning is found in subjects such as chemistry, geology and physics. In technical education this mode of learning is found in the applications of academic subjects to such fields as medicine, engineering and information technology. In informal education this mode of learning is found in practical, skill-based courses. In our everyday lives, this is "how-to" learning.

We need to be careful, however, and not think of instrumental learning as being at the lower, less complex end of some kind of hierarchy of learning. As we have seen, instrumental learning encompasses understanding and engaging with the complex world that modern science has given us. Equally, we engage in instrumental learning when we learn how to deal with the legal environment, or the economic environment or the political environment. In this categorization, we see the learning as instrumental if our interest is in managing the "environment" as if it were inanimate, and as if the people who inhabit that environment were objects. Our relationship to our world is that of subject to objects.

We engage in *interpretive learning* in order to understand and come to grips with the human condition. We learn about people, about how we organize ourselves, about how we relate and communicate, and about symbolic interaction and the social construction of meaning. The "rules" governing interpretive learning are different from the rules of instrumental learning. We learn to solve problems not by the application of "scientific" logic but by talking things through and seeking consensus. In the world of academic disciplines interpretive learning is found in the descriptive social sciences such as sociology and anthropology, and in history, literature and theology. In the world of informal education this mode of learning is found in communication skills and "personal growth" workshops and liberal or "enrichment" adult education courses. In our everyday lives this is learning about living as social beings in our social world. Our relationship to our world is that of subject to other subjects.

We engage in *critical learning* in order to understand what makes us tick. We examine our subjective world. We examine the psychological and cultural histories that make us what we are. In critical learning we solve problems by seeking to identify and analyze what motivates us, what drives us, and what constrains and inhibits us. In this mode of learning we foreground segments of our lifeworld. We can do this by opening ourselves to insight, or by using the more rational process of teasing out the ideas, assumptions, values and ideologies which we have constructed our lives on. Once identified, we can set about changing the ideas, assumptions, values and ideologies which no longer suit us. Again the "rules" are different. Despite being apparently a very personal endeavor, critical learning is a political act. It makes us less susceptible to hegemonic control. It helps us see through ourselves and so become better at seeing through others. It helps us understand the history of our thinking and so enables us to change our thinking. In the world of academic disciplines this kind of learning can be found in the critical social sciences such as psychoanalysis, in the critiques of ideology and the philosophy of science, and in some forms of political and cultural studies. In the world of informal education this kind of learning can be found in courses and workshops that involve a reflexive examination of cultural norms and the values and assumptions that underpin them. In our everyday lives this is the learning we do every time we try to separate out "truth" from "ideology." Our relationship to our world is that of subject to self.

Learning and Action

Action can lead to learning and learning to action, but the relationship between the two is not always there. Myles Horton said, "You only learn from the experience you learn from" (interviewed in Moyers, 1981). It is possible for experience to teach us little or nothing, as we may finally, ruefully recognize after having made the same mistake over and over. Horton is arguing that there is a need for someone—oneself, a partner, a friend, a colleague, an educator—to intervene and help the learning happen. Understanding the three modes of learning can help us make that intervention.

Rarely will one mode of learning happen in isolation, but we can enter a situation intending to focus on a particular mode. There will be times when we need to include very instrumental learning in what we do. An educator working with street kids will help them learn how to protect themselves physically from overzealous arrest by the police and will equip them with the information and skills necessary to deal with the legal environment if they are brought to court. There will be times when we intervene with the intention of encouraging learning mainly in the interpretive mode, as the trade union educator will do when running a session on preparing for a negotiation. And there will be times when we intervene with the intention of facilitating critical learning, using a metaphor exercise, say, or dialogic discussion.

Critical teaching and learning are often associated with Freire's principles and practices. Freiran educators could spend weeks or months in preparation, listening and learning, devising specific materials and then engaging with a group of learners in a lengthy, reflexive process. But critical learning can also occur suddenly, by chance, and as a part of another activity altogether. We can enter an educational event intending to facilitate mainly instrumental and interpretive learning but be presented abruptly with an opportunity to shift the learning into the critical mode. Someone makes an unthinkingly racist comment. Instead of challenging the speaker, we can ask "Where does that idea come from?" And in the discussion which follows we may be able to make the point that every idea, every opinion, every prejudice has a history. If someone says to us, "I never thought of it like that," we might be able to ask, "Well, how *did* you see things?" and together dispassionately deconstruct the abandoned viewpoint. Having got the person to recognize that the abandoned viewpoint was unthinkingly adopted from peers or subtly imposed by someone else, we may then be able to turn her or his attention to the newly adopted viewpoint and critically examine that as well.

Of course, there will be times when we intervene intending that the learning take place in all three modes. The organizers of a forum theater event would expect there to be instrumental and interpretive learning in the planning and mounting of the event, and they would hope for critical learning during the event itself. An understanding of the different modes would enable the Joker to guide the whole event, encouraging an outcome which would be a fusion of learning and action.

When Pitika Ntuli sent me an e-mail giving me permission to use the story in the way I have he gave little away, but I imagine he was amused. After all, I have made a lot of his taking the microphone and saying his few words. But it was a remarkable moment and, if we subject it to just a little more analysis, we can see that it was also a coherent educational event. It was organized. Ntuli had invited the Shembes to take part in the festival. It had a structure. There was a beginning in the form of the opening blast of the trumpets, a middle in the form of the mesmeric dance, and an end in the form of Ntuli's impassioned debriefing. And the event had an educational purpose, or was given one when Ntuli intervened. Because their performance had been so different from the rest of the festival, the Shembes provided a rupture in the day, making the familiar experience of being on that field in front of that stage starkly explicit. The ordinary became extraordinary, and Ntuli took control of the moment, renaming the event as a celebration of a shared humanity. He made us, the audience, look at ourselves and our world anew. He located the event in a collective striving to construct a society based on trust and love. And he offered us the opportunity to join with him in trying to bring that society about.

Part Five

DEFIANCE
AND MORALITY

16

CONSTRUCTING MORALITIES

I am coming to the end of this discursive book. I have found myself talking about vineyards, Gandhi, the love life of two philosophers, problem-solving models, anarchy in the streets of Paris, cricket, forum theater, jelly and ice cream. But there has been a thread of argument running through the book: I have proposed that activist educators and learners examine and understand rebelliousness, that we find ways of turning that rebelliousness into defiance, that we teach and learn how to choose defiance, and that we examine and understand the different forms of defiance we can choose from. In this final part of the book, I will examine how we can try to make our choices morally good ones, and I will argue that we can set about teaching and learning how to do that by telling stories.

A Moral Challenge

In the previous chapter I presented the three categories of action fairly dispassionately, taking my lead from Dalton (1996) and McAllister (1992), neither of whom expressed preferences when they presented their various categories of participation. But I did say that moving from conventional action to confrontational action involves entering a twilight area between legality and illegality, and that moving from confrontational action to violent action involves stepping across significant legal and moral boundaries.

I have written some of this book while living in France, and I was talking to a French activist near the thirtieth anniversary of the passage of the first of two laws through French parliament that effectively legalized abortion. She talked of the struggle over the years leading up to the passage of these two laws and she referred particularly to a manifesto which was published in a prominent French current affairs weekly, *Le Nouvel Observateur*, on April 5, 1971 and signed by 343 women. The women became known as *les trois cent quarante trois salopes*. This translates roughly as "the 343 'whores' or 'bitches,'" but neither word captures the meaning of *salope* precisely. In everyday modern French people use the word as a spontaneous oath in response to a woman who has exasperated them, tricked them or defied them. The women who signed the manifesto publicly acknowledged that they had all either had an illegal abortion or helped someone have an illegal abortion. Amongst the women were national figures like the philosopher Simone de Beauvoir, the actress Delphine Seryge, and the lawyer Gisèle Halimi. But there were many signatories who were less well known, and many who were completely unknown on the public stage. Each woman admitted to an act vigorously condemned by many, and defied the authorities to prosecute her for breaking the law. The manifesto "passed into posterity" (Zancarini-Fournelle, 2004, 211) as a turning point in the campaign. The women confronted the law, no one was arrested and the momentum created by the manifesto carried the campaign forward, resulting in the passage of the laws three years later.

The activist told me that the women's movement had been divided over the manifesto, some arguing that openly admitting to having had abortions would alienate many and so work against their cause. Others sought the confrontation. History had proved the confrontationists right, she said. She smiled, gave a shrug of her shoulders, and added that *la douceur*, gentleness, did not always work. Sometimes *la rupture*, resistance or disruption, were needed to make things happen. The smile and the shrug were very French. They were not dismissive of the matter, as might have been the case in an English-language context. They were acknowledgements of the enormity of the moral challenge activists can face.

Innate and Constructed Moralities

There is a debate about whether we are born with a sense of morality or whether we develop one as we live our lives. On the one side there are some, like Peter Jarvis (1997, 165), who contend that our morality is "pre-knowledge," there within us both before and somehow apart from knowledge, "beyond cognitive reason." He associates morality with desire, which he maintains "lies beyond the realm of education." Bauman seems in sympathy with this idea when he suggests that it is the "moral competence" of the members of society which makes society possible. A moral capacity comes first, society next:

> Rather than reiterating that there would be no moral individuals if not for the training/drilling job performed by society, we move towards the understanding that it must be the moral capacity of human beings that makes them so conspicuously capable to form societies and against all odds to secure—their happy or less happy— survival [Bauman, 1993, 34].

In the extreme form of this view, our moral sense is an instinct, given to us genetically by some force of nature, by the fates: when we act morally, we are acting according to intuition. Mark Mason, while not subscribing to this view himself, suggests that for those who do there are analogies between moral phenomena and love. Moral phenomena are spontaneous. They are not a product of reason or reflection. Just as a gesture of love would cease to be love if it were the result of an instrumental decision based on a calculation of likely profits and losses, so a moral act would cease to be moral (Mason, 2001, 56).

Morality, in this view, is nonrational or even prerational. It is not something that can be learned, nor is it something which can be subject to examination, appraisal and reconstitution. We can examine, appraise and reconstitute codes of ethics because these are sets of guidelines or rules agreed to by some group or community or congregation of people and so are social constructs. But we cannot examine, appraise and reconstitute the moral sense that may lie behind them. Ethics may be the province of education but not morality.

On the other side of the debate is the contention that, if our consciousness is constructed in interaction with our social and physical worlds, then so is our conscience. Our moral sense is part of the lifeworld, in part constructed by our culture, in part constructed by our own experiences within that culture and so, if you like, a deeply embedded, personalized code of ethics. For the most part, in the course of our ordinary lives, our sense of morality will remain unexamined and will influence our actions in the way the myriad components of our lifeworld influence our lives, without our considering them or even being conscious of their existence.

However, just as with other parts of our lifeworld, we can foreground our moral sense. We can, so to speak, take our conscience out and examine it, appraise it and, if need be, set about reconstituting it. We can think about the decisions we take and the judgments we make, and about the feelings of satisfaction or guilt we experience in the course of our engagement with other people. Through reflection, reading and conversation with others, we can appraise our decisions, look for the reasons why we judged this act good and that act bad, and seek explanations for our feelings of satisfaction and guilt. We can assess and change the values which inform our decisions, judgments and feelings and so take on full responsibility for the development of our moral sense.

Camus (1954, 54) offers us no alternative. Driven by a longing for happiness and reason we find ourselves face to face with "the benign indifference of the universe." There is no meaning so we must find meaning for ourselves. There is no Being or Purpose to provide us with moral guidance (just violet light and a hum, according to Vonnegut) and so the onus is on us to construct our own morality. Devising our own morality becomes an act of defiance in the face of the absurd.

Sartre, too, offers us no alternative. Objects and actions have no value in themselves but are given value by virtue of our choosing them. If we strive to live consciously, then we are continually making choices. And in making choices we ascribe value and so create and recreate our own morality. Devising our own morality becomes an act of defiance in the face of those authorities who want to affix moral values for us.

Teaching Morality

If our moral sense is constructed, then it can be taught. Morality is the province of education, not in the sense that we must promote a particular ethical code, but in the sense that we can help ourselves and others learn how to critically examine and construct our own moral sense. Depending on our own beliefs and interpretations of various theories, we can defy the fates, the absurd, or the authorities.

However, even though we can take responsibility for our own morality in theory, in reality we all too often operate according to moral codes which we have learned uncritically. I have talked above about foregrounding our conscience but I suspect that few of us actually do so. We talk often enough about acting "according to our conscience" but do not go on to ask "What is conscience?" and "Where does my conscience come from?"

If we are to teach and learn morality, we need to ask questions like these. We and our learners need to develop not just our rational and imaginative consciousness but also our moral consciousness. We need to go through what Freire (1972a) calls "conscientization," the term he applied to the change he intended to bring about in learners through his dialogic teaching and learning. Freire's "conscientization" is often interpreted as the process of learners changing status from objects to subjects. Ideally, the learners move from a fatalistic consciousness to a critical consciousness. Through dialogue, through the processes of naming and renaming, through the use of authentic language, through the critical analyses of their worlds, they come to understand the ways in which their thinking has been constrained by their social, political and cultural contexts. From inaction and passivity they move to a praxis, a fusion of critical reflection and action. They set about changing their thinking, and acting as independent agents both within and on their contexts.

Some interpretations of conscientization stress the political transformation in the process, and it undoubtedly can involve that, but the word was used in radical "para-Christian" movements in Brazil in the 1950s and early 1960s (Jarvis, 1987, 266), and Freire makes clear in his writing that the word, while taking on his political dimensions, should retain its moral dimension as well. He does this through his allusions to the Christian faith. For example, he requires those who commit themselves to the oppressed to "experience their own Easter" (Freire, 1985, 122). In saying this Freire is not promoting a Christian morality above any other but using a device from his own culture to alert us to the idea that truly conscientized teachers and learners remake themselves. They come to understand the moral as well as the social, political and cultural forces which have constructed their consciousness. They foreground the principles according to which they judge actions to be good or bad, subject those principles to critical examination, and set about changing them where they deem a change necessary. Morality as intuition dies, and morality as conscious engagement rises in its place.

Techniques

How, without proselytizing, do we teach and learn morality?

We can use techniques such as metaphor, critical-incident analysis, literature, mind mapping and other modes of self-reflection which transformative educators employ to help learners examine and revise their psychological and cultural assumptions. Some of those assumptions will have a moral dimension, and so some of the process of transformative learning will be moral learning. We can use the dialogic techniques employed by Freiran educators. As we have seen, these educators are concerned with helping people become capable of making their own personal, political and moral decisions. We can use the more conventional academic methods some critical educators may use to help people analyze power and make the moral and political decision to struggle against injustice. In a sense all educational activity can be an exercise in moral learning, and good educators will be aware of this.

But I am ducking the issue if I leave it at that. When I engage with other people with the express purpose of teaching morality, I tell them I am going to shift the emphasis from the abstract concept of morality to the more practical activity of making moral choices. I then present the three categories of conventional, confrontational and violent action and invite personal accounts and discussion. Everyone present has been involved in some kind of conventional action, if only voting in an election. (Voting is compulsory in Australia.) I ask them what other kinds of conventional action they have taken. Was the action successful? Is that as far as they have gone? Who, I ask, has been involved in confrontational action? Was the decision to move from conventional action to confrontational action difficult? Did they make a considered decision or just do it? If they did think about it, then upon what criteria did they base their decision? Was the action successful? But just a minute, what do we mean by successful? And, by the way, was anyone arrested? Would anyone present make the move from confrontational action to violent action? Are there any circumstances at all under which anyone would consider violent action justified?

This discussion can be a confronting one. Australia is a multicultural country and people in adult classes can have various and difficult histories. Some will have fled their countries of origin and arrived as refugees, some welcomed, some egregiously unwelcomed by current Australian authorities. Some will have left situations of complete social upheaval and breakdown. Some will have been the recipients of violence, and some may have engaged in violence themselves. At the outset the discussion may well be about a conventional campaign, for more open space in the city, say, but it may easily move on to confrontational action outside a refugee detention center in outback Australia, or to violent repression, invasion, revolution or resistance in Chile, Vietnam, West Papua, Cambodia, Lebanon, Fiji, Palestine, Bosnia, East Timor, Afghanistan or Iraq.

Violence and "Violent" People

Usually, in response to the discussion, some people state adamantly that they would never engage in violent action. I respond by saying that I, too, find violence repugnant and that I normally find the people who advocate violence repugnant. Then I talk about one, two or three particular people who have entertained violence and whom I do not find repugnant. I try to break the deadlock in our discussion, the silence, by using stories.

The first person is a friend who worked for an international trade union body in a country where work conditions could be draconian and the rights of workers were few. The sons of the owner of one particular factory raped the women workers more or less at will. Two women complained publicly to my friend, disappeared the next day, and have never been seen again. "Why," my friend asked with tears in his eyes, "when there is violence against us, it is all right, but when we consider violence in return, we are condemned?"

The second person is Nelson Mandela. When he was released from prison towards the end of 1989 Mandela emerged a gray-haired, elderly man with the authority of his years of commitment, struggle and imprisonment behind him. He alone, or so it seemed, was capable of uniting South Africa, of bringing the white oppressors and the other, oppressed races together to form a new South Africa, of preventing bloodshed and mayhem, and of forging a transition government that would lead to a new nation. He was charismatic. He was forceful yet gentle. He was the great peacemaker. Yet, as a much younger man at his trial in 1964, this great peacemaker explained why he had moved from nonviolent action to violent action in his pursuit of justice for his people. He said that for years the white oppressors had remained unmoved by rational, legal and moral argument, or by nonviolent demonstrations and resistance. He described four kinds of violence—sabotage, guerilla warfare, terrorism and revolution—and presented them as stages in the escalation of violent struggle. He explained how he and his comrades had chosen to engage in sabotage as "the first method" because it did not involve any loss of life, and to exhaust this form of action "before taking any other decision" (Mandela, 1994, 167). The implication is clear. They would contemplate escalating their action if sabotage failed to move their oppressors. Face to face with those oppressors in court, with no expectation of anything other than severe retribution from the state, Mandela calmly justified violence.

The third person is Gandhi and about him, I say, there can be no doubt. He was a man of peace, and at the core of any action he took was a commitment to nonviolence. I tell the story of the salt march. I then say that before the salt march Gandhi wrote to the viceroy of India, promising him that no English people would be hurt. I explain that Gandhi always warned authorities beforehand of what he intended to do, and that we can interpret this feature of the satyagraha as a nicely crafted combination of confrontation and courtesy. But there is a further interpretation. By 1930 Gandhi fulfilled a role close to that of guru to people like Jawaharlal Nehru of the Indian National Congress, was revered by people in cities and towns across India and was considered close to being a god by hundreds of thousands of peasants (Woodcock, 1972). Gandhi's letter to the viceroy can be read in another way. "Mess with me," he was saying, "and all of British India will be in flames." If we redefine violent action as damage to property and injury *or the menace of injury* to people, then it is my contention that Gandhi was engaged in violent action. The salt march marked an escalation in the kind of action he took.

17

STORYTELLING

Gathering Stories

If, as Sartre suggests (1984, 530), each time we express our own freedom we impinge on somebody else's, then every action we take has a moral dimension. For activists and activist-educators this proposition will be particularly true since we are trying to force or resist change. Each action we take will involve some kind of moral choice. Hard-and-fast rules to help us make these choices are impossible to lay down. But we *can* tell stories.

We can tell the stories of people, like Mandela and Gandhi, who have made the decision to escalate from one form of action to another. We can go looking for stories of people who have engaged in political, social and community action in places as different as, say, Portugal (Lima and Guimaraes, 2004), Nigeria (Umar, 1993) or Nicaragua (Miller, 1985). We can draw on the stories of activist-educators like Horton (1990) who have confronted and helped others confront violence. We can draw on our own experience and tell our own stories. And we can take events like the attack on the World Trade Towers in New York in 2001 and the attack on Iraq in 2003, examine our responses and recast those responses as stories by asking questions such as "How did you react?" and "What have you done since?" In this kind of teaching and learning the educator presents morality in terms of challenge rather than regulation, and helps the learners amass a large number of stories so that each time they are confronted with moral choices they will have a body of their own and others' experiences to draw upon.

Using Stories

Telling stories is a magical way of teaching, and listening to stories a magical way of learning. We know this from our childhood. All but the most deprived were told stories at home and at school. At home we gave meaning to our family through story. There were the favorite stories, which were like legends, about Uncle Clarrie or Grandmother. There were the stories a parent told us as children about our own exploits when we were too young to remember. And there were the shared experiences which we told and retold for the pleasure of it, and which reinforced our family bonds. At school our teachers entertained, distracted, thrilled, calmed and educated us by telling us stories. In adulthood we continue to communicate and give meaning to our lives through the telling of stories, in the pub, over dinner, in idle conversation and in formal presentations. Our religions are constructed on stories, from the Australian indigenous people's "dreaming" to the myths of classical Greece to the stories told about and attributed to Jesus to the stories of the *Ramayana* to the stories of Islam. Some narrative therapists talk of "storying ourselves into existence." This kind of therapist gets clients to tell and retell the stories of their lives, describing and interpreting their roles and reactions differently, and so changing their understanding of themselves (Monk and others, 1997). People like Mike Kaye (1996) and Stephen Denning (2001) see storytelling as a way to describe, consolidate and bring about change in organizations. And some postmodern writers would have us understand all social experience in terms of story, in terms of what Jean-François Lyotard (1984) has called "meta-narratives."

Story and Language

If we are to use stories well, we need to think about the language in which we tell the stories. I will talk about the English language here, but I do not intend to suggest it is better than any other language. It is simply the language I know best, the language I use the most, and the one I am writing this book in. I should also acknowledge that some sociolinguists want us to talk more about language use and the users of language than about any particular language as an entity. But I am unreconstructed on this point. I think the English language does exist as an entity despite (or maybe because of) its many variations across the globe, and that this entity has characteristics we can identify, discuss and celebrate.

At the base of English is Anglo-Saxon, a Germanic language which gives us a vocabulary of short, sharp uncompromising words. So the American rock singer Melissa Etheridge can write the line "I feel the slap and the sting of the foul night air" and we do almost feel the slap and the sting. To that Anglo-Saxon base have been added words and structures from the scholarly Latin of the Middle Ages and then from the scientific Latin of the seventeenth and eighteenth centuries, giving us the tools for argument and precision. To that Anglo-Saxon base have also been added words and structures from French, first when the Normans invaded England, then when the Renaissance brought the languages of Italy and France to England, and then when the Royal Court returned to England from France at the time of the Restoration. The influxes of French have given English the language of government, of relationship and love, and of theory and abstraction. To these varied influences were added words and new and different nuances of expression from the languages of the countries that were parts of the British Empire.

Influences have come into the English language but, from the sixteenth century on, the English language has traveled out from England. It has been given various and often very different colors and character by other English-speaking countries in North America, the Caribbean, the Indian subcontinent, Africa, Malaysia, the Philippines, Oceania, Australia and New Zealand. In the last century English took on the role of the major international language, and continues to be daily influenced by people from non-English-speaking countries who adapt and develop it as they use it in their international affairs. A research section in the European firm of Matra, located outside Paris and made up of German and French staff, used English as their working language. The language was flexible enough to let them introduce occasional French and German words, specialist words and shorthand phrases only they would understand.

Amidst all these variations a standard English has emerged. I went to see a Jamaican film in London and was relieved that the film carried subtitles. The characters spoke in Jamaican English, and without the subtitles I would have found it impossible to understand. Some years later I was in Jamaica and was approached by three men in a street in Kingston. They were speaking amongst themselves in the patois that had confounded me in the film but they quickly shifted to standard English in order to offer me high-quality dope. I used the same standard English to courteously refuse. To lessen the impact of my refusal I also used standard English to chat to them about the current cricket test match being played in Kingston between the West Indies and Pakistan, and the four of us parted on amiable terms.

English is comfortable with practical matters. In this it remains stubbornly Anglo-Saxon. English can deal eminently well with abstraction, but we speakers of English prefer to have that abstraction accompanied by a practical example. A French text can deal entirely with abstractions. (French is the only other language I can speak and read in, and in a pretty ham-fisted way at that.) The French reader, usually educated at school in philosophical discourse, will be comfortable with abstractions. Translated into English, the text can become inaccessible, not because the ideas are less clearly expressed but because the English-speaking reader will yearn for examples. This gap between the two languages and the two modes of expression is wonderfully illustrated in Toril Moi's book *Sexual/Textual Politics* (1988). In it she examines the texts and ideas of prominent English-speaking and French-speaking feminists and, incidentally as it were, shows the huge differences in style, expression and content between the writings of, say, Virginia Woolf and Simone de Beauvoir, or between Kate Millet and Luce Irigaray.

We speakers of English want ideas expressed in practical terms. We want abstractions converted into concrete analogies. We want images of the material world. We want the philosopher to say something like this: "The existentialist idea of the absurd is rather like someone walking purposefully along a pier at night, not knowing when they will fall off the end into the water and not knowing why." We can see that. We can hear it. We can feel the slap and the sting of the spray as the wind whips it up off the water. At the end of the day what we really want is a story.

Kinds of Storytelling

English is the meeting point between two kinds of storytelling. Its Germanic origins give us dark and powerful northern stories peopled with archetypal figures, terrible gods and supernatural forces, and heroes of extraordinary physical prowess and endurance. Relationships derive from heroic and awesome action. The Romance influences give us the stories of courtly love, no less robust in their own way, but couched in relationships. The action, both physical and affective, derives from these relationships. We can see this northern, influence in Shakespeare's *Macbeth*, in which supernatural forces prey upon Macbeth's flawed character to bring this great warrior crashing down into a mire of murder and self-destruction. And we can see the courtly influence from southern Europe in Shakespeare's *Romeo and Juliet*, no less disturbing and tragic in its end, but with its story driven by a passionate and entrancing love, ignited at first sight in the very recognizably human minds and bodies of the two central characters.

If we use story, then, we have fine traditions to draw upon. Indeed, it might be worth revisiting *Macbeth* and *Romeo and Juliet* in preparation. For my money they are the plays with the strongest stories. In *Macbeth*, the evil portrayed in the witches at the very outset leaves us in no doubt about the eventual outcome. So we watch with a kind of fascinated dread as Shakespeare unfolds his story in horrid, lurid, inevitable detail. The killing starts and it continues, and we look on as Lady Macbeth sinks into madness, and as Macbeth's lust for power becomes a crazed mixture of defiance and despair. In *Romeo and Juliet* the storytelling is radically different. There is youth and passionate love and therefore hope. The initial love, despite all the difficulties, is consummated and grows even stronger. We are allowed to witness this and are made to yearn for Romeo and Juliet's happiness. As the events unfold we are buoyed by hope and, until the very last scene when Romeo drinks the poison, nothing is inevitable.

Teaching and Learning Through Story

A story needs to be woven into our teaching and learning. It needs to come out of the points we are making or the ideas we are examining and it needs to lead back into them.

We can start a story by identifying a problem or asking a question. In the beginning phase of a story we should locate the events in time and place and, as the "characters" appear, we should give them identities by indicating their positions or roles or occupations or relationships to one another. Names are not necessary but the listeners need to be able to quickly recognize, identify with or form an attitude to "the factory manager" or "the disgruntled parent" or "a drunk wending his way home." The middle of the story is the narrative in which, step by step, action by action, fact by fact, we take our listeners from the unknown to the known. The narrative needs to be driven along by a tension of some kind. If the outcome is inevitable, then the steps towards that inevitability should produce that sense of dreadful fascination in the listeners. People should want, yearn, to know *how* the inevitable will come about. If the outcome is open, then the listeners should be buoyed by hope. *Please let this happen. Please do not let that happen.* Sometimes we can stop and use the uncompleted story as a trigger for discussion, asking the listeners questions like "What do you think will happen?" "What do you want to happen?" and "What would you do to make that happen?" or "What would you do to stop this from happening?" And the story needs an end, in the form of a discussion of the problem and a search for solutions, or with the problem resolved and another more challenging problem raised. In the business of teaching and learning the job of a good story is to leave the listeners thinking, and we will rarely want to leave the listeners replete or with a sense of finality, as some plays and films and books do.

Remembering and Forgetting

Stories are memories, but in the telling of them they become a tangle of memory and imagination. We take a story out of the continuous flow of existence and immediately alter it by giving it a beginning, middle and end. Sometimes we will make a story out of a number of memories because to recount all of them separately would be time-consuming and tediously repetitive. Sometimes we will invent the story. Invented stories are imagined memories. They are told in the past tense just like "real" stories. And if they echo real memories, then they are stories of events *which could have happened* and so they will carry a supertruth. In a sense our culture is "a palace of memories" (Ricoeur, 2000) which storytellers enter and where they make their selection, compiling, summarizing, copying, editing and altering as they go. The "palace" contains the collective memories of our family, community, country, nation and humanity, in the forms of traditional and urban myths, stories and songs, nursery rhymes, gossip, literature, theater and films.

There are good memories and bad ones. There are stories worth remembering and, although it may sound paradoxical at first, there are stories worth forgetting. I listened to French philosopher Alain Finkielkraut one evening in Paris. He and two other philosophers took part in a panel discussion, held in a large church and eagerly listened to by some eight hundred people. Finkielkraut talked of *la pédagogie de la mémoire* and *la pédagogie de l'oubli*. Again it is difficult to translate these phrases. If I say "the pedagogy of remembering" and "the pedagogy of forgetting," I focus on the actions of remembering or forgetting and lose the additional qualities of the abstract and the universal that are contained in the phrases if I leave them in French. Finkielkraut explained these concepts with reference to the Holocaust. He argued that it would be tempting to see the modern-day European Union as countries coming together because of their common cultures, because of their centuries of shared memories. But the opposite was the case. Modern Europe, he argued, grew from the sentiment "Never again." It was constructed upon the story of the Holocaust which was to be acknowledged and, by creating the union, expunged and forgotten. The terrible reminders during the breakup of Yugoslavia that such violence and inhumanity were still possible in Europe made the union all the more urgent. Rather than being centuries old, modern Europe was as new as the most recent commitment to construct a joint future, and its roots, its identity, were to be found not in the past but in this future.

We may not always think on the scale Finkielkraut does, but adult educators and trainers do make use of the two pedagogies in a number of ways, without necessarily naming them. In the course of facilitating experiential learning we ask people to recall events from their own lives, and then compare and analyze them in the course of the learning. We ask people both to remember and to forget when we debrief a role play. And elsewhere (Newman, 1999) I described how, after a long and divisive strike at a paper mill in a small Australian country town, the union required management to pay a number of trainers to run workshops in which strikers, strikebreakers and townspeople talked out their experiences, put remaining bitternesses aside and began reconstructing a sense of community.

18

RELATIVE AND FOUNDATIONAL MORALITIES

Another Debate

Through stories we can help people remember and forget, we can raise people's consciousness and we can teach morality. But building a stock of stories to draw upon is a haphazard business, and if we do it uncritically we may include stories which mislead and obfuscate as well as help. We need, at the very least, to receive the stories with "a reflective skepticism" (Brookfield, 1987, 21–23), weighing them against our own knowledge and experience and being alert to the explicit and implicit values they may carry. But we will need to go further. We will need to evaluate the stories and to grade them in some way, and this leads to another debate, this time between those who maintain that all morality is context-bound and therefore relative (we cannot grade the stories), and those who maintain that there are a number of foundational moral values which will prevail irrespective of context (we can grade the stories).

The sides in this debate are not so clear. Most social theorists would agree, however, that the debate is located in a world where there is increasing diversity and accelerating change. Some commentators use strong, near-apocalyptic language. Giddens talks of "a runaway world of dislocation and uncertainty" (Gidden,1994, 3), and of "double-edged risk" and "crumbling traditions" (Giddens, 2000, 21, 22). "Chaos and contingency," Bauman tells us (1995, 24), "are back with a vengeance." And Jane Kenway and Elizabeth Bullen (2000, 266) provide evidence of intellectual confusion in their list of more than thirty terms used to denote theories of the contemporary, ranging from "the age of anxiety" and "the age of rage" to "the end of history" and "the end of Reason" to "the risk society" and "casino capitalism."

We are told that in this late-modern, high-modern or post-modern age there has been a loss of foundational concepts upon which we can construct our lives. In traditional societies we knew our positions and the roles we were expected to play. But the authority of the agencies which provided us with these certainties— God, the state, our community and our family—has been weakened. We are faced with a multitude of both trivial and significant choices which people in traditional societies simply did not have to make: what food to eat, what clothes to wear, what education to choose for our children, what occupation to follow, and what spiritual, political and intellectual beliefs to espouse. Now we encounter potential disorientation daily (Giddens, 1994, 83–85; Giddens, 2000).

This loss of foundational concepts is accompanied by a loss of a sense of society. Using information technology we can make things happen at a distance, and our social experience becomes detached and vicarious. Giddens (1994, 247) talks of "an ethos where . . . the mechanisms of economic development substitute for personal growth and for the goal of living a happy life in harmony with others and with nature." Bauman says that instead of striving for a harmonious life, we buy things, and he makes this scathing assessment of the process:

> Individual needs of personal autonomy, self definition, authentic life or personal perfection are all translated into the need to possess, and consume, market-offered goods. This translation, however, pertains to the appearance of use-value of such goods, rather than the use-value itself; as such it is intrinsically inadequate and ultimately self-defeating, leading to momentary assuagement of desires and lasting frustration of needs [Bauman, 1989, 189].

Our age is marked by anxiety about the potentially catastrophic environmental, economic and political dangers we have created.

Bauman argues (2001, 186) that our growing awareness of these dangers goes hand in hand with a growing impotence to deal with them. Giddens sees this paradox as creating a debilitating self-doubt. In the process of seeking and applying new knowledge we create a need for more, but when we look for an authority on a given topic we are confronted instead by a proliferation of authorities, many with radically different opinions. This perpetual revision of knowledge and our loss of faith in the experts cause us to doubt the value of knowledge itself. And once we doubt the knowledge upon which we conduct our lives we lose confidence in who we are, and we experience an ontological insecurity (Giddens, 1991, 194–196; Giddens, 2000, 52).

Amidst this uncertainty, isolation and doubt, morality is lost. Mark Mason (2001, 48) maintains that along with an insecure identity comes a diminished sense of responsibility and a tendency to act "with scant regard for the human or moral consequences." Fritz Oser (1999, 232) suggests that many people have all but abandoned moral responsibility and consider that "economic rationality and imperatives, the judicial system, and cultural achievements" provide sufficient guides and mechanisms to regulate our social system.

Moral Relativism

In place of moral absolutes has come a moral relativism. This has occurred in the context of globalization. Because of international trade, economic migration and the displacement of refugee populations, we now have large multicultural cities across the world in which people of widely differing customs, religions, and moral codes come together. Mass media and worldwide electronic communication systems have put us in contact with societies both subtly and significantly different from our own. As a result we are presented with "a plethora of options as to the ultimate source of the good and the right" (Mason, 2001, 49).

In its extreme form, moral relativism leads us to believe that anything goes and that acceptable behavior is simply behavior which conforms with one's culture. Certainly moral relativism can foster qualities such as tolerance, respect and humility, and Oser argues that to consider different moral belief systems equally legitimate seems, at first glance, to be a "democratic attitude." But he goes on to say that "in morals, equalising means paralysing" (Oser, 1999, 234); moral relativism cannot help the person who must decide whose side she or he is on.

Mason (2001, 52, 59–60) makes the point that if all moral codes have the same merit, then the only meaningful criterion for making a choice will be the efficacy of that choice. Does it work? And the only significant point of reference would be the self of the person making the choice. Does it work for me? After all, "If no ultimate moral right can be defended, why should I not exploit others for my own ends?"

Looking for Absolutes

Confronted by the shortcomings of moral relativism, a number of theorists have gone looking once again for a morality guided by foundational concepts. Cox (1995) appears to return to the traditional authorities of community and household for her ideas of civil society and social capital. Trust would appear to be a foundational concept in her thinking and so a significant element in any choice or action we might judge right or good.

A civil society constructed on trust, like any utopian vision, provides us with an ideal to strive for and a standard against which to evaluate our actual state of affairs. But trust is a concept without texture or degree. We either trust or we do not. And there is something passive in the act of trusting. When we put our trust in someone, whether it is our doctor, the principal of our children's school or an international relief worker, we can all too easily let that other person take control. At the end of the day, trust strikes me as a drab and unenergetic concept upon which to build a brave new moral world.

Giddens also uses the concept of a utopia, but he has two bob each way. He enjoins us to adopt a framework of "utopian realism." This is a beguiling concept. He calls it "realism" because it involves us adopting a critical outlook in which we "grasp actual social processes" and "suggest ideas and strategies which have some purchase." And he calls his realism "utopian" because, in an increasingly reflexive social universe where we are constantly examining possible futures, "models of what could be the case can directly affect what comes to be the case" (Giddens, 1994, 249–250). Like Finkielkraut, Giddens is suggesting that our roots lie in the future.

Kenway and Bullen (2000, 270) describe Giddens's utopian realism as "a politics of hope grounded in a strong sense of the possible" and argue that the framework invokes notions of autonomy, responsibility, solidarity and dialogue. These four concepts have a foundational feel to them. Autonomy and responsibility imply a duty to express one's own independence of being and to respond openly and fairly to the independence of being of others. Solidarity and dialogue carry the idea of respect for the Other, in the form of a commitment to collective action and to egalitarian communication. I like the framework and can see how all four notions could contribute to making an act a moral one. But the utopian realism, which is meant to provide the act with a purpose, smacks too much of compromise. Just how much of our utopian dream must we abandon to strategies which will have some purchase? Just how pragmatic do we have to be? If for even a moment we consider a principle negotiable, then in the heat of action we may well find we have jettisoned it and are left floating on a postmodern sea without any moral anchors.

Giddens (1994, 93) also talks of generating an "active trust," and at first glance this might seem to answer my worries about the unenergetic nature of the trust the civil societarians put their faith in. However, if I use the idea of active trust with reference to relationships in the private domain, there is an internal contradiction. We either trust someone or we do not. If I must work at trusting someone, it can only be because I do not trust that person. Giddens himself talks of active trust in the public domain, of building trust "from below" and linking the state to the "reflexive mobilisation of the people," using the concept somewhat in the way Cox uses the concept of social capital. But the idea of active trust carries a half-truth and, as a result, offers false expectations. Mobilizing people into groups of active citizens can certainly generate trust, but this form of facilitated social encounter can also produce justified dislike and distrust. We do not necessarily love our neighbors. Nor do we have to. Distrust can be as activating a force as trust. It puts us on our guard, makes us think hard, and can motivate us to form dynamic solidarities with like-minded people. There are people who cannot be trusted and active *dis*trust, that is, a determination never to take things on trust alone, can be a motive to action, and a morally justified stance.

Morality, Reason and Prereason

Bauman gives the impression that he sees morality solely in terms of instinct. "Morality," he tells us, "is not safe in the hands of reason." What makes the self moral is

> that unfounded, non-rational, un-arguable, no-excuses-given and non-calculable urge to stretch towards the other, to caress, to be for, to live for, happen what may [Bauman, 1993, 247].

Possibly because of this elated element in Bauman's discourse, Mason (2001) describes Bauman as an "intuitionist." Certainly Bauman's use of the word *urge* suggests some kind of spontaneous, almost biological force, but he most definitely is not suggesting that we are born essentially good (or bad), nor that we are blessed with an intuitive understanding of what is good or evil, right or wrong. "In fact," he says, "humans are morally ambivalent" (Bauman, 1995, 10).

Bauman describes morality in terms of a situation we find our-selves in:

> Well before we are taught and learn the socially constructed and socially promoted rules of proper behaviour, and exhorted to follow certain patterns and to abstain from following others, we are already in a situation of *moral choice* [Bauman, 1995, 1].

The situation is "primal":

> Morality does not need codes or rules, reason or knowledge, argu-ment or conviction. It would not understand them anyway; moral-ity is "before" all that [Bauman, 2001, 175].

Bauman argues that we are presented with this choice in our very first encounter with the Other. We find ourselves in a condi-tion of *being-for*. We are faced with the challenge of responsibility for the Other and answerability to the Other. This face-to-face encounter is "naive," producing a moral impulse which "precedes speech"(Bauman, 2001, 175). We are "ineluctably—*existentially*—moral beings" (Bauman, 1995, 1). In saying this Bauman differs from Sartre, who argues that the Other's gaze makes me an object amongst other objects and so drains my world away from me. Bauman (1993, 78) maintains that it is through "stretching myself towards the Other that I become unique." In my union with the Other, I take on my identity as a moral being. "I am I in as far as I am for the Other."

Bauman (1993, 77) sees morality in terms of our responsibility for and answerability to the Other, irrespective of what I might know of the Other or of what the Other might do for me. He main-tains that the Other need do nothing to earn my responsibility, and in saying this he adopts a position analogous to that of Camus. In Camus' case, it is in my encounter with the silence of the universe that I come to understand that I must construct my own morality. In Bauman's case, it is in the encounter with the silence of the

Other. To his interpretation of moral phenomena as primal, spontaneous and nonrational, then, Bauman (1993, 247) adds the foundational concept of this "un-arguable, no-excuses-given and non-calculable" responsibility.

In his idea of a primal encounter with the Other, Bauman sees the Other as pure. He talks of "the tremendous encounter with the Other as a *Face*," and contrasts this with encounters with others wearing the "masks" of class and stereotype and acting out roles, driven by different, potentially conflicting interests and motives. The possibility of bad faith and fraud "crawls in" and "the innocent confidence of moral drive" is replaced by "the unquenchable anxiety of uncertainty" (Bauman, 2001, 179). Morality then, Bauman seems to be saying, is a site for struggle. We form our morality in encounters with an idealized concept of purity and with the everyday realities of bad faith and fraud.

Conflict and Dignity

Oser, an educationalist, adopts a more realistic view of the Other as the starting point for developing his ideas of moral education. He sees the Other as significant precisely because she or he is different, classified differently, "incommensurable." He acknowledges that this requires of us a tolerance and that this in its turn can lead to the dangers of moral relativism. One way out of this trap is to go beyond "mere tolerance" and require a "fighting culture" of fair play. This allows us to concentrate on the arenas of conflict. We are not required to accept the opposite view or belief or interpretation, but "to acknowledge the dignity of the other side" (Oser, 1999, 235).

Oser's ideas are attractive. He accepts that there will be sides, and so he allows me to have people I dislike and may even hate. Bauman acknowledges these conflicts as well but seems to regret them and to blame them for the loss of innocence and the advent of fraud and uncertainty. In Oser's vision, conflicts of interest are part of the order of things, along with a proactive kind of fair play and the foundational respect for dignity. This is a nice mix of the pragmatic and the ideal. In my search for the good or right act I do not have to consult or emulate some model of a pure encounter, but I do have to respect my enemy.

An Ethics of Integrity

Mason, another educationalist, also places an emphasis on respect for dignity, but significantly it is a respect for ourselves as well as for others. He decries the current conditions in which there is "a loosening of the bonds of local community, and hence a diminished sense of moral responsibility in our primary relationships" (Mason, 2001, 62). He suggests that "meaning, purpose and fulfilment" may be reestablished in the interconnected domains of our self and our relationships. A person living an authentic life respects her or his own being. We may take strength simply in who we are. Equally, a person living an authentic life respects the being of others. We nurture relationships "that in turn nurture us," and in the company of others we counter the existential dread of being utterly alone (Mason, 2001, 65).

A respect for our own being implies a willingness to be responsible for our own actions. And a respect for the being of others implies an acceptance of moral demands originating from outside ourselves. Mason takes these themes of respect and responsibility and proposes "an ethics of integrity." This ethics is "constituted by the principles of respect for the dignity of our and each other's being, and the acceptance of responsibility for the consequences of our moral choices" (Mason, 2001, 59).

Mason argues that his ethics of integrity can be interpreted as a "dialectical" morality in that it is sensitive to both foundational and nonfoundational moral positions. The concept of commitment, open to objective evaluation, for example, sits in tension with the more subjective idea of face-to-face responsibility (Mason, 2001, 62). The implications are significant. In adhering to an ethics of integrity, Mason appears to be telling us, we would be applying an integrity whose internal contradictions invited constant critical scrutiny. Such an integrity would be open to revision and so remain vital and dynamic.

19

HATING AND LOVING

What can I offer the learner-activist who has to make moral choices? How do I construct my own morality in order to do this? Giddens, Bauman, Oser and Mason all give me ideas. I want, for example to find foundational concepts upon which I and my learners can rely. I want to identify primal, "intuitive" urges which we can then develop as one might develop a natural aptitude. I want to recognize conflict as part of the moral order of things. I want to maintain a respect for others. And I want to develop a morality with a dynamic tension in it which impels us into action.

The trouble is that Giddens, Bauman, Oser and Mason also leave me disappointed. The concepts around which they construct their thinking, such as responsibility, dignity and integrity, may be admirable but they have something of the same effect on me as the concept of trust has. They are worthy but dull. They have that static, almost passive feel to them. The words themselves are nouns rather than verbs. Even when the word can be used as both a noun and a verb, as is the case with *trust*, the writers tend to use it to denote a state, quality or condition rather than an action. Dreadful though this may be to say about someone who writes with the élan of Bauman, all the writers quoted above give me the impression of scrabbling around in the foothills of the debate. I grow impatient with them and want the passion of Camus who scaled the mountain and stood there shouting defiantly into the infinite. But Camus, too, ultimately disappoints. He urges us to be defiant, yes, but in the face of meaninglessness.

I came across an essay by William Hazlitt (2004), originally published in 1826 and called "The Pleasure of Hating." The title is shocking. That we should enjoy hating is a disturbing idea. The essay itself, like everything Hazlitt wrote, is elegant, passionate, wickedly witty in places and deadly serious in others. Hazlitt was one of the great English radicals of his age, a social and literary commentator of genius, and his essay has given me the courage to choose hate as one of the two themes in my ideas on morality. And at roughly the same time I came across a book by Alain Finkielkraut called *La sagesse de l'amour* (The Wisdom of Love). I had heard Finkielkraut speak and wanted to try reading him. The opening passage of his book gave me the courage to choose love as the other theme in my ideas on morality.

Of course there are terrible disadvantages in using the ideas of hate and love. They have been rendered unutterably maudlin by our popular culture. They have been used for malign purposes by religious fundamentalists. They have been reduced to banality by bikies (and Robert Mitchum playing a crazed preacher) who have the words tattooed across the fingers of their clenched fists. And they have been so devalued in colloquial speech that we can now use them to express mild approval as in "I love that dress," or even milder disapproval as in "I hate this flavor of ice cream."

But there are also advantages. Love and hate can be acts, emotions or conditions. They are simple and forceful transitive verbs. *I love her. He hates me.* They can be nouns expressing profound feelings. *There was hate in his eyes.* They can be nouns that mark out the conditions of a relationship. *They were wonderfully in love.* Love and hate can be interpreted in different ways. They can be seen as "primal," "intuitive" even, in that we experience, learn and express love and hate in our very early encounters with our social and physical world. And they can be seen as "universal" or "foundational" in that they are states of being experienced by virtually everyone. All but the most miserably deprived have experienced some kind of love, and all but the most repressed have experienced some moment of hate.

Love and hate are radically different but reflect and rely on each other. Neither one would be the generative or destructive force it is if the other did not exist. These two "urges," these two foundational forces in our lives, sit in uneasy dialectical relationship with each other, mediated by our own actions and relationships, by the mass media, by our culture and by the various so-called social norms set by our political leaders, our churches and our many and various role models and "moral guardians."

Hate

Neither Hazlitt nor Finkielkraut talks of hate and love in banal or maudlin terms. Hazlitt sees hate as a great motivator:

> Nature seems (the more we look into it) made up of antipathies: without something to hate, we should lose the very spring of thought and action. Life would turn to a stagnant pool, were it not ruffled by the jarring interests, the unruly passions of men [Hazlitt, 2004, 105].

And he sees hate as an enduring force in our lives:

> Pure good soon grows insipid, wants variety and spirit. Pain is bitter-sweet, which never surfeits. Love turns, with a little indulgence, to indifference or disgust: hatred alone is immortal [Hazlitt, 2004, 105].

We need to beware the hyperbole of a popular essayist, but Hazlitt's writing and ideas have endured, and in his high and merry style he is telling it how he sees it. Hazlitt opens his essay with the description of a spider crawling across the matted floor of the room in which he is writing. He lifts the matting to let the spider escape, is glad to get rid of the intruder, and shudders at the recollection of it after it has gone. Hazlitt remarks that "a moralist a century ago" would have crushed the spider to death but that his "philosophy has got beyond that." He goes on:

I bear the creature no ill-will but still I hate the very sight of it. The spirit of malevolence survives the practical exertion of it. We learn to curb our will and keep our overt actions within the bounds of humanity, long before we can subdue our sentiments and imagination to the same mild tone. We give up external demonstration, the *brute* violence, but cannot part with the essence or principle of hostility. We do not tread upon the poor little animal in question (that seems barbarous and pitiful!) but we regard it with a sort of mystic horror and superstitious loathing [Hazlitt, 2004, 104].

Hate and anger are closely connected. Anger can underpin hate. Hate can express itself in anger. In looking at ways in which we can both benefit from hate yet learn to curb it, Hazlitt anticipates by 170 years the distinction that Diamond (1996) draws between rage and anger. Hazlitt makes the distinction between a hate that spills into brute violence and a hate that inspires us to action, between a spontaneous hatred and a calculated loathing. Just as with anger, all but the most sudden and spontaneous hate can be controlled. We can simulate it and disguise it. We can vary it in kind. To revisit Diamond's image for anger, we can adjust its intensity as if we were operating a dimmer switch. Again like anger, hatred can be put to use.

Hazlitt himself does not reject unbridled hate. On the contrary, he delights in it:

The wild beast resumes its sway within us, we feel like hunting animals, and as the hound starts in his sleep and rushes on the chase in fancy, the heart rouses itself in its native lair, and utters a wild cry of joy, at being restored once more to freedom and lawless, unrestrained principles [Hazlitt, 2004, 107].

But Hazlitt is clear that this is all "in fancy," a state to be enjoyed as a satisfying dream can be. We can savor our hate and the imagined actions it might spur us on to. And we can use it to spur us on to real action, but that real action, that "overt" action, is to be kept "within the bounds of humanity" (Hazlitt, 2004, 104). Hazlitt hated the spider and the idea of the spider after it had gone, but he lifted the matting to let it escape. Our hate, he tells us, can be savage, but our response to it must be civilized.

Hazlitt tells us to be fearful of hate in the hands of the fanatic. He expresses wonder at a fire-and-brimstone preacher in the London of his day, a Mr. Irving, who was "like a huge Titan, looking as grim and swarthy as if he had to forge tortures for all the damned!" And he goes on:

> What a strange being man is! Not content with doing all he can to vex and hurt his fellows here "upon the bank and shoal of time," where one would think there were heart-aches, pain, disappointment, anguish, tears, sighs, and groans enough, the bigoted maniac takes him to the top of the high peak of school divinity to hurl him down the yawning gulf of penal fire; his speculative malice asks eternity to wreak its infinite spite in, and calls on the Almighty to execute its relentless doom [Hazlitt, 2004, 108]!

And there's the rub. Hate in the hands of the reasonable person may be one thing, but in the mouths and hands of bigoted maniacs it will be another. Finkielkraut (1984, 148), in his book on love, also writes briefly on "the hatred of the Other," and in that section he cuts to the chase in the first sentence and makes reference to the demonic hatred Hitler and his Nationalist Socialists had for the Jews. There were no redeeming features in that hatred.

Love

If I am to use hate as an essential element in my ideas on morality, I will need to include ways of curbing, controlling and setting limits to it. I will need to find a way to prevent myself, and others I put these ideas to, from becoming bigoted maniacs.

I believe we can do this by using love. But I do not want to suggest that love be used as some straightforward kind of counterbalance. Love and hate can be placed in relationship to each other but, at the risk of saying the obvious, they are emotions, acts and states of being too complex, too variable and too uniquely themselves to be seen as direct opposites, or of equal force to one another. Hazlitt claims that hate will outlast love. Louis Aragon, who wrote a sublime love poem to his wife, Elsa Triolet, towards the end of her life, would surely say the opposite. Nor do I want to propose that we use love as some kind of antidote, whether in the naive form found in popular songs—"all you need is love"—or in the spiritual form found in some religions. Most certainly I do not want to suggest that we go through the emotionally perilous and potentially self-destructive business of trying to love our enemies.

Love has internal inconsistencies in the way that hate does not. Finkielkraut opens his book with these words:

> There is a word in numerous languages which denotes at the same time the act of giving and the act of taking, charity and greed, generosity and covetousness—it is the word *love*. Paradoxically, the passionate desire a person has for complete gratification, and a selflessness without reserve come together in the same term. We speak of love as both the apotheosis of self-interest and as a concern for the Other pushed to its extreme [Finkielkraut, 1984, 11; my translation].

We can see this fusion of the desire to take and the willingness to give in two people making ardent sexual love. An absorption in self-gratification, in one's own senses and one's own pleasure combines with a care for the other and an intense concern for the other's pleasure. And we can see this two-way nature of love manifested terribly in the breakdown of relationships as well. We give our respect to people we love and we desperately want their respect in return. If we do not get it, there is an aching, intolerable lack. When people we love turn away from us, we either literally or metaphorically tear at their person, trying to turn them back to us, trying to force our love on to them, and trying grasp a love for us out of them.

Love and Abandon

I have talked of calculated hate, but can I do the same with love? Bauman argues not. In an essay entitled "Does Love Need Reason?" he disassociates love from reason, just as he disassociated morality from reason, arguing that reason and love "fear" each other, "speak different languages" and "seldom produce a tolerable *modus vivendi*" (Bauman, 2001, 168). If we take the example of sexual love, we might be tempted to agree. After all, we often use the word *abandon* to describe a state of passion, and the implication is that we have discarded all reason and given ourselves over to this other, different thing called love.

Bauman argues that love is disassociated from reason in the following ways. Love is about value; reason is about use (Bauman, 2001, 164). That is, love is concerned with an inherent quality while reason concerns itself with what is practicable to the user. Love and reason "have radically different horizons"(Bauman, 2001, 166). That is, love is both "infinite" and "indefinite," while reason is concerned with events tied to time and place. And love is concerned with solidarity for the Other while reason is concerned with loyalty to the self (Bauman, 2001, 167).

Just as he does with morality, Bauman describes love in terms of an encounter, if needs be an utterly selfless one, with "the naked face" of the Other:

> To love . . . means to value the other for its otherness, to wish to reinforce it in its otherness, to protect the otherness and make it bloom and thrive, and to be ready to sacrifice one's own comfort, including one's own mortal existence, if that is what is needed to fulfil that intention [Bauman, 2001, 165–166].

In his own inimitable way, Bauman paints love as a pure, and exigent, moral force.

Rational Love

But in another way, again associated with his particular mode of argument, Bauman misrepresents love badly. Early on in his essay he says, "Reason and love do not really converse—more often than not they shout each other down," and further on "As a defendant at the tribunal of reason, love is bound to lose its case" (Bauman, 2001, 163–164). Bauman is writing of love as he would of a person, presenting love as the actor rather than the act, and this is anthropomorphic nonsense. Love is not the actor. There are people involved. *People* do the loving, and they love *something* or they love *someone*.

Immediately Bauman's disassociation of reason from love is less easy to justify. I can love a painting. I am not talking here of liking a painting but of loving it, of feeling moved and excited by it, of having to look at it again and again, so that it becomes a significant part of my emotional and intellectual experience, part of my life, part of me. As I look at it, I will not only enjoy the painting and the feelings it arouses in me but I will try to understand why I enjoy it. To do this I may compare this painting with others, read about it, consult with others who like or dislike it and so, in effect, engage in my own research. Reason and love are in harmony here. And I can love a person. In passion we may let go of reason but passion is often followed by moments of repose and, as my own experience and countless novels and films tell me, in those moments of repose we can find ourselves looking at our lover and thinking about why we love her or him so much. We savor our love, linger over it, reflect on it and find our reasons for it.

Louis Aragon looked at his wife with whom he had shared a profound love for some thirty years, and wrote this wonderful poem. It is in French and I am going to quote it in full. I dare not translate it, but I will talk a little about what I think it says:

Mon sombre amour d'orange amère
Ma chanson d'écluse et de vent
Mon quartier d'ombre où vient rêvant
         Mourir la mer

Mon doux mois d'août dont le ciel pleut
Des étoiles sur les monts calmes
Ma songerie aux murs de palmes
         Où l'air est bleu

Mes bras d'or mes faibles merveilles
Renaissent ma soif et ma faim
Collier collier des soirs sans fin
         Où le coeur veille

Dire que je puis disparaître
Sans t'avoir tressé tous les joncs
Dispersé l'essaim des pigeons
         A ta fenêtre

Sans faire flèche du matin
Flèche du trouble et de la fleur
De l'eau fraîche et de la douleur
         Dont tu m'atteins

Est-ce qu'on sait ce qui se passe
C'est peut-être bien ce tantôt
Que l'on jettera le manteau
         Dessus ma face

Et tout ce langage perdu
Ce trésor dans la fondrière
Mon cri recouvert de prières
         Mon champ vendu

Je ne regrette rien qu'avoir
La bouche pleine de mots tus
Et dressé trop peu de statues
         A ta mémoire

> *Ah tandis encore qu'il bat*
> *Ce coeur usé contra sa cage*
> *Pour Elle qu'un dernier saccage*
> > *Le mette bas*
>
> *Coupez ma gorge et les pivoines*
> *Vite apportez mon vin mon sang*
> *Pour lui plaire comme en passant*
> > *Font les avoines*
>
> *Il me reste si peu de temps*
> *Pour aller au bout de moi-même*
> *Et pour crier-dieu que je t'aime*
> > *Tant*

[Aragon, 1959, 41-43]

The poem is dense with imagery hinting at age and beauty and weakness and strength. There is joy, panic, calm and wistfulness. Nature, both majestic and intimate, is evoked. In a moment of existential fervor, Aragon cries out for his throat to be cut and for his blood, his wine, to be carried to his loved one for her pleasure. But the angst in this cruel image gives way to calm, and to the most beautiful expression of regret for something not yet lost. As always translation is difficult, and the last stanza carries a subtle mixture of ordinary and extraordinary language, but in it Aragon expresses dismay that he has so little time left to cry out, "I love you so much."

Aragon's poem is passionate yet it is a passion which has been written down and so thought about in the writing. It is an expression of feeling and a product of reasoning. Only a person who has really considered how language works could take a banal phrase like "I love you so much" ("je t'aime tant") and give it back all its original force. Bauman's contention (2001, 163) that "reason and love do not really converse" simply cannot survive the onslaught of this kind of evidence.

Relating Love to Hate

Into the equation with hate I want to bring a love which has that fusion of self-interest and selflessness that Finkielkraut sees, the pure and primal moral force that Bauman sees, and the application of passionate reason which I find in Aragon's poem. As a lead-in, I want to tell one more story.

I first heard of the philosopher Rick Turner when I was visiting South Africa some years ago. Turner had taught at the University of Natal in Durban during the 1960s and into the 1970s. He had written his book *The Eye of the Needle* in 1972 and revised and republished it in 1973. The book was highly critical of the then racist apartheid government of South Africa. In court proceedings to which he had been called as a witness and which were ostensibly unconnected with his book, Turner was "banned" for five years. In the South Africa of the day, banning was akin to house arrest. Turner could not work, go to places of work or town centers or meet more than one person at a time. One evening in 1978, near the end of his banning, Turner went to answer a knock on the front door of his house and was shot through the head and died instantly. It has been generally accepted that he was assassinated by the country's "security" forces. He was thirty-eight.

I was in South Africa some eighteen years after Turner's death and I was struck by how present he still was in the minds of those who had known him. Several people talked to me about him. The education officer of the National Union of Metalworkers told me he thought Turner's book had played a significant part in motivating black trade unionists. A white academic talked with reverence of Turner's teaching and offered me copies of notes from Turner's lectures. A colleague in the center where I was briefly located on study leave talked of Turner with tears in her eyes. She told me that his ideas and his book had been a major influence in regenerating resistance to the apartheid regime. Everyone who mentioned him did so with such affection that, if I had not known, I would have assumed he had died in the last few weeks.

I went looking for a copy of *The Eye of the Needle* and found one in a secondhand bookshop in a Durban suburb. There were two people behind the counter, one black and one white. The black man served me, went looking for the book, found it and brought it back to the counter. The white man joined him and took responsibility for wrapping the book. The moment was remarkable. One man wrapped the book slowly, doing it perfectly. The other man watched, motionless, in silence. When the man had finished wrapping the book, he looked up and said, "I was at Rick's funeral." Again I had this uncanny impression that Turner had only just died. I paid, said my thanks and left, carrying away this book which had been handled with so much love.

Turner's story is a terrible and wonderful one: terrible because he made choices, took action, defied a hateful regime and lost his life as a result; wonderful because he made choices, took action, defied a hateful regime and was loved for the choices he made and the actions he took.

My Response

In my adult education practice I have used a range of learner-centered activities and been involved in projects where a degree of control was handed over to the learners. Early on in this book I talked about designing a course to do just this. But for the most part I have been reluctant to relinquish my authority as teacher. When I worked as a trainer within the trade union movement, I conducted training on the clear understanding that, no matter how participatory the course might be in its process, the collective objectives of the trade union movement, or of the particular union I was working for, took precedence over the interests, needs and demands of the individual course participants. When I went on to teach in a university, I assumed that I must retain some authority. I might aim to make my classes democratic but I also had a responsibility, if only dictated by the assessment procedures, to be the teacher. And when I worked with activists, I assumed they had invited me because they wanted to hear some of the things I had to say.

In its most reductionist form, this approach means that sometimes when I am asked a question I will answer using my position as the teacher to privilege my views over others. And so when I spoke about different categories of action and was asked: "Well, how do *you* choose between one category or another?" I told my story of buying Rick Turner's book and then went on to say something like this:

There are hateful people who do hateful things, who exploit and oppress and will not let other people grow. These people are our enemies, and we have every right to hate them. Some say we should let go of our hatred but I believe we should exult in it, nurture it, and use it to motivate ourselves and others to take bold and decisive action. Of course, hatred can send us careering out of control. It can make us as loathsome as our enemies. To avoid this happening I believe we should look to the Other, to others, to people whose integrity we respect. And I believe that we should make every effort at every turn to earn the love of these people with the choices we make and the actions we take. Hate *for* the hateful should be our motivating force. Love *from* the people we respect should be our goal, our guide, and our source of moral authority.

Postscript

As I finished writing this book, American, British, Australian and other troops still occupied Iraq. Bombings and kidnappings continued. An Italian journalist had been kidnapped by one of the insurgent organizations but was released into the hands of Italian security officers. They were driving to Baghdad airport to put the journalist on a plane home when American forces opened fire on their car, killing one of the Italian security officers and wounding the journalist. Allegations were made that the shooting was not a mistake. The journalist herself suggested as much from her hospital bed in Italy. In *The Australian* on March 8, 2005 she was reported as saying that the Americans did not approve of negotiations for the release of hostages and that she may well have been their target. Confusion, distrust, fear and barbarity. Bauman talks of chaos, Giddens of a runaway world. It is easy to lose heart.

We were due to leave Paris in a couple of days, and my partner and I wandered out of our apartment and into the streets, ending up at the Place des Vosges. This is a square of magnificent houses in red brick and cream plaster, built in the early seventeenth century, enclosing a garden. The houses overhang the pavement, their first floor supported by thick pillars, creating a cloisterlike arcade which runs around the square. In one part of the arcade some twenty musicians were performing. Most were in their twenties, with a few in their thirties or forties. Three were playing cellos, and the rest violins or violas. Some had music stands and scores, others were playing from memory. The concert, if that is what it was, had an impromptu feel to it. A woman violinist counted the group into each piece, but there was no conductor and no one made any announcements or introductions. The group played bouncy, joyful music, by Vivaldi and Mozart mainly. Some of the playing was rough around the edges but the acoustics were excellent and it was thrilling to stand inside the arcade, close to the musicians, and let the music envelop us. During a brief break my partner asked one of the violinists who they were, and he said they were mostly students, with a sprinkling of professionals. There was a standard repertoire, and they simply turned up on Sundays and played, for the pleasure and for the practice.

On the far side of the square there were more musicians, this time a blues band, made up of a bassist, two guitarists and a harmonica player who also sang. They were all men in their fifties, and when the singer announced the next song he spoke French with an Anglo accent. They were called the Wedding Band, he said, but were equally ready to play at divorces. They were very good and a considerable crowd listened. Again the acoustics in the arcade were excellent. The band swapped instruments around a bit. One of the guitarists changed to saxophone, and for one number the other guitarist played a ragged and raucous trombone.

Further down the arcade was a hat shop which spilled out onto stalls on the pavement. There was a mirror against one of the pillars and somebody trying on a hat turned away from it and asked my partner how the hat looked. She responded, and another couple of people joined in the conversation. We all laughed at the spontaneous encounter. Beautiful surroundings, fine music and easygoing civility—a world worth defying the doomsayers, barbarians and bigots for.

References

Adam-Smith, P. *The Anzacs*. Melbourne: Thomas Nelson Australia, 1978.

Allman, P. "Paulo Freire's Education Approach: A Struggle for Meaning." In G. Allen, J. Bastiani, I. Martin, and J. K. Richards (eds.), *Community Education*. Milton Keynes, England: Open University Press, 1987.

Allman, P. *Critical Education against Global Capitalism: Karl Marx and Critical Revolutionary Education*. London: Bergin & Garvey, 2001.

Anstey, M. *Negotiating Conflict: Insights and Skills for Negotiators and Peacemakers*. Kenwyn, South Africa: Juta and Co., Ltd., 1991.

Aragon, L. "Je t'aime tant." *Elsa*. Paris: Gallimard, 1959.

Arendt, H. "Communicative Power." In S. Lukes (ed.), *Power*. Oxford, England: Blackwell, 1986.

Argyris, C. *On Organizational Learning*. Oxford, England: Blackwell, 1999.

Argyris, C., and Schön, D. A. *Organizational Learning II: Theory, Method, and Practice*. Reading, Massachusetts, U.S.A.: Addison-Wesley, 1996.

Ayer, A. J. *Language, Truth, and Logic*. Harmondsworth, England: Penguin, 1971. (Originally published 1936.)

Bauman, Z. *Legislators and Interpreters: On Modernity, Post-Modernity, and Intellectuals*. Cambridge, England: Polity Press, 1989.

Bauman, Z. "Modernity and Ambivalence." In M. Featherstone (ed.), *Global Culture: Nationalism, Globalization, and Modernity*. London: Sage, 1990.

Bauman, Z. *Intimations of Postmodernity*. London: Routledge, 1992.

Bauman, Z. *Postmodern Ethics*. Oxford, England: Blackwell, 1993.

Bauman, Z. *Life in Fragments*. Oxford, England: Blackwell, 1995.

Bauman, Z. *The Individualized Society*. Cambridge, England: Polity Press, 2001.

Boal, A. *Theatre of the Oppressed*. London: Pluto, 1979.

Boud, D., and Walker, D. *Experience and Learning: Reflection at Work*. Geelong, Australia: Deakin University Press, 1991.

Branch, T. *Parting the Waters: Martin Luther King and the Civil Rights Movement, 1954–63*. London: Macmillan, 1988.

Brookfield, S. *Developing Critical Thinkers: Challenging Adults to Explore Alternative Ways of Thinking and Acting*. Milton Keynes, England: Open University Press, 1987.

Brookfield, S. "Using Critical Incidents to Analyze Learners' Assumptions." In J. Mezirow and Associates, *Fostering Critical Reflection in Adulthood: A Guide to Transformative and Emancipatory Learning.* San Francisco, U.S.A.: Jossey-Bass, 1990.

Brookfield, S. *Becoming a Critically Reflective Teacher.* San Francisco, U.S.A.: Jossey-Bass, 1995.

Brown, B. E. *Protest in Paris: Anatomy of a Revolt.* Morristown, New Jersey, U.S.A.: General Learning Press, 1974.

Camus, A. "L'Hôte." In *L'Exil et le royaume, nouvelles.* Paris: Gallimard, 1957.

Camus, A. *The Rebel.* (A. Bower, trans.) London: Hamish Hamilton, 1953. (Originally published 1945.)

Camus, A. *The Stranger.* (S. Gilbert, trans.) New York: Vintage Books, 1954. (Originally published 1942.)

Camus, A. *The Myth of Sisyphus.* (J. O'Brien, trans.) London: Penguin, 1975. (Originally published 1942.)

Collier, K. "Once More With Feeling—Identification, Representation and the Affective Aspects of Role-Play In Experience-Based Education." In J. Rolfe, D. Saunders, and T. Powell (eds.), *Simulation and Games for Emergency and Crisis Management.* London: Kogan Page, 1998.

Collier, K. "Finding A 'Forum' for Debriefing Role-Play in Adult Education." In D. Saunders and J. Severn (eds.), *Simulations and Games for Strategy and Policy Planning.* London: Kogan Page, 1999.

Collier, K. "Spotlight on Role-Play: Using Theatre Arts to Interrogate the Theory and Practice of Role-Play in Adult Education." Unpublished Ph.D. thesis, Faculty of Education, University of Technology, Sydney, 2005.

Congreve, W. *The Way of the World.* London: Nick Hern Books, 1995.

Cox, E. *A Truly Civil Society: 1995 Boyer Lectures.* Sydney: ABC Books, 1995.

Crowther, J., Galloway, V., and Martin, I. (eds.) *Popular Education: Engaging The Academy.* Leicester, England: NIACE, 2005.

Dallmayr, F. "The Discourse of Modernity: Hegel, Nietzsche, Heidegger, and Habermas." In M. Passerin d'Entreves and S. Benhabib (eds.), *Habermas and the Unfinished Project of Modernity.* Cambridge, England: Polity Press, 1996.

Dalton, R. *Citizen Politics.* Chatham, New Jersey, U.S.A.: Chatham House, 1996.

Danaher, G., Schirato, T., and Webb, J. *Understanding Foucault.* Sydney: Allen and Unwin, 2000.

Darwin, C. *The Expression of the Emotions in Man and Animals.* Chicago: University of Chicago Press, 1965. (Originally published 1872.)

de Botton, A. *Philosophy: A Guide to Happiness*, part 3: "Seneca on Anger." London: Channel 4 Television, 2000.

Dean, J. "Civil Society: Beyond the Public Sphere." In D. Rasmussen (ed.), *The Handbook of Critical Theory.* Oxford, England: Blackwell, 1996.

Denning, S. *The Springboard: How Storytelling Ignites Action in Knowledge-Era Organizations*. Boston, U.S.A.: Butterworth-Heinemann, 2001.

Deshler, D. "Metaphor Analysis: Exorcising Social Ghosts." In J. Mezirow and Associates, *Fostering Critical Reflection in Adulthood: A Guide to Transformative and Emancipatory Learning*. San Francisco, U.S.A.: Jossey-Bass, 1990.

Diamond, S. A. *Anger, Madness, and the Daimonic: The Psychological Genesis of Violence, Evil, and Creativity*. Albany, New York, U.S.A.: State University of New York Press, 1996.

Drucker, P. "The Effective Decision." In Peter F. Drucker and others, *Harvard Business Review on Decision Making*. Boston, U.S.A.: Harvard Business School Press, 2001.

Feenberg, A., and Freedman, J. *When Poetry Ruled the Streets: The French May Events of 1968*. Albany, New York, U.S.A.: State University of New York Press, 2001.

Finkielkraut, A. *La sagesse de l'amour* [The wisdom of love]. Paris: Editions Gallimard, 1984.

Fisher, R., and Ury, W. *Getting to Yes*. London: Hutchinson, 1983.

Firkins, P. *The Australians in Nine Wars: Waikato to Long Tan*. London: Pan Books, 1973.

Fogler, H. S., and Leblanc, S. E. *Strategies for Creative Problem Solving*. Englewood Cliffs, New Jersey, U.S.A.: Prentice Hall, 1995.

Foley, G. (ed.). *Understanding Adult Education and Training*. Sydney: Allen and Unwin, 1995.

Foucault, M. *The History of Sexuality*, vol. 1: *An Introduction*. (R. Hurely, trans.) Harmondsworth, England: Penguin, 1978.

Foucault, M. *Power/Knowledge: Selected Interviews and Other Writings*. (C. Gordon, ed.) New York: Pantheon, 1980.

Freire, P. *Cultural Action for Freedom*. Harmondsworth, England: Penguin, 1972a.

Freire, P. *Pedagogy of the Oppressed*. Harmondsworth, England: Penguin, 1972b.

Freire, P. *The Politics of Education*. (Donaldo Macedo, trans.) South Hadley, Massachusetts, U.S.A.: Bergin and Garvey, 1985.

Gammage, B. *The Broken Years: Australian Soldiers in the Great War*. Canberra: Australian National University Press, 1974.

Giddens, A. *Modernity and Self-Identity: Self and Society in the Late Modern Age*. Stanford, California, U.S.A.: Stanford University Press, 1991.

Giddens, A. *Beyond Left and Right: The Future of Radical Politics*. Stanford, California, U.S.A.: Stanford University Press, 1994.

Giddens, A. *Runaway World: How Globalization Is Reshaping Our Lives*. New York: Routledge, 2000.

Gildea, R. *France Since 1945*. Oxford, England: Oxford University Press, 1996.

Goatly, A. *The Language of Metaphors*. London: Routledge, 1997.

Gonczi, A. (ed.). *Developing a Competent Workforce*. Adelaide, Australia: National Centre For Vocational Education and Research, 1992.

Gramsci, A. *Selections from the Prison Notebooks of Antonio Gramsci*. (Q. Hoare & G. N. Smith, eds.) New York: International Publishers, 1971.

Greenland, H. "Paris in the Spring." *Sydney Morning Herald, Good Weekend Magazine*, May 9, 1998, 16-20.

Griffith, T. R. "Introduction." In W. Congreve, *The Way of the World*. London: Nick Hern Books, 1995.

Habermas, J. *Knowledge and Human Interests*. (J. J. Shapiro, trans.) London: Heinemann Educational, 1972. (Originally published 1968.)

Habermas, J. *The Theory of Communicative Action*, vol. 1. (T. McCarthy, trans.) Cambridge, England: Polity Press, 1984. (Originally published 1981.)

Habermas, J. *The Theory of Communicative Action*, vol. 2. (T. McCarthy, trans.) Cambridge, England: Polity Press, 1987. (Originally published 1981.)

Hazlitt, W. *The Pleasure of Hating*. London: Penguin, 2004. (Originally published 1826.)

Heller, J. *Catch-22*. London: Corgi, 1964.

Hopkins, G. M. "The Windhover." In *The Faber Book of Modern Verse* (M. Roberts, ed. Revised by D. Hall.) London: Faber and Faber.

Horton, M. *The Long Haul*. New York: Doubleday, 1990.

Husserl, E. *Cartesian Meditations: An Introduction to Phenomenology*. The Hague: Kluwer Academic Publishers, 1995. (Originally published 1950.)

Jarvis, P. (ed.). *Twentieth-Century Thinkers in Adult Education*. London: Croom Helm, 1987.

Jarvis, P. *Ethics and Education for Adults*. Leicester, England: NIACE, 1997.

Kaye, M. *Myth-Makers and Story-Tellers: A Guide for Effective Managers and Communicators*. Sydney: Business and Professional Publishing, 1996.

Kellner, D. "Introduction." In A. Feenberg and J. Freedman, *When Poetry Ruled the Streets: The French May Events of 1968*. Albany, New York, U.S.A.: State University of New York Press, 2001.

Kenway, J., and Bullen, E. "Education in the Age of Diversity: An Eagle Eye's View." *Compare*, 2000, *30*(3), 265-273.

Lewis, A. *Portrait of a Decade: The Second American Revolution*. New York: Bantam Books, 1965.

Lima, L., and Guimaraes, P. (eds.) *Adult Education in Portugal*. Braga, Portugal: University of Minho, 2004.

Lyotard, J.-F. *The Postmodern Condition: A Report on Knowledge*. Manchester, England: Manchester University Press, 1984.

MacKinnon, S. "The Cape York Heads of Agreement: Expanding Green Strategies-Negotiation as a Model for Creating Change." *Wilderness*, 1998, *153*, 9-11.

MacKinnon, S. "Emancipatory Learning and Social Action: Implications for the Environment Movement." *New Zealand Journal of Adult Learning*, 2003, *31*(2), 53-71.

MacKinnon, S. "Expanding Green Strategies: Learning in and from Cape York to Create Change through Negotiation." Unpublished Ph.D. thesis, Faculty of Education, University of Technology, Sydney, 2004.

Mandela, N. *The Struggle Is My Life*. Western Cape, South Africa: Mayibye Books, 1994.

Marquis, D. "warty bliggens the toad." *Archy and Mehitabel*. London: Faber and Faber, 1963.

Mason, M. "The Ethics of Integrity: Educational Values beyond Postmodern Ethics." *Journal of Philosophy of Education*, 2001, *35*(1), 48-69.

Mayer, B. "The Dynamics of Power in Mediation and Negotiation." *Mediation Quarterly*, 1987, 16, 75-85.

McAllister, I. *Political Behaviour: Citizens, Parties and Elites in Australia*. Melbourne: Longman Cheshire, 1992.

McIntyre, J. "On Becoming a Meditator: Reflections on Adult Learning and Social Context." In P. Willis and B. Neville (eds.), *Qualitative Research Practice in Adult Education*. Melbourne: David Lowell Publications, 1996.

McMillan, J. F. *Twentieth-Century France: Politics and Society, 1898–1991*. London: Arnold, 1992.

Merquior, J. G. *Foucault*. London: Fontana Press, 1991.

Mezirow, J. "A Critical Theory of Adult Learning and Education." *Adult Education*, 1981, *31*(1), 3-27.

Mezirow, J. *Transformative Dimensions of Adult Learning*. San Francisco, U.S.A.: Jossey-Bass, 1991.

Miller, V. "The Nicaraguan Literacy Crusade: Education for Transformation." In C. Duke (ed.), *Combating Poverty through Adult Education*. London: Croom Helm, 1985.

Moi, T. *Sexual/Textual Politics*. London: Routledge, 1988.

Monk, G., Winslade, J., Crocket, K., and Epston, D. (eds.). *Narrative Therapy in Practice: The Archaeology of Hope*. San Francisco, U.S.A.: Jossey-Bass, 1997.

Morphet, T. "Richard Turner: A Biographical Introduction." In R. Turner, *The Eye of the Needle: Towards Participatory Democracy in South Africa*. Johannesburg: Ravan Press, 1980. (Originally published 1973.)

Moyers, B. "Adventures of a Radical Hillbilly." *Bill Moyers' Journal*. New York: WNET/Thirteen, 1981.

Neville, B. *Educating Psyche: Emotion, Imagination and the Unconscious in Learning*. Melbourne: Collins Dove, 1989.

Newman, M. *The Third Contract: Theory and Practice in Trade Union Training*. Sydney: Centre for Popular Education, 1993.

Newman, M. *Defining the Enemy: Adult Education in Social Action*. Sydney: Centre for Popular Education, 1994.

Newman, M. *Maeler's Regard: Images of Adult Learning*. Sydney: Centre for Popular Education, 1999.

Oser, F. "Can a Curriculum of Moral Education Be Postmodern?" *Educational Philosophy and Theory*, 1999, *31*(2), 231-236.

Plato. *Phaedrus*. Indianapolis, Indiana, U.S.A.: Bobbs-Merrill, 1975.

Rasmussen, D. (ed.). *The Handbook of Critical Theory*. Oxford, England: Blackwell, 1996.

Ricoeur, P. *La mémoire, l'histoire, l'oubli* [Memory, history, forgetting]. Paris: Editions du Seuil, 2000.

Rogers, B. *A.J. Ayer: A Life*. London: Chatto & Windus, 1999.

Russo, J. E., and Schoemaker, P.J.H. *Winning Decisions: How to Make the Right Decision the First Time*. London: Piatkus, 2002.

Sartre, J.-P. *Being and Nothingness*. (H. E. Barnes, trans.) New York: Washington Square Press, 1984. (Originally published 1943.)

Schön, D. *The Reflective Practitioner*. London: Temple Smith, 1983.

Schön, D. *Educating the Reflective Practitioner*. San Francisco, U.S.A.: Jossey-Bass, 1987.

Segal, S. "The Existential Conditions of Explicitness: An Heideggerian Perspective." *Studies in Continuing Education*, 1999, *21*(1), 73-89.

Sharp. G. *Gandhi as a Political Strategist*. Boston, U.S.A.: Porter Sargent, 1979.

Sternberg, R. J., and Davidson, J. E. (eds.). *The Nature of Insight*. Cambridge, Massachusetts, U.S.A.: MIT Press, 1995.

Tavris, C. *Anger*. New York: Simon and Schuster, 1982.

Thompson, J. *Learning Liberation: Women's Response to Men's Education*. London: Croom Helm, 1983.

Thompson, J. "Adult Education and the Women's Movement." In T. Lovett (ed.), *Radical Approaches to Adult Education*. London: Routledge, 1988.

Thompson, J. *Words in Edgeways*. Leicester, England: NIACE, 1997.

Thompson, J. *Women, Class and Education*. London: Routledge, 2000.

Turner, R. *The Eye of the Needle: Towards Participatory Democracy in South Africa*. Johannesburg: Ravan Press, 1980. (Originally published 1973.)

Umar, A. "The Protest Tradition in Nigerian Adult Education: An Analysis of NEPU's Emancipatory Learning Project (1950–1966)." *Convergence*, 1993, *36*(4), 19-32.

Usher, R., Bryant, I., and Johnston, R. *Adult Education and the Postmodern Challenge*. London: Routledge, 1997.

Vonnegut, K. *Slaughterhouse-Five*. London: Triad/Granada, 1979. (Originally published 1969.)

Weber, M. *Economy and Society: An Outline of Interpretive Sociology* (multiple translators.) New York: Bedminster Press, 1968. (Originally published in German, in different forms, 1922, 1925, 1947, 1956.)

Welton, M. (ed.). *In Defense of the Lifeworld: Critical Perspectives on Adult Learning*. Albany, New York, U.S.A.: State University of New York Press, 1995.

Willis, P. *Inviting Learning: An Exhibition of Risk and Enrichment in Adult Education Practice*. Leicester, England: NIACE, 2002.

Woodcock, G. *Gandhi*. London: Fontana/Collins, 1972.

Youngman, F. *The Political Economy of Adult Education and Development*. London: Zed Books, 2000.

Zancarini-Fournel, M. "Notre corps, nous-mêmes [Our bodies, ourselves]." In E. Gubin, C. Jacques, F. Rochefort, F. Studer, F. Thebaud, and M. Zancarini-Fournel, *Le siècle des féminismes* [The century of feminisms]. Paris: Les Editions de l'Atelier/Editions Ouvrières, 2004.

Index

Problems: using commonsense logic to address, 75; decision making to solve, 75–79; principal interventions, 89–90; school caretaker, 87–89
Protest, 224–225

R

Rage, 51–54, 276
Rasmussen, D., 4
Rational discourse, 75
Rational love, 280–282
Rational self-reflection, 152–155
Reason: applied to morality/moral action, 268–270; as concerned with loyalty to self, 279; love as being disassociated from, 279–280; love as rational, 280–282
Rebelliousness: channeling dismay into, 48–49; cultural, 17–21; defiance as instilling purpose in, 61; focusing anger to inspire, 49–51; frustration leading to, 43–47; political, 21–23; rebellion and, 24–30; revolution and, 31–37; systemic, 23–24
Relationships: impact of rupture on, 216–217; negotiating, 149–152; phenomenological reflection on, 155–157
Renaming/naming, 207–210
Respect, 271–272
RESPONSIBILITIES (problem-solving model), 90, 93fig
Responsibility to other, 269–270
Revolution: rebelliousness and, 31–37; violent activism escalated to, 253
Ricoeur, P., 261
"The Right," 72
Rogers, B. A., 200
Role play, 144–146, 198–204
Romeo and Juliet (Shakespeare), 259–260
Rosemount Resource Centre (Northern Ireland), 57
Rowlatt Act (1919) [India], 33
Rupture, 216–217
Ruskin College (Oxford), 57
Russo, E., 75, 76, 83

S

La sagesse de l'amour (The Wisdom of Love) [Finkielkraut], 274

Sartre, J.-P., 4, 25, 62, 65–66, 163–164, 165, 207, 249, 255
Satyagraha resistance (India), 31–32, 33–37
Schoemaker, P., 75, 76, 83
Schön, D., 91, 154, 155
School caretaker problem, 87–89
"Second Chance for Women" course, 56–57
Segal, S., 166, 215, 216, 217, 218, 219
Self: duality of identity and, 147–149; idea of multiple and discontinuous, 148–149; moral, 268; reason as concerned with loyalty to, 279; shame of, 164–165
Self-identity: duality of self and, 147–149; sustaining of, 4
Self-reflection: action from, 219; encouraging, 157–158; phenomenological, 155–157; pondering, 157; rational, 152–155
Semistructured social movements, 235–236
Seneca, 52, 187
September 11, 2001, 7, 255
Seryge, D., 246
Sexual/Textual Politics (Moi), 258
Shakespeare, W., 194, 259–260
Sharp, G., 31, 32, 36, 37
Shembe Church (South Africa), 221, 222–223, 230, 241
Shongweni Resources Reserve, 221
Slaughterhouse-Five (Vonnegut), 182
Slogans, 61
Snowden (fictional character), 176–177
Social action, 231–232, 233–234
Social capital, 228
Social movements: kinds of, 234–237; U.S. civil rights, 21–23, 226. See also Action
Sonnets: as art form, 188–189; flouting conventional structure of, 191–193; standard structure of Elizabethan, 187–188; "warty bliggens, the toad" (Archy), 191–193; "The Windhover" (Hopkins), 189–190
South Africa: apartheid of, 230, 283; Awesome Africa music festival of, 221–223, 241–242; Mandela's

DATE DUE

GAYLORD			PRINTED IN U.S.A.